IN THEIR
OWN WORDS

IN THEIR OWN WORDS

Women and the Story of Nauvoo

CAROL CORNWALL MADSEN

Deseret Book Company
Salt Lake City, Utah

Opposite: Nauvoo the Beautiful, from an old lithograph

Credits

All photographs and illustrations courtesy LDS Church Archives except the following: page 13, courtesy Museum of Art at Brigham Young University; page 108, courtesy Georgia Whipple Hammond; page 161, from Henry Hendricks Family History; page 214, courtesy Utah State Historical Society; page 257, *Relief Society Magazine,* March 1917, p. 132.

Library of Congress Cataloging-in-Publication Data

In Their Own Words: Women and the Story of Nauvoo / Carol
   Cornwall Madsen.
       p.   cm.
   Includes index.
   ISBN 0-87579-770-9
   1. Women, Mormon—History—19th century—Sources. 2. Mormon
Church—Illinois—Nauvoo—History—19th century—Sources. 3. Nauvoo
(Ill.)—Church history—19th century—Sources. 4. Illinois—Church
history—19th century—Sources. I. Madsen, Carol Cornwall, 1930–
BX8615.I3F35   1993
289.3'082—dc20   93–41762
                                                                          CIP

Printed in the United States of America

10   9   8   7   6   5   4   3   2   1

To those women
"whose lives were chapters of sacred history to be read
and followed by those who came after."
(Zina Diantha Huntington Young)

CONTENTS

CONTENTS

REMINISCENCES

PREFACE

On a wall in St. Oswald's Parish Church in the Lake District village of Grasmere, England, is a brief memorial to Laetitia Pritchard, who died in 1827: "Her life was devoted to the offices of Charity, the claims of Friendship, and the duties of Religion." When I read this inscription, I was struck by its familiarity. Not only did it describe the virtues of Laetitia Pritchard of Grasmere, England; it also identified personal qualities and patterns of relationship evident in the personal narratives of Mormon women in nineteenth-century Nauvoo. Friends, community, and Church were the binding force of their Nauvoo experience. Their writings are their testament to the strength of these attachments.

But only in such broad sweeps of characterization can we discern a "model" of Mormon womanhood. As their writings attest, there is no single image. Their individuality is one of the most compelling features of their writings. Not only do they exhibit varying levels of literary competency and style; they also reflect a variety of responses to the dynamic events that made up their life in Nauvoo. They all, however, shared a need to write, to transpose their life into language. Their personal accounts are literary self-portraits, representations of the inner and outer reality of their authors' lives, realities that together formed their conscious worlds. The reader will find them always emotionally articulate if not always grammatically so, but they all valued their experiences to the point of permanently inscribing them.

My dilemma in preparing this volume was deciding which documents to select from the plethora of materials available. Nauvoo was pivotal in the lives of early Mormon women, and many chose to memorialize that period in some written form. I chose the documents for this volume primarily for the range of experience they reflected and the different perspectives from which they were written. I believe that somewhere within that range of experience and perception can be heard the silent voices of those who, for their own reasons, did not leave a written record. Moreover, as individual as each account is, there are commonalities that enable us to generalize about women's Nauvoo and to sketch at least an outline of what it was like to be a Latter-day Saint woman at that time. While some of the accounts suggest the spiritual tensions that ultimately divided the Church in Nauvoo, the focus of this volume is on those women who maintained their faith in the mission of Joseph Smith and willingly transferred it to the calling of Brigham Young as his successor. Those who followed other paths have different stories to tell.

Understandably, these women were selective in what they recorded, and the reader (and the historian) must always recognize the historical limitations of personal discourse. We discover as we read of their lives, however, that their humility was not always self-generated, but that surviving the physical and spiritual challenges of Nauvoo and retaining their faith in a beleaguered religion were occasions for gratitude, not pride. Because of their strong community identity, their sense of collective spiritual destiny, and their participation in a movement of universal claim, their writings escape the narrow egocentrism of many personal narratives.

The twenty-five women whose writings comprise this volume found their lives transformed by conversion to Mormonism and shaped by their experiences thereafter. The voices we hear as we read these documents are clearly their own, expressing patterns of living from their own perspectives and in their own vernacular. Their narratives serve as analytical categories through which we can better understand a past wherein gender boundaries were both fixed and fluid, and their relationships both autonomous and affiliative. They write of a female world given cohesiveness by the common female rituals of birthing, nurturing, caring for, and supporting those "others" who came within their circle of attachment. But they were not immune to their social matrix. The private and the public continually intersect.

The rhythm of their private worlds was inescapably measured by the cadence of the religious community in which they lived.

Their texts interweave many strands of experience and thought: family and friends, religion, material struggles, sorrow, self-appraisal, and faith, the generative power that fueled and directed their lives. The design that emerges is unique to each writer as she gives greater or lesser prominence to each thread of experience. Religion, however, is the current that runs through them all. To study their writings is to discover the meaning of religion and the power of faith in the lives of women. Faith in divine providence was the lens through which the whole of life was viewed, dictating their thought and behavior as well as belief. Mary Ann Stearns, for example, clearly distinguished between becoming a Mormon—that is, accepting membership in the Church—and becoming a Latter-day Saint, or allowing her religion to transform her very nature and her way of relating not only to deity but to the world about her.

Though I cannot claim family kinship with these women or with any of the women of Nauvoo, I recognize them as spiritual kin and can claim my own place in the community of faith that nourished and guided them. They were women who lived life fully, whose clarity of vision infused the uncertainties and challenges with a transcendent meaning. "Our wounds were seared over with wisdom," Bathsheba W. Smith affirmed, as she reflected on her early Church experiences. "Pain gave birth to patience, and our martyred Saints rose, peradventure our best petitioners in the courts above."[1] These are words not casually chosen. They came from her soul's deepest resources and reflect truths that only experience can confirm.

In bringing these narratives together, I hope they will speak to the reader as they have to me. The disclosure of these women's lives, as they perceived them to be, brings woman's experiences in from the edges of history and enables us to bridge the silence that has separated us, as women, from our past. Perhaps anticipating that chasm of separation, several women agreed to write their life histories in 1880 as a "memorial" to the jubilee anniversary of the Church, designating them to be read at the one-hundredth anniversary of the Church.[2] An interesting provision to which all of them agreed was included at the end of Mercy Fielding Thompson's life story: "This is designed for my oldest female Descendant, if such should be living at the time this will be brought forth. If no such individual can be found, I design it to be handed to the oldest Female descendant of Martha Ann Smith Harris, my Sister's Daughter, Daughter of Hyrum and Mary [Fielding] Smith."[3]

What prompted these women to write their histories and then leave them specifically to their female descendants? Were they afraid that their accounts and their lives, left to the vagaries of time or chance, would travel only the byways of history, their experiences lost or ignored by a later generation? Or did they somehow want to link their lives with the lives of those who could most knowingly understand and share their stories, thereby preserving the chain of experience that connects one generation to another? Perhaps they understood that women ofttimes hear their own voices in the voices of other women, and hoped they would be heard across the generations. This volume is an attempt to reflect the spirit of their desire and to reaffirm the reality of our spiritual heritage. How better to claim that legacy than to allow these women to speak to us in their own words?

A note about the documents: As far as possible, the spelling and sentence structure of the original documents have been preserved, changes made only to facilitate reading and comprehension. Occasionally square brackets have been used to designate words completed or added for the sake of clarity. For those documents taken directly from typescripts, spelling and grammar have been standardized, leaving intact any peculiarity of word choice or expression. An awareness that nuances of personality can be lost if too much standardization is applied has guided the decisions in altering the texts in any way.

NOTES

1. *Woman's Exponent* 34 (January 1906): 41.

2. Mary Jane Mount Tanner, "Autobiography" (1837-1880), photocopy of typescript, LDS Church Archives.

3. Mercy Thompson Papers, Daughters of the Utah Pioneers Collection, LDS Church Archives.

INTRODUCTION

Faith and Community

FAITH AND COMMUNITY

After the Latter-day Saints were driven from Missouri in 1839,[1] the new gathering place, or "cornerstone of Zion," the Prophet Joseph Smith declared, was to be established on a promontory of Illinois land, then known as Commerce, that jutted out from the eastern banks of the Mississippi River. The swampy land on the river's edge—the flats, as they were called—gave rise to a plague of disease and death that struck almost every family on arrival, and yet they streamed into the new city from all directions, believers who, Eliza R. Snow affirmed, "seemed to have been held in reserve to meet the occasion, for none but Saints full of faith, and trusting in the power of God could have established that city."[2]

For those escaping the trials of Missouri, Nauvoo was a city of hope, a place to regroup and start again. To religious seekers, drawn to Nauvoo from the eastern and southern states and Canada by the pull of the gospel, Nauvoo was to be their "city on a hill," the fulfillment of a long religious quest. And for those who gathered from abroad, Nauvoo was their city of promise, offering hope and relief from their economic and spiritual impoverishment. But above all, Nauvoo was the City of Joseph, named for the prophet whose latter-day revelations drew these disparate people together and united them as Latter-day Saints. "I [will] gather mine elect from the four quarters of the earth," the Lord revealed through Joseph Smith in 1830, "even as many as will believe in me, and hearken unto my voice." (D&C 33:6.) They came to Nauvoo to prove the strength of their belief in the Lord and of their conviction that he had indeed called them from out of the world through a living prophet. "I was willing to come and gather," declared Jane Manning James, because "I was certain he

3

[Joseph] was a prophet. . . . I saw him back in old Connecticut in a vision, saw him plain and knew he was a prophet."[3]

Unlike many frontiers, Nauvoo reflected a family settlement pattern, the ratio of women and men nearly at parity.[4] It could not have developed so rapidly without the presence and commitment of the women who settled there. Yet possibly only three women of this period could claim instant name recognition among Latter-day Saints today: Emma Smith, Eliza R. Snow, and Sarah M. Kimball. These three constituted a nascent corps of "leading sisters," respected as such because of either their relationship to a Church leader, like Emma Smith's, their economic or social position, like Sarah Kimball's, or their talent, like Eliza R. Snow's.

However, thousands of other women were also engaged in the process of kingdom-building during the seven-year period that marked the Church's presence in Nauvoo.[5] They too had heard the voice that called them out of the world. One of them, whose name is little known, was Nancy Tracy. "You knew the voice of the good shepherd," she was reminded in her patriarchal blessing, ". . . and when He came to gather His sheep, you recognized His message and received it with joy and gladness."[6] Thousands of other women committed themselves at conversion, as did Priscilla Staines, to lay their "idols all upon the altar" and "set out for the reward of everlasting life, trusting in God."[7]

The hardships they encountered did not seem to offset that commitment. Mary Field Garner's mother was typical. She lost her husband and two daughters after reaching Nauvoo but entertained no thought of abandoning her resolve to be numbered among the Saints. "We did not complain," Mary wrote. "We were too thankful to be at Nauvoo with the other Saints of God, and to be associated with our prophet and leader, Joseph Smith, and listen to his teachings."[8]

Though these women were seemingly preoccupied with the continuous challenges of housing shortages, scarcity of commodities, and ubiquitous disease, they wrote predominantly religious narratives, recorded accounts of lives mandated and justified by the spiritual epiphany that brought them to Nauvoo. It is as though in the recital of their daily struggles they gave testimony to the greater truth that informed their lives, the restoration of the gospel of Jesus Christ and their part in that important movement. Thus it is that in the presence of so much adversity, their accounts are remarkably free of self-pity or regret. "I did not put my hand to the Plough to look backward," Electa Williams responded when her husband's parents offered a home and security if they would return to Michigan.[9] For her, the time of decision had passed.

Faith in the reality of the restoration and Joseph Smith's prophetic calling had brought them to this gathering place despite its inhospitable environment. But adversity seemed to nurture faith and create a tightly woven society, interdependent and self-defined. These new Latter-day Saints were building more than a city. They were establishing the cornerstone of Zion to be ready to receive all who would gather to Joseph's city, willing to confront the challenges that would make them saints in deed as well as in name. Mary Ann Stearns Winters was under no illusion that "sainthood" came with baptism. "I am a 'Mormon' in every fibre of my being," she insisted, but "I have never yet claimed to be a Latter-day Saint. . . . I am trying to live to that end."[10]

The initial contrast between Commerce and the cities they had left was startling to many newcomers. The swampy flatlands, forested bluffs, and sparse settlement were not inviting. "Nauvoo the Beautiful" was little more than a hope in the beginning.[11] Nor were the prospects of finding shelter and food any more encouraging. Sharing became the law of survival. There were few self-sufficient families. Cooperation and neighborliness were not just amenities; they were essentials. From necessity, families shared the shanties and small log cabins that started to rise among the few existing houses.

And there was no distinction between the "leading families" and the others. Material challenges faced them all equally. Bathsheba Smith remembered that after her marriage to George A. Smith, they lived with his parents on the Iowa side of the Mississippi, living in three different small log cabins, all with leaky roofs and smoking chimneys, before renting a room from some friends. Finally they acquired a lot in Nauvoo with a small log house on it. Despite George's home improvements, Bathsheba claimed it to be "the worst looking place"

View of Nauvoo from the Nauvoo Militia parade grounds

they had lived in, but it had the inestimable advantages of possessing neither a leaky roof nor a smoking chimney.[12]

Some of the other Missouri outcasts, including the families of several of the apostles, found temporary shelter across the river in Montrose, Iowa, and other small settlements nearby. While their husbands served missions to Great Britain, the apostles' wives attempted to maintain life in the deserted ruins of the old Fort Des Moines, each family occupying a single barracks room. When addition of a new baby increased Mary Ann Young's need for space, Leonora Taylor and her children gave up their room and moved in with Sarah Pratt. Phebe Woodruff lived with the Smoot family until she and Leonora decided to share quarters. Better housing always seemed to remain just out of reach.

In the meantime, the fort at least provided shelter, though sickness, loneliness, and shortages left the women physically and emotionally on edge. "I never needed more grace, patience or your prayers than I do at present," Leonora wrote to her husband, John Taylor.[13] The women's resilience and inner resources, as well as their material and emotional support of each other, carried them through the worst of their circumstances. Eventually, Leonora Taylor and Mary Ann Young were able to move across the river to a little better housing in Nauvoo, while Phebe Woodruff decided to go to stay with relatives in the East.

Despite a frenzy of building in Nauvoo, housing could not keep up with the flood of newcomers, mainly converts from Great Britain. British immigrant Ellen Douglas might have wondered about the wisdom of bringing her family to Nauvoo when she first arrived in 1842, but she was delighted to find a small house to rent, especially since she had prayed "that we might have one to ourselves for there is 3 or 4 families in one room, and many have to pitch their tents in the woods or anywhere they can for it is impossible for all to get houses when they come in for they are coming in daily."[14]

The stream of immigrants continued to swell the population even after the Prophet's death in 1844, stretching the building limits of the burgeoning city. In a letter to fellow apostle Wilford Woodruff in April 1845, George A. Smith reported the lack of housing, "even a room to rent," unhappy news for "the immense Emigration coming in the Spring."[15]

Hannah Pitt Kington and Jane Benbow and their husbands were among the British Saints who found the pull of the gospel compelling enough to uproot their ordered English lives and gather with the Church in Nauvoo. Better off than many of their fellow emigrants, they found that Nauvoo did not offer the material resources to create the comfortable circumstances they had left behind. Nevertheless, they had cast their lot with the Saints and were determined to stay with them.[16]

The Crookstons also found Nauvoo materially disappointing. Their house was "very poor with a leaky roof," and Robert Crookston, an artisan, had to settle for work in an adobe yard to support his family. Soon afterwards, however, like so many of his fellow immigrants, he caught the dreaded malaria and died, followed by his two young sons. Left to fare for themselves, his wife and daughter found it difficult to continue on alone "in that hovel on the Mississippi shore." "It was very hard to accustom ourselves to conditions," wrote young Ann Crookston, "after having been used to a comfortable home in England."[17]

As "deputy husbands," some women took up tasks for which they were often little prepared, when death, sickness, or Church duties prevented their husbands from assuming their usual familial roles. Drusilla Hendricks enlisted the help of her friend Melinda Lewis to chink and plaster her new log house, which had been hastily "throwed together by the Brethren" because of her husband's disabling injury in the skirmish at Crooked River in Missouri.[18] Lydia Partridge had to finish her house herself when her husband, Bishop Edward Partridge, died suddenly before completing it.[19] And Louisa Pratt, whose husband, Addison, had purchased lumber for a frame house before he was called to serve a mission to the Society Islands, was left "to get it put up and covered." Her account of constructing and furnishing the house shows a resourceful and competent woman at work eagerly preparing a home for a husband who would never live in it.[20]

As a missionary "widow," Bathsheba Smith managed alone by working out an exchange with her in-laws. She did housework and sewing for her husband's family and recorded blessings for her father-in-law, Patriarch John Smith, while they in turn plastered her half-finished house, supplied her with meal and flour, and tended to her other needs. She earned sufficient means during her husband's absence to furnish her house comfortably in preparation for his return.

If making a home of a hovel or building a home themselves was one daunting challenge women faced in the early years of Nauvoo, feeding their families was another. While some families had the means to secure enough land to plant gardens or pasture livestock, many did not. Moreover, flour was always in short supply, and so cornmeal became the staple of most diets. Stretching a cupful of cornmeal or a small bunch of greens to feed a family of hungry children required ingenuity. Mary Garner's mother managed to feed her six children for several weeks with only a pint of cornmeal a day, while Mary Rollins Lightner gave painting lessons to Julia Murdock, Sarah Ann Whitney, and others in exchange for some needed household commodities.[21] Cooperation minimized the household deficiencies so many women faced.

Since few women had access to kitchen gardens, many of those who did shared both their garden space and their produce. New immigrants, like Ann Pitchforth, often brought to Nauvoo precious seeds and plant cuttings, which they shared or exchanged for the household necessities they lacked.[22] Such reciprocal arrangements not only created strong networks among the women of Nauvoo, but also helped to bolster the city's faltering economy.

The traditional household division of labor dissolved under the tremendous economic challenges and high mortality of Nauvoo. Women became instant providers when sickness and death struck down the traditional breadwinners. Historically they turned to their domestic skills to support themselves and their families. Sarah Southworth learned to braid straw hats in a boarding school in Nauvoo, and after her marriage she supplemented the family income by making and selling them for a dollar each to passengers on the steamships that came in and out of Nauvoo.[23] Hannah Ells used the *Times and Seasons* to advertise her millinery business, which she operated in Samuel Bennett's home, where she also lived.[24] Drusilla Hendricks took in sewing and washing and reluctantly went out "on public days" to sell her homemade gingerbread, "this showing," she wrote, "that necessity is the mother of invention."[25]

When Ann Crookston lost her father and two brothers, she and her mother had to become self-sufficient. Ann traveled to Chicago to find work, returning to Nauvoo just as the Saints were preparing to leave in 1846. She and her mother lacked sufficient provisions for the long trek, so both took what work they could find. "She [mother] could do very fine hand sewing and I was able to get a little housework," Ann remembered, "but there was no choice in the matter and we were glad to get anything we could to help make an outfit for the journey which we expected to make."[26]

Taking in boarders helped Mary Ives to make ends meet for a while, but when business dropped off, she came under the "painful necessity of going from this place to work where ever I can find I can work for provisions but it is verry hard to get clothing more particular Flannel unless one has the money."[27]

Women developed other economic strategies, such as trading networks—exchanging a spool of fine cotton thread for a piece of pork, a blanket for a sack of flour, or a son's labor for a cow. The unequal possession of common household goods and the lack of money elevated bartering and trading to the primary means of commercial exchange in frontier communities. Through this informal, domestic mercantile operation, women demonstrated their expertise and value in the economic life of the community. These interdependent family clusters characterized the cooperative spirit that sustained Nauvoo's rapid growth.

Prized heirlooms and family memorabilia were reluctantly included in the pool of possessions to be sold or exchanged. Only when no other options appeared did Louisa Pratt give up her silver teaspoons to acquire a bushel of apples.[28] And fifteen-year-old Ann Crookston and her mother reached desperation before they were willing to part with their family silverware. Sent out to sell the spoons, Ann was delighted when the first person she offered them to accepted and pressed a dollar bill into her hand. But she was even happier when he told her to "buy what she needed with the dollar and take the spoons back home to her mother." Her benefactor turned out to be Joseph Young, Brigham's brother.[29]

Lack of provisions prompted Matilda Streeper to advise her brother to stock up before making the journey to Nauvoo. "It is a hard place to get things," she wrote, "and don't depend on getting dry goods or housing goods on the rode for you can get them beter at home and haf plenty of provisin when you start and lay in your grocries at saint luis."[30]

Along with sewing, housekeeping, and boarding guests, teaching provided an income for several self-dependent Nauvoo women. It required a degree of literacy not possessed by all of Nauvoo's adults. Eliza R. Snow, Zina D. H. Young, Louisa Barnes Pratt, and Emmeline B. Wells were among Nauvoo's teachers, all having had varying degrees of education. Their schools were informal, generally small, and irregular, but the schools helped educate the growing populace even as they provided a living for the teachers. These occupations not only enabled women to meet their own economic needs, but also provided necessary services to the community before such services were institutionalized. Economic necessity blurred the distinction between the private and the public as women worked both in and out of their homes, performing both paid and unpaid labor for their families' welfare.

Throughout American history, settling new communities always disrupted traditional patterns of family work and relationships. This social dislocation was exacerbated by the heavy physical toll inherent in the harsh environment of early Nauvoo. Moreover, building both a temporal and a spiritual community imposed extraordinary personal demands. The influx of European converts, along with converts from the United States and Canada, provided a numerical and psychological boost to the new community, but it taxed Nauvoo's resources to provide work, food, and homes for the new settlers.[31] Old skills had to be abandoned when they proved useless in a new setting, and new ways of supporting families had to be employed. Men, women, and children were all engaged in finding ways to sustain themselves and their community even as they were adjusting to a new way of life as Latter-day Saints.

Unfortunately, because of the swampy conditions in Nauvoo, sickness became a rite of passage for settlers. Each week the *Nauvoo Neighbor* published the names of those who had succumbed to the deadly malaria, along with a litany of other ailments that attacked the populace.[32] As traditional caregivers, women carried much of the burden of these debilitating diseases, often while suffering from their symptoms themselves. "We were now a family of invalids," Sarah Allen exclaimed when she followed her husband and children into the sickbed, her body shaken with chills and fever. "It was very difficult to hire a nurse," she wrote, "and as difficult to keep one on account of so much sickness, so I had to be my own nurse."[33]

When the entire Woolley family were bedridden with chills and fever, they paid money "for every pail of water brought into the house," more than a few pails needed to quench the thirst of a family of eight. When Rachel Woolley felt the chills coming back some time later she "stamped her feet and said most emphatically, three times[,] I won't have another chill, and I didn't nor haven't had one of that kind up to the present time [1881]." Perhaps others should have tried her remedy.[34]

Women nursed their neighbors as well as their families. Little Margaret Judd remembered going with her mother "around among [our] sick neighbors nursing and helping them," fully expecting the neighbors would do the same for them if needed.[35] Elizabeth Kirby, a young widow from Canada, found nursing financially disappointing but dependable employment.[36] Immigrant Mary Ann Maughan scarcely had time to unload her luggage before she was called to nurse William and Caroline Pitt, fellow Saints from England, who were suffering from the ague. When her husband was bedridden from the complaint for a year, Mary Ann claimed that it "was the hardest one of my life, as I had to provide for a family of eight in the best way I could."[37] Even Charlotte Haven, a highly critical non-Mormon visitor to Nauvoo, acknowledged the selfless service of two Mormon midwives who attended the birth of her nephew. "A kind heart in this place," she observed, "can always be active."[38]

If life in Nauvoo was often physically and emotionally draining, it also offered camaraderie and social exchange. Like other community builders, Nauvoo residents brought their own forms of amusement, and games, sports, musicals, dramas, and dances reflected southern, eastern, New England, Canadian, and British customs and traditions. Homes were the first social centers, but after Joseph Smith completed the Mansion House, it became the setting for many spirited social gatherings.[39] Outdoor events such as visiting circuses and other amusements attracted thousands to the grove, situated just below the temple hill, where Latter-day Saints gathered in the summer months for religious meetings. In the style of the revivalist camps, they sat on makeshift benches, on the ground, on their horses, and in their wagons, listening to two- and three-hour sermons by the Prophet Joseph and other leaders. When the Prophet spoke, time passed quickly for listeners like Elizabeth Howe, who vividly recalled that his words "thrilled my whole being."[40]

But for style and pageantry, nothing could match the mustering of the Nauvoo militia and its parades. Performed on the prairies near Joseph Smith's farm east of the city, the troops gathered for inspection to the accompaniment of at least one and often two bands. Emma Smith rode beside her husband, who was smartly outfitted in a uniform befitting his position as lieutenant general, their horses colorfully decorated and plumed. "The Prophet was a very dignified looking man," Mary Field Garner recalled, "and in his uniform of General of the Nauvoo Legion he was noble and kingly looking. His voice was clear and distinct and he could take command of his men in a very intelligent way. We were proud to call him our leader at all times."[41] Emily Partridge thought the Prophet looked "grand on his big black horse 'Charley' and dressed in his uniform as Lieutenant General." She

Joseph Smith mustering the Nauvoo Legion, from a C. C. A. Christensen painting

remembered Emma accompanying him either on horseback or in a carriage. "Emma looked well on a horse," she recalled. "She was a large and noble looking woman. She generally rode the chestnut horse, 'Joe Duncan.'"[42]

Cruising the Mississippi on the Church-owned steamship *Maid of Iowa,* ordinarily used to bring immigrants to the city, offered respite on a hot, muggy summer evening. Dancing parties on deck and picnics aboard were a feature of the summer itinerary for many Nauvoo residents. But the river was more than a scene of summer excursions and winter skating. For many, it was the heartbeat of the city, bringing the steamships to Nauvoo with goods, mail, and passengers and then carrying the ships away loaded with cargo and travelers destined for other ports. The freight they deposited was sustenance for the growing city, but their human cargo was its life.

The river landings were the most important social centers of Nauvoo. The arrival of new converts, the return of long-absent missionaries, and the reunion of families and friends long separated made the landings, one at the south end of Main Street near the Nauvoo House and the other at the north end of town, scenes of excitement and

*Nauvoo dock, one of the steamboat landings in Nauvoo,
located at the south end of Main Street*

expectation. Mary Bennett's joy at reaching Nauvoo mirrored the feelings of most of the new converts. After six hard weeks on the Atlantic, the Bennetts and the other immigrants traveling with them finally reached New Orleans, only to find the *Maid of Iowa* embargoed and lashed to the wharf. Mary, a woman of wealth in England, provided the money to lift the embargo, outfit the steamer, and secure a crew to enable the travelers to continue their journey. During the five-week passage upriver, they encountered insults and persecutions, a furious gale, loss of steam power, mob threats at several ports, and a nearly fatal fire on board. Word of their difficulties preceded them, and a large welcoming crowd gathered at the dock in anticipation of their arrival, Joseph Smith among the number. When the boat finally docked, Joseph made his way to Mary Bennett and blessed her for "so materially aiding the saints."[43]

Seeing the Prophet for the first time was a notable experience recorded by many immigrants. New convert Mary Alice Lambert was thrilled to recognize him without introduction as the steamboat arrived at the Nauvoo landing. "I knew him the instant my eyes rested upon him, and at that moment I received my testimony that he was a Prophet of God," she wrote.[44] Priscilla Staines was certain she would recognize him at first glance and was gratified that her intuition was verified when the man she had settled upon instantly boarded the boat and made himself known to the travelers as the Prophet.[45]

Returning to the city after a period away from it was almost as moving an experience as seeing Nauvoo for the first time. Several days before reaching the city, on her return from a visit to relatives in Maine, Louisa Follett expressed her longing "to gaze on[c]e more on the beloved City of the Saints . . . and to meete in the assembly of the Saints and again be privileged with hearing the words of eternal life." After arriving safely "at the Stone House [a hotel near the ferry landing] where we met with a most cordial welcome from our friends and relatives," she traveled to the temple site where she viewed with "wonder and amazement the magnificence of that beautiful Struc-ture." She had visited "Babylon" for the last time, she said, hoping never to return.[46]

But even as the Nauvoo landings heralded seasons of joy and reunion, they also initiated periods of loneliness, the partings, some permanent, engraving their images on saddened hearts. The landing at the end of Water Street was inked in the memory of Emmeline Har-ris when she said good-bye to her husband of little more than a year as he boarded a boat to go "downriver" to find work. She little dreamt she was bidding him good-bye forever. "Here I was brought to this great city by one to whom I ever expected to look for protection," she wrote a few months later, "and left dependent on the mercy and friendship of strangers."[47] Louisa Pratt also viewed the river as a scene of sorrow. With unrestrained weeping, she and her four young daugh-ters stood on one of Nauvoo's landings to bid farewell to their husband and father, leaving to fulfill a Church mission to Tahiti. They would not meet again until they were all in Utah, five long years later.[48] Lucy and Jane Walker and their eight siblings, whose mother had died soon after they arrived in Nauvoo, also watched their father travel out of their lives in answer to a mission call.[49] Like Emmeline Harris, these and the many other divided families looked to their own resources and the compassion of others in the absence of their traditional providers.

In such instances, women's emotional needs became as great an incentive as their material requirements for developing friendship networks. Their faith and conviction were contagious, buoying up lagging spirits while testifying of their commitment to the work of the restoration, whatever the sacrifice. Women's traditional ritual of visiting served as a powerful agent of female community in Nauvoo. Their personal writings map the territory of this female world in all its dimensions. Sarah Kimball and Rachel Ivins formed a lifelong friendship in Nauvoo that survived Rachel's temporary disaffection and return to New Jersey in 1844. Jane Richards recounted her friendship with Julia Farnsworth, the kind, helpful, motherly way of Mrs. Leavitt, the intelligence and kindness of Jenetta Richards, "respected by everybody." She treasured her special relationship with other apostles' wives—Vilate Kimball, Leonora Taylor, and Phebe Woodruff.

Visiting linked not only individuals but also families in ever-widening spheres of association and affiliation. The Riches, Hubbards, and Kimballs, for instance, found themselves neighbors in Nauvoo and immediately created a small community of their own. On one side of the Riches were the Hubbards, who had aided Charles and Sarah Rich upon their arrival in Nauvoo. On the other side lived Vilate Kimball, in the small log cabin her husband had hastily built for her before leaving for England with the other apostles. "We soon became strong friends to each other," Sarah wrote, "and we felt for each others interest." If the Riches "had any nice things to eat that [Vilate] did not have we shared it with her," Sarah remembered, "and she did the same by us." They all experienced "many trying circumstances together," taking "solid comfort together." Vilate opened her small home for meetings in which her family, the Riches, Hubbards, and other neighbors worshipped together. "We then, as a people were united and were more like one family than like strangers," Sarah wrote.[50]

Midwives, such as Patty Sessions and Zina Young, visited others almost daily, entering into the lives of many families in their round of duties. They served as a common point of connection among Nauvoo families. They also found time to visit solely for sociability. Scarcely a day passed that Zina Young did not visit or receive someone—women friends or family members who came together just to visit. Patty Sessions and Lucy Mack Smith became great friends, exchanging visits regularly. Mother Smith often stayed with Patty while Patty's husband served a mission in the eastern states.

Elizabeth Ann Whitney recounted another kind of kinship that developed among some Nauvoo women. Only a minority of women encountered the principle of plural marriage in Nauvoo, some immediately rejecting it, while others were converted to the doctrine. One of the earliest women to engage in plural marriage, Elizabeth Ann found it to be a positive experience and learned much about her sister Saints that she had not known. "Instead of my opinion of women being unfavorable or my feelings unkindly," she wrote, "I am more favorably disposed to women as a class, learning more of the true nature of woman-kind than I ever could without this peculiar experience."[51]

As if their compassionate service, social visits, and Relief Society meetings were not enough, women also gathered in informal groups for prayer and spiritual uplift.[52] Their reciprocal visits and spiritual gatherings interwove many strands of the social fabric of Nauvoo, binding and unifying the community in an informal social structure based on women's traditional modes of relating to each other and to their communities. Their writings indicate that family and friends often blended into a single "kinship" network, binding women together in ties of mutual support and companionship. A common faith and shared experience strengthened those bonds. "Behold how lovely it is for Friends to dwell together in unity," Zina Young effused. "O God," she prayed, "ever let union Prevail."[53]

Visiting did more than link women together in social networks and create a strong collective identity, however. The webs of relationships that developed among women also helped to shape the society in which they lived.[54] Before the institutionalization of such services, women provided health and welfare assistance, instituted and maintained cultural and educational programs, and created social and recreational activities. Often, the success of their domestic economy determined the survival of a settlement and, certainly, that of their own families. The extent to which women were willing and able to render such service determined the quality of life in the community.

Small, informal alliances of women frequently burgeoned into citywide collectives, extending the reach of their service. In Nauvoo, for instance, the Relief Society began with a small group of women who were all connected as neighbors, relatives, or fellow boarders with Emma Smith or with other founding members. Soon membership grew to reflect a broad section of the Mormon community, expanding the reach of their affiliative ties in a mutual aim to improve Nauvoo's material and moral welfare. Similarly, from the women who received the temple ordinances from Joseph Smith in Nauvoo came a small sisterhood of temple workers that expanded with the building of each new temple in the West. Upon reaching the Salt Lake Valley in 1847, Eliza R. Snow sent back to her sister temple workers who waited in Winter Quarters a short poem that anticipated the continuation of their temple service, concluding with the lines: "Come along, you holy women, / And your blessings here impart."[55]

Because of the dramatic impact of temple worship on that first generation of Latter-day Saints, the women who were authorized to minister to their sisters in the temple were esteemed as holy women and formed the heart of the growing network of women endowed in the House of the Lord. Such religious service, along with their visiting and task-oriented groups, involved women in both the material and the spiritual life of the community, their overlapping networks proving to be an important cohesive element.

The features that most distinguished the religious experiences of Nauvoo women from those of other women of their time were the unique principles and practices of Mormonism. More compelling than the demanding rituals of daily living, and often serving as an antidote to them, was their immersion in the life of the spirit. The spiritual meetings that gathered families and neighbors together in each other's homes intertwined the religious with the familial. "I never missed a meeting when it was in my power to go," Elizabeth Kirby recalled, remembering especially the prayer meeting when "Sister Wheeler sang in tongues and the gift of interpretation was given to me."[56] Non-Mormon Charlotte Haven attended several of these Sunday evening cottage meetings and found each time "the room well filled" and the meetings "orderly" though unstructured, everyone "at liberty to speak."[57]

The merging of their everyday and religious lives developed among the women strong spiritual as well as social kinships. Manifestations of the Spirit, as experienced by Elizabeth Kirby, were quiet demonstrations of a unity of faith, expressed within the sanctuary of friendship. Spiritual gifts gave witness to the true gospel, and its restoration brought an inevitable renewal of these spiritual entitlements. Dependence on faith endowed the most homely act with a supernal significance, and in the presence of untreatable illness, many turned to this restorative power.

Elizabeth Ann Whitney was one of several women set apart by Joseph Smith "to administer to the sick and comfort the sorrowful" through the power of faith, a service that she provided throughout her long life and that won her the honored title "Mother Whitney."[58] Always steadfast and wise from experience, she was often sought after for counsel and guidance. Drusilla Hendricks turned to Mother Whitney when she was undecided about how best to provide for her family. Feeling that Mother Whitney had special spiritual insight because she "had had her endowments," Drusilla asked for direction and received spiritual confirmation from Elizabeth Ann of her desire to go to St. Louis to earn money for needed supplies.[59] Abigail Leonard also drew on this reserve force of spiritual power when she called in the sisters to administer to a young British convert with whom she shared her home. "They came, washed, anointed, and administered to her," Abigail wrote, noting that the young woman's health speedily returned.[60]

The slowly rising temple merged the temporal and the spiritual. Not only was it becoming a visual focal point of the flourishing city, as it rose high on the bluffs overlooking the river, but even more—it was the spiritual focus of the people.

The laying of the cornerstones on April 6, 1841, was a grand affair since it also marked the anniversary of the organization of the Church. The celebration began with an early review of all the companies of the Nauvoo Legion. When Joseph Smith arrived in his full regalia as lieutenant general, the women of Nauvoo presented him with a "beauti-

*Sketch of the
Nauvoo Temple
by Amelia Stevens
Tronslot (ca. 1848)*

ful silk National flag," the ceremony duly hailed by the firing of cannon. The procession then continued on to the temple ground, where a large crowd awaited the service.[61] There could be no doubting the commingling of the worldly and the heavenly in such an event, the pomp and ceremony of the secular world evoked to underscore this significant occasion of the spiritual.

Everyone had a stake in completing the temple and found ways to be included in its construction. As men took their turns building it, setting every tenth day aside to work on it in the beginning, women contributed clothing for the workers and their families, shared their homes with the builders, and offered tithes and other contributions.[62] Many women, Louisa Decker remembered, "sold things that they could scarcely spare" to get money toward its construction, her mother selling her best china dishes and fine bed quilt "to donate her part."[63] Widow Elizabeth Kirby gave the only possession she had with which, she said, she would grieve to part: her husband's watch. "I gave it," she explained, "to help build the Nauvoo Temple and everything else I could possibly spare and the last few dollars that I had in the world, which altogether amounted to nearly $50."[64]

By November 1841 the temple baptismal font was in use, but another four years passed before any other rooms were in service. Rather than diminishing enthusiasm, the death of Joseph Smith before the temple was finished inspired the Saints to press for its full completion. Finally, in October 1845, it was far enough along to house a church conference, and by the next month the attic story was ready to be dedicated.[65]

Their assistance in building a holy edifice was not unique to LDS women, but what was to transpire within temples was a distinctive expression of their religious belief. Unlike the sacred rituals of other religious groups, the temple ordinances, the most sacred of Mormonism's religious rites, required women's participation to receive the ordinances for themselves and to act as officiators and as proxies for others. The restoration of temple worship meant that they would experience the sealing powers of the priesthood, linking husbands and wives in eternal marriage and binding families together from generation to generation;[66] it meant that they would enter into the covenants and receive the keys that would lead them to exaltation; and it also meant that they would themselves perform their portion of those saving ordinances, officiating at the temple alongside their brethren.[67]

Emma Smith was the first woman to receive the ordinances. She, in turn, administered the initiatory rites to other women, including Bathsheba W. Smith, who felt privileged to receive them from the Prophet's wife and "to be led and taught . . . by the prophet himself who explained and enlarged wonderfully upon every point."[68] Bathsheba later became a lifelong temple worker and served as matron of the Salt Lake Temple.

Another early participant was Mary Ellen Kimball, who, when she saw the temple for the first time, admired its beauty both within and without, feeling "a reverential awe knowing [it] to be the temple of God built by revelation." Deeply moved by the physically and spiritually empowering promises of the initiatory ordinances administered to her by her sister wife, Vilate, she was overwhelmed by a sense of "love and admiration" for her. "I know her to be a Saint," Mary Ellen wrote. "No one could fill that position so well without the spirit of our Saviour to assist them to do it."[69]

Louisa Barnes Pratt also found the temple and its ordinances to be an important spiritual addition to her life. After receiving her own endowment, she longed to stay in the temple throughout the day to keep hold of the spirit she felt there, but the press of numbers prevented her. Many visits followed, however, and she was delighted to go through "the stately edifice and examine the varied apartments, the architecture of which was dictated by the wisdom of God."[70]

It was through their ministrations in these holy places that many women most felt their connection to the sacred work of the restoration and experienced the spiritual power and holy calling of religious service. In receiving and administering the saving ordinances of the gospel, they found new ways to show their discipleship to the Savior. Noting the devoted temple service of Eliza R. Snow, Emmeline Wells recalled that she was one of the first women who "ministered in the [Nauvoo] Temple in the holy rites that pertain to the house of the Lord as priestess and Mother in Israel to hundreds of her sex."[71]

Eliza R. Snow and Vilate Kimball were only two of thirty-six women who have been identified as ordinance workers in the Nauvoo Temple, working around the clock during the winter of 1845-46 to administer the rites to as many women as possible before the exodus. "I worked in the Temple every day without cessation until it was closed," recalled Elizabeth Ann Whitney, another one of the thirty-six. "I gave myself, my time and attention to that mission."[72] Dozens of other women washed the clothing and prepared the food that physically sustained the workers.[73]

Elizabeth Ann Whitney's pleasure in temple service was exceeded only by the joy she felt in giving birth to the child who, she explained, was the first to be "born heir to the Holy Priesthood and in the New and Everlasting Covenant in this dispensation." Having been sealed to her husband by the Prophet Joseph just a few months before, Elizabeth Ann treasured the knowledge that her daughter was the first child to receive that cherished birthright in this dispensation.[74]

The purpose of the gathering, Joseph Smith explained, was to build a temple wherein one could learn the way and receive the ordinances leading to exaltation. Thus, the temple has always been the focal point of LDS worship. Before the Mormon exodus from Nauvoo in 1846, more than five thousand men and women were able to receive their endowments and other blessings in the Nauvoo Temple. Yet many who had left homes and loved ones to gather with the Saints were unable to receive these ordinances in Nauvoo, having to postpone that experience until temples were built in the West.[75]

For members of the Jolly family, the temple formed their primary experience in Nauvoo. Sarah Pippen Jolly's husband and sons answered the call to give all of their time to building the temple, the family surviving on little more than corn bread and water for long periods of time. "But it was good," Sarah recalled. "I don't complain. I had the privilege of going through the temple with my husband so I am paid for all of my trouble."[76]

This same spirit guided the Saints' decision to formally dedicate the temple even though they had abandoned Nauvoo before it was totally completed. A private dedication occurred the evening of April 30, 1846, and the public dedicatory services took place during the following three days. Few of those already on the trail to Winter Quarters returned for the dedication, but one who did was fourteen-year-old Elvira Stevens. Orphaned in Nauvoo and traveling west with her sister and brother-in-law, Elvira crossed the Mississippi three times to attend the services, the only member of her wagon company to do so. "The heavenly power was so great," she wrote, "I then crossed and recrossed to be benefitted by it, as young as I was."[77] Elvira had not yet received the temple ordinances, but the spiritual power of the edifice itself and the circumstances of its dedication remained prominent memories of her brief and troubled life in Nauvoo.

Adding to the rich spiritual dimension of the lives of these Nauvoo women were their patriarchal blessings. Though personal and individualized, the blessings were also universal in their spiritual investment, declaring to women their royal lineage in the house of Israel and assigning them specific spiritual tasks and privileges. Along with the temple endowment, patriarchal blessings revealed additional ways for women to express their faith in the Savior and their service to his church. The blessings confirmed the women's place "within the grace of the covenant," and their participation in the blessings of Abraham. Many were promised wisdom, inspiration, knowledge, and spiritual power to influence and bless the lives of their families and associates.

Like the revelation given to Emma Smith in 1830 (D&C 25),[78] these blessings charged women to "teach, instruct, and counsel." The women were also admonished to use their faith to bless the sick, rebuke the adversary, and discern evil for the benefit of their families.[79] Consider the promises given to Elizabeth Barlow Thompson. The patriarch told her she would receive all of the "blessings of mother Sarah of old." These included "a renewed gift of wisdom, knowledge, light and understanding" and, she was told, "many will come to thee for counsel and advice and they shall go away happy and contented." The patriarch, recognizing that she was a woman close to the Spirit and willing to extend the reach of her nurturing, further said to her: "You will have great influence with thy sex for good . . . the young and rising generation [shall] come to thee for advice and instructions and thou shalt bless them and they shall bless thee."

Such promises were not confined to the Nauvoo period. In 1876 Martha Riggs, like many others, was blessed that she would "become mighty in the midst of thy sisters . . . and thou shall have a knowledge by which thou shall teach the Daughters of Zion how to live, for it shall be required unto thee from the heavens." These promised experiences of spiritual reciprocity characterized women's relationships within the Church, and such exchanges of support, instruction, and blessing not only strengthened their sense of sisterhood but also bound them together in shared testimony of God's ruling hand in their lives.

Besides receiving gifts of "wisdom, knowledge, and light" to benefit the community of Saints, women whose family ties had been severed at their conversion found solace in the knowledge that they would "stand as a savior in the midst of [their] father and mother's house." A salve to many aching hearts was the promise that because the women chose to embrace the gospel of Jesus Christ, they would be instruments in reuniting their families in an eternal union through the ordinances of the temple.[80]

The bonds of spiritual kinship that embraced the women of Nauvoo were strengthened and expanded on March 17, 1842, when Joseph Smith organized the Relief Society. "I have desired to organize the Sisters in the order of the Priesthood," Sarah Kimball remembered his saying when she presented her proposal for a charitable society. "I now have the key by which I can do it," he said. "The organization of the Church of Christ was never perfect until the women were organized."[81] The Relief Society was thus perceived as more than a facility for charity or a commission of moral stewardship. It was to be an integral part of the Church, giving women a distinct ecclesiastical identity.

Like a spiritual magnet, the new organization drew women into membership in ever-increasing numbers, some even ferrying across the river from Montrose to attend its meetings.[82] Before its final session in Nauvoo in 1844, it numbered nearly thirteen hundred members. In looking after the material and spiritual needs of the community, it provided an institutional seal to the solicitude that already informed the relationships of the women of Nauvoo.[83] Its rapid growth bespeaks their strong desire to preserve those relationships and to give definition to the strong female community of shared belief and commitment.

Joseph Smith's spiritually charged sermons to the members of the Relief Society instilled in them a powerful sense of their worth as women as well as Latter-day Saints. He had a broad vision of woman's role in the restoration and desired to teach them how they "would come in possession of the privileges & blessings & gifts of the priesthood" that accompanied the restoration of the gospel.[84] The Nauvoo minutes, which inspired and guided the women of the Church for several generations, indicated his hope to make "of the Society a 'kingdom of priest[esses]' as in Enoch's day, as in Paul's day," affirming its connection with the ordinances of the temple.[85] The minutes tell of his delivering to the sisters the keys of knowledge and intelligence, interpreted as both temporal and spiritual, and his encouragement of their

"Benevolence, the Spirit of Relief Society," photo of a bronze plaque by Avard Fairbanks for the Relief Society centennial memorial campanile in Salt Lake City

expression of the gifts of the Spirit, all of which gave them a sense of full citizenship in the restored church.[86]

Nancy Tracy recalled the power of those sermons: "He was so full of the Spirit of the Holy Ghost that his frame shook and his face shone and looked almost transparent."[87] Temple worship, their patriarchal blessings, and the lofty mission of the Relief Society transformed the physical and emotional claims on their lives into a transcendent vision of their part and potential in the great work of restoration.

The Prophet Joseph's death, like his life, emerged as a rallying point for the faithful. Stunned by the news from Carthage, Joseph's followers were at first transfixed in disbelief. The recorded memories of the tragedy distill the confusion and anxiety that followed into one dominant emotion, an overwhelming sense of irretrievable loss. "The mourning of the saints . . . baffles description," recalled Elizabeth Howe Hyde.[88] "Every heart is filled with sorrow, and the very streets of Nauvoo seam to morn," agreed Vilate Kimball, in a letter to her absent husband, Heber.[89] Zina Young noted the enormity of the loss to the Saints of their leaders: "In one day . . . fell the Prophet and Patr[i]arch of the church of the Lat[t]erday Saints," she wrote, "the kind husbands, the affectionate Father, the venerable statesman, the Friends of man kinde, by the hand of a ruthless Mob mixed with desenters."[90]

Joseph's death imposed a strange request upon young Elizabeth Jane Bybee of Carthage. The townspeople had tried unsuccessfully to remove the bloodstains from the room in Carthage jail where the murders had occurred. "They thought that if a Mormon girl came and scrubbed the floor," Elizabeth recalled, "the stains would come out. They came for me, but neither I, or any of the other girls would go."[91]

Memorialized in verse by some of Mormonism's finest poets, the tragedy evoked private poetic expression, such as Louisa Follett's simple but moving stanza: "Oh Illinois," she wrote, "thy soul has drunk the blood, / Of prophets martyred for the Cause of God. / Now Zion mourns—she mourns an earthly head. / The prophet and the Patriarch are dead."[92]

The events leading to and following the martyrdom of Joseph and Hyrum Smith have been rehearsed in every Mormon history book. But only those who experienced them can fully express their meaning in human, rather than institutional, terms. Joseph Smith was the source of authority and symbol of authenticity for the Church. As its Prophet he was also Christ's representative on earth and his people's spiritual center. His death thus became another time of decision for some. But the sifting process left a strong corps of believers in the principles he had taught in Nauvoo, followers who were "more united than ever before," Zina Young observed. "The faithful are determined to keep the law of God," she affirmed, " . . . to finish the temple . . . and claim the blessings that had ben promised to us as a people by Joseph, A Man of God, and I believe after Gods own hart."[93]

Zina Young knew that the temple would be the focus of the Church's last years in Nauvoo. It was central to the faith and represented the culmination of Joseph Smith's ministry. Dedicating themselves to its completion was affirmation of their faith in the slain

Prophet and their testimony to the divinity of his mission. Work on it continued despite the growing rumblings of anti-Mormons.

Those who lived outside Nauvoo were the first to note the discontent when the murder of Joseph failed to decimate the Church. Harassment turned to violence as houses and crops were burned and lives threatened. "Days of watching and nights of terror" dominated the lives of Mormons in the settlements, wrote Mary Jane Mount Tanner, and many began to move into Nauvoo. As non-Mormons took over the vacated houses, she lamented that the homes of the neighbors with whose children she had played were filled with strangers.[94]

Mary Field Garner was only a child when the Prophet died, but the events that followed remained deeply etched in her memory. Because the six Field children and their widowed mother were among those too poor to begin the long westward journey when the Church left Nauvoo in February 1846, they felt the full force of mob violence the following summer. They watched the mobbers desecrate the temple, ransack and burn homes, and hold mock baptisms in the river. Finally driven from the city, the Fields decided to remain on Nickerson Island across from Nauvoo for the winter, returning to the city the next spring when peace was finally restored. "We were glad to be back in our beloved Nauvoo where we could have food and shelter," Mary wrote. But it was not the same. "We were lonely for the other Saints and our leaders, and the place seemed so quiet and deserted, for the spirit of love and unity had gone with the Saints."[95]

It was three years before the Fields were able to leave, Mary's mother having remarried while Mary worked for a friend in a neighboring village to help raise sufficient money. When all was ready, Mary's stepfather suddenly died, leaving her mother once again the sole caretaker of her children. Harnessing all of their resources, material and emotional, the family finally made their way to the Salt Lake Valley. Her faith was clearly the driving force in the life of Mary Garner's mother, compensating her for the tremendous personal loss and physical struggle she experienced after becoming a Latter-day Saint.

The "battle of Nauvoo," recounted in many of the reminiscences in this volume, left other widows and orphans in its wake, most of them bereft of personal goods as well. The Saints were leaving Illinois much as they had arrived seven years earlier, taking with them little more than their faith. That faith would take them to another gathering place, another "cornerstone of Zion," another region to regroup and build again. But it would be different from Nauvoo. The seven years spent by the Saints in Nauvoo, wrote Eliza R. Snow, "is a history that never will, and *never can* 'repeat itself.'"[96]

How can such steadfastness be explained? There were always alternatives, and there were those who opted for them. But the women in this study stayed the course. Maybe Phebe Chase best expressed the conviction that sustained them. In a letter to her unconverted children she wrote: "The Lord has blest us in obeying his command in gathering with the saints and helping on the work of the latter-day w[h]ich you think is not the work of the lord[,] but my children it is the work of the lord for no man ever could bring about so great and so marvelous a work."[97]

The inexplicable power of faith perplexes reason. It neither invites nor warrants intellectual understanding, for it functions in a realm that cannot be reached by empirical means. The study of the soul, as one historian wryly noted, has not yet become the subject of historical inquiry. But whether as believers or unbelievers, historians cannot fully come to terms with the experience of women of the past without acknowledging the dominant place of religion in their lives. It has defined them as women and structured their social and familial roles. The quality of faith, however, is less yielding to analysis. Deeply embedded in one's psyche, it is elusive and resistant to the scholar's inquiry. But its effect is clearly discernible. As a powerful motivation in the lives of individuals, it cannot be relegated to the periphery of the human story, however indefinable it may be to the scholar.

No intellectual exercise is necessary to recognize that faith was the impelling force that brought the women of this volume to the Church and bound them to it. None of them doubted God's overruling power, and heaven, to them, held this life's unfulfilled promises and the rewards of the faithful. This volume is a testament to the compelling power of faith.

It was inevitable that their collective faith would create strong bonds of community among them, especially when their "faith and their work were so in tune with [their] every day lives," as one woman remembered.[98] Bonded by a shared stewardship and enfolded and linked by the covenant of the gospel, they found that their sisterhood, the sense of community that unified and embraced them, was not an end in itself. Rather, it became the means to maintaining a collective identity and toward creating a base of support and strength from which they would meet the demands and challenges of establishing the Church and living the restored gospel.

Zina Young, a natural agent of female community, resonated with the power of this solidarity. "It is a blessing to meet together," she wrote after one of the many women's gatherings she attended. "The Spirit of God is here, and when we speak to one another, it is like oil going from vessel to vessel."[99] Perhaps we too can experience the blessing and uniting power invoked by that image and feel their deep sense of shared faith and loving community as these women speak to us from out of their own writings.

NOTES

1. With the intention of making Independence, Missouri, its central headquarters, The Church of Jesus Christ of Latter-day Saints (Mormon) had moved, from its beginnings in 1830 in New York, to Ohio and thence to Missouri. Conflict between the Mormons and the Missourians led Governor Lilburn W. Boggs to formally order the expulsion of the Mormons, who were forced to find refuge in Quincy, Illinois, in 1838–39 before settling the river town of Commerce, which they renamed Nauvoo.

2. Eliza R. Snow, "Sketch of My Life," 12, microfilm of holograph, LDS Church Archives, Salt Lake City, Utah. Original in Bancroft Library.

3. "Joseph Smith, the Prophet," *Young Woman's Journal* 16 (December 1905): 553.

4. James E. Smith, "Frontier Nauvoo, Building a Picture from Statistics," *Ensign* (September 1979): 17–19. See also Susan Easton Black, "New Insights Replace Old Traditions: Membership of the Church in Nauvoo, 1839–1846," 8–9, unpublished paper in possession of author.

5. Two recent publications have begun to rectify the omission of such women from history. See Jill Mulvay Derr, Janath Russell Cannon, and Maureen Ursenbach Beecher, *Women of Covenant: The Story of Relief Society* (Salt Lake City: Deseret Book, 1992), and Richard Neitzel and Jeni Broberg Holzapfel, *Women of Nauvoo* (Salt Lake City: Bookcraft, 1992).

6. Patriarchal blessing given to Nancy Naomi Alexander Tracy by O. N. Liljenquist, June 27, 1891, found in "Life History of Nancy Naomi Alexander Tracy Written by Herself," 74–75, Special Collections, Harold B. Lee Library, Brigham Young University, Provo, Utah.

7. Quoted in Edward W. Tullidge, *The Women of Mormondom* (New York: Tullidge & Crandall, 1877), 288.

8. Mary Field Garner, "Autobiography," typescript, LDS Church Archives; also in Special Collections, Harold B. Lee Library, Brigham Young University, Provo, Utah. A variant account is in Kate B. Carter, comp., *Our Pioneer Heritage*, 20 vols. (Salt Lake City: Daughters of Utah Pioneers, 1964), 7:406–14.

9. "Autobiography of Electa C. Williams," in the papers of Emily Stevenson, microfilm of typescript, LDS Church Archives.

10. "Reminiscences of Mary Ann Stearns Winters," typescript, LDS Church Archives, original in private possession.

11. Helen Mar Whitney, "Scenes in Nauvoo," *Woman's Exponent* 10 (July 15, 1881): 26.

12. Bathsheba Smith, "Reminiscence," holograph, LDS Church Archives.

13. Leonora Cannon Taylor to John Taylor, September 9, 1839, original in John Taylor Collection, LDS Church Archives; also edited by Ronald K. Esplin and published under "Sickness and Faith: Nauvoo Letters," in *BYU Studies* 15 (Summer 1975): 425–34.

14. Ellen Douglas to Father and Mother, June 2, 1842, Nauvoo, Illinois, typescript, in Martha Deseret Grant Boyle Collection, LDS Church Archives.

15. George A. Smith to Wilford Woodruff, April 13, 1845, Nauvoo, Illinois, holograph, LDS Church Archives.

16. John Benbow and Thomas Kington, with their wives, were among the 999 United Brethren who converted almost en masse to Mormonism. Both were substantial yeoman farmers and leaders in their church and community. Both contributed to the emigration of many Latter-day Saints in the 1840s. Their wives had each received small legacies from their fathers, which they contributed toward the publication of the Book of Mormon, *Millennial Star*, and a British hymnbook. See James B. Allen, Ronald K. Esplin, and David J. Whittaker, *Men with a Mission, 1837–1841: The Quorum of the Twelve Apostles in the British Isles* (Salt Lake City: Deseret Book, 1992), 124, 151, 248.

17. "A History of Ann Welch Crookston," typescript, LDS Church Archives.

18. Drusilla Dorris Hendricks, "Historical Sketch of James Hendricks and Drusilla Hendricks," 24, typescript, LDS Church Archives.

19. Emily Dow Partridge Young, "Incidents in the Life of a Mormon Girl," 50–51,

typescript, LDS Church Archives. See also "Eliza Marie Partridge Lyman," and "Emily Dow Partridge Young" in Carter, *Our Pioneer Heritage* 19:255–58, 262–64.

20. "Journal of Louisa Barnes Pratt," in Kate B. Carter, comp., *Heart Throbs of the West,* 13 vols. (Salt Lake City: Daughters of the Utah Pioneers, 1947), 8:228–29.

21. "Autobiography of Mary Rollins Lightner," typescript, Special Collections, Harold B. Lee Library, Brigham Young University, Provo, Utah.

22. Ann Pitchforth provided seeds for Leonora Cannon's small garden, in exchange for which Leonora willingly shared the mature produce. Ann Hughlings Pitchforth to her parents, May 1845, Nauvoo, Illinois, Special Collections, Harold B. Lee Library, Brigham Young University, Provo, Utah.

23. "A Sketch of the Life of Mrs. Sarah Burbank," from *Pioneer Journals,* typescript, Special Collections, Harold B. Lee Library, Brigham Young University, Provo, Utah.

24. *Times and Seasons* 2 (October 1, 1841): 566.

25. Drusilla Hendricks, "Historical Sketch," 24.

26. "A History of Ann Welch Crookston."

27. Mary Ives to Parents and Friends, c. 1840, in Amos L. Underwood Correspondence, 1831–1853, photocopy, LDS Church Archives.

28. "Louisa Barnes Pratt," in Carter, *Heart Throbs of the West* 8:228.

29. "A History of Ann Welch Crookston."

30. Matilda Streeper to her brother, March 28, 1844, photocopy of holograph, LDS Church Archives.

31. For data on British immigrants see Richard L. Jensen, "Transplanted to Zion: The Impact of British Latter-day Saint Immigration upon Nauvoo," *BYU Studies* 31 (Winter 1991): 76–87.

32. For a detailed analysis of the subject of death and disease in Nauvoo, see M. Guy Bishop, Vincent Lacey, and Richard Wixon, "Death at Mormon Nauvoo, 1843–1845," *Western Illinois Regional Studies* 19 (Fall 1986): 70–83.

33. "Sarah Beriah Fiske Allen Ricks," in Carter, *Our Pioneer Heritage* 11:138.

34. Rachel Emma Woolley Simmons, "Reminiscences and Journals, 1881–1891," holograph, LDS Church Archives.

35. Margaret Gay Judd Clawson, "Rambling Reminiscences of Margaret Gay Judd Clawson," holograph, LDS Church Archives.

36. Elizabeth Terry Kirby Heward, "A Sketch of the Life of Elizabeth Terry Heward," typescript, 13, 15, LDS Church Archives.

37. "Journal of Mary Ann Weston Maughan," in Carter, *Our Pioneer Heritage* 2:363, 370.

38. Charlotte Haven, "A Girl's Letters from Nauvoo," February 19, 1843, Nauvoo, Illinois, as printed in *The Overland Monthly* (San Francisco), December 1890, 622–24.

39. Helen Mar Whitney gives a detailed account of some of the social activities of

Nauvoo in "Scenes and Incidents in Nauvoo," *Woman's Exponent* 11 (November 15, 1882): 90.

40. Elizabeth Howe Hyde, in Myrtle Stevens Hyde Collection, microfilm, LDS Church Archives.

41. Mary Field Garner, "Autobiography."

42. Emily Dow Partridge Young, "Diary and Reminiscence," February 1874–November 1899, typescript, LDS Church Archives.

43. This incident is recounted in at least three sources: Jannetta Platts Rigby, "Biographical Sketch of Mary Ann Bennett Kay Burrup," microfilm, LDS Church Archives; "Priscilla Mogridge Staines," in Tullidge, *The Women of Mormondom*, 289–91; Helen Mar Whitney, "Scenes and Incidents in Nauvoo," 90.

44. *Young Woman's Journal* 16 (December 1905): 554.

45. "Priscilla Mogridge Staines," in Tullidge, *The Women of Mormondom*, 291.

46. Louisa Follett, Diary, September 7, 1845, typescript, LDS Church Archives. The original manuscript is located at the State Historical Society of Iowa.

47. Emmeline B. Wells, Diary, February 20, 1845, Special Collections, Harold B. Lee Library, Brigham Young University, Provo, Utah.

48. Journal of Louisa Barnes Pratt as quoted in Kenneth W. Godfrey, Audrey M. Godfrey, and Jill Mulvay Derr, *Women's Voices: An Untold History of the Latter-day Saints, 1830–1900* (Salt Lake City: Deseret Book, 1982), 13–14.

49. Lucy Walker Smith Kimball, "Autobiography," photocopy of holograph, LDS Church Archives.

50. "Journal of Sarah Pea Rich," typescript, 18–19, copy in possession of author.

51. Elizabeth Ann Whitney, "A Leaf from an Autobiography," *Woman's Exponent* 7 (January 1, 1879): 115.

52. "Patty Sessions," *Woman's Exponent* 13 (November 15, 1884): 94–95.

53. Zina Diantha Huntington Jacobs, Nauvoo Diary, March 10, 1845, and November 17, 1844, as quoted in Maureen Ursenbach Beecher, "'All Things Move in Order in the City': The Nauvoo Diary of Zina Diantha Huntington Jacobs," *BYU Studies* 19 (Spring 1979): 313. The original diary is in the LDS Church Archives. See also pages 69–87 in this volume.

54. An extended discussion of the community value of female visiting among Quaker women is Nancy Tomes, "The Quaker Connection: Visiting Patterns among Women in the Philadelphia Society of Friends, 1750–1800," in Michael Zuckerman, ed., *Friends and Neighbors: Group Life in America's First Plural Society* (Philadelphia: Temple University Press, 1982), 174–95. The parallels with Mormon women's religiously based community life are striking.

55. Eliza R. Snow, "Come to the Valley," *Poems: Religious, Historical, and Political,* 2 vols. (Liverpool: F. D. Richards, 1856), 1:188.

56. Elizabeth Terry Kirby Heward, "A Sketch," September 6, 1843, 13.

57. Charlotte Haven, "A Girl's Letters from Nauvoo," 627.

58. Elizabeth Ann Whitney, "A Leaf from an Autobiography," *Woman's Exponent* 7 (November 15, 1878): 91.

59. Drusilla Hendricks, "Historical Sketch," 25.

60. As quoted in Tullidge, *The Women of Mormondom,* 169. The ritual of washing and anointing was frequently utilized by women in early days for healing, for childbirth, and in temple worship. Because of its association with the temple, it came to be performed exclusively within temples. See Derr, Cannon, and Beecher, *Women of Covenant,* 220–21.

61. Joseph Smith, *History of the Church,* 7 vols. (Salt Lake City: Deseret News, 1949), 4:326–29.

62. "Nauvoo Temple," *Woman's Exponent* 10 (September 1, 1881): 53. See also "Boston Female Penny and Sewing Society," *Times and Seasons* 6 (March 1, 1845): 820, and 6 (March 15, 1845): 847, which notes that one thousand dollars had been collected by Mercy Thompson and Mary Fielding Smith in the penny subscription drive.

63. Louisa Decker, "Reminiscences of Nauvoo," *Woman's Exponent* 37 (March 1909): 41–42.

64. Elizabeth Terry Kirby Heward, "A Sketch," 13.

65. Don F. Colvin, "A Historical Study of the Mormon Temple at Nauvoo, Illinois," master's thesis, Brigham Young University, 1962, 141–42. See also "Nauvoo Temple," *Woman's Exponent* 10 (September 1, 1881): 53.

66. Widow Elizabeth Kirby worried that she "could not obtain her blessings as she was," since she had not been married "for time and eternity" to her first husband, so she decided that "the best thing she could do" was to marry her husband's hired hand, John Heward, who had come to Nauvoo from their native Canada to assist her after her husband died. They were married by Hyrum Smith. Elizabeth Terry Kirby Heward, "A Sketch," 15.

67. At a Relief Society conference in Juab Stake in 1879, President John Taylor explained this partnership: "Our sisters should be prepared to take their position in Zion. Our sisters are really one with us, and when the brethren go into the Temples to officiate for the males, the sisters will go for the females; we operate together for the good of the whole, that we may be united together for time and all eternity." "Relief Society Conference, Juab Stake," *Woman's Exponent* 8 (June 1, 1879): 2.

68. "Latter-day Temples," *Relief Society Magazine* 4 (April 1917): 185–86.

69. Mary Ellen Kimball, Journal, holograph, LDS Church Archives.

70. "Louisa Barnes Pratt," in Carter, *Heart Throbs of the West* 8:235.

71. "Pen Sketch of an Illustrious Woman," *Woman's Exponent* 9 (October 15, 1880): 74. In earlier days, the term "mother in Israel" was often applied to women who contributed exceptional service to the Church or through their teaching, counseling, and blessing others. The term "priestess" was commonly used in the nineteenth century to denote female temple workers.

72. Elizabeth Ann Whitney, "A Leaf From an Autobiography," *Woman's Exponent* 7 (February 15, 1879): 191.

73. For more contemporary details relating to the Nauvoo Temple, see Helen Mar Whitney, "Scenes and Incidents in Nauvoo," *Woman's Exponent* 12 (June 15, 1883): 9–10. A historical account of women's relationship to the temple in the nineteenth century is Carol Cornwall Madsen, "Toward a New Understanding: Mormon Women and the Temple," in Maureen Ursenbach Beecher and Lavina Fielding Anderson, *Sisters in Spirit* (Urbana: University of Illinois Press, 1989), 80–110.

74. Elizabeth Ann Whitney, "A Leaf from an Autobiography," 191. Elizabeth Ann recalls the month as January in this account, although family genealogy puts the date as February 17, 1844.

75. Jensen, "Transplanted to Zion," 83–84.

76. Sarah Pippen Jolly, "Reminiscences," LDS Church Archives.

77. Elvira Stevens Barney, "Ruins of the Nauvoo Temple," comments on postcard pictures of the temple sketched by her sister, LDS Church Archives.

78. A blessing given to Emma Smith in 1834 by her father-in-law reconfirmed the endowment of "understanding" and "power to instruct thy sex." Emma Smith Papers, Archives, Reorganized Church of Jesus Christ of Latter Day Saints, typescript copy in possession of author.

79. See specifically the blessing of Abigail Hall by Isaac Morley, March 21, 1846, Nauvoo, Illinois, and the blessing of Margaret M. Martin by James Adams, July 7, 184? (not clear), Bancroft Library, University of California at Berkeley. See also Elizabeth Ann Whitney, "A Leaf from an Autobiography," *Woman's Exponent* 7 (November 15, 1878): 91. A longer treatment of the value of women's patriarchal blessings in defining their spiritual roles is Carol Cornwall Madsen, "Mothers in Israel: Sarah's Legacy," in Marie Cornwall and Susan Howe, eds., *Women of Wisdom and Knowledge* (Salt Lake City: Deseret Book, 1990), 179–201.

80. Blessing given to Pamela Elizabeth Barlow Thompson by Patriarch Israel Barlow, n.d., LDS Church Archives; blessing given to Martha A. Riggs by Zebedee Coltrin, November 11, 1876, LDS Church Archives; blessing given to Anna Ballantyne by William Smith, Nauvoo, 1845, RLDS Church Archives, typescript copy in possession of author; blessing given to Lydia Savage by Patriarch Lorenzo Hill Hatch, Woodruff, Arizona, March 31, 1900, LDS Church Archives.

81. Sarah M. Kimball, "Early Relief Society Reminiscences," March 17, 1882, Relief Society Record, 1880–1892, LDS Church Archives.

82. "Autobiography of Electa C. Williams," in the papers of Emily Stevenson, microfilm, LDS Church Archives.

83. The death of her husband and thirteen weeks of illness left Ellen Douglas unable to sew clothing or provide other household necessities for her children. Encouraged by a friend to apply to the Relief Society for help, she was overwhelmed at the response. "They brought the wagon and fetched me such a present as I never received before from no place in the world. I suppose the things they sent were

worth as much as 30 shillings." Ellen Douglas to Father, Mother, Sisters and Brothers, Nauvoo, Illinois, April 14, 1844, typescript, LDS Archives.

84. Smith, *History of the Church* 4:602. See also Derr, Cannon, and Beecher, *Women of Covenant,* especially 39–58.

85. In 1906, General Relief Society President Bathsheba W. Smith recalled that Joseph Smith had given the sisters in Nauvoo "instructions that they could administer to the sick and he wanted to make us, as the women were in Paul's day, 'A kingdom of priestesses.' We have the ceremony in our endowments as Joseph taught." "Relief Society Reports [Pioneer Stake]," *Woman's Exponent* 34 (July August 1906): 14.

86. *History of the Church* 4:602; Nauvoo Relief Society Minutes, April 28, 1842; Dean C. Jessee, *The Papers of Joseph Smith,* vol. 2, Journal, 1832–1842 (Salt Lake City: Deseret Book, 1992): 378–79.

87. "Incidents, Travels and Life of Nancy Naomi Alexander Tracy," 24–25.

88. Elizabeth Howe Hyde, brief autobiographical information, in Myrtle Stevens Hyde Papers, microfilm of typescript, LDS Church Archives.

89. Vilate Kimball to Heber C. Kimball, June 30, 1844, as quoted in Ronald K. Esplin, "Life in Nauvoo, June 1844: Vilate Kimball's Martyrdom Letters," *BYU Studies* 19 (Winter 1979): 238. See also pages 138–39 of this volume.

90. Zina Jacobs, Diary, in Beecher, "'All Things Move in Order in the City,'" 292. See also pages 69–87 in this volume.

91. Elizabeth Jane Bybee Smith, "Reminiscences," microfilm of typescript, LDS Church Archives.

92. Louisa Follett, Diary, July 21, 1844, typescript, LDS Church Archives.

93. Zina Jacobs, Diary, in Beecher, "'All Things Move in Order in the City,'" 298, 305. See also pages 69–87 in this volume.

94. Mary Jane Mount Tanner, Diary, typescript notes, LDS Church Archives.

95. Mary Field Garner, "Autobiography." Fanny Young Murray, who also remained, wrote to her sister that Nauvoo "looks like a grave yard," and she hoped to leave it soon. See "Fanny Young Murray to Vilate Young," June 3, 1846, LDS Church Archives.

96. Eliza R. Snow, "Sketch of My Life," 12.

97. Phebe Chase to her children, ca. 1840–1842, in Charles Marsh Correspondence, photocopy, Nauvoo Restoration, Inc., LDS Church Archives.

98. Paraphrased statement of Emmeline B. Wells, from Annie Wells Cannon, "Mothers in Israel," *Relief Society Magazine* 3 (February 1916): 68.

99. Minutes of the Senior and Junior Co-operative Retrenchment Society, October 4, 1874, LDS Church Archives.

IN THEIR OWN WORDS

DIARIES

❧

"In the City of Saints"

"IN THE CITY OF SAINTS"

"A woman's diary," historian Judy Lensink asserts, reflects "a supersubtle design, similar to a quilt's, made up of incremental stitches that define a pattern."[1] The pattern is always unique and may not necessarily conform exactly to the lived life, being the diarist's daily reinvention of it as she selects and arranges and weaves together the information she records. The very act of writing synthesizes the countless rituals and occurrences that comprised the author's day and gives them both permanence and significance.

A woman and her diary. In some minds, the words might conjure up the romantic nineteenth-century image of a woman sitting alone in her room at the close of day before her writing desk, pen and diary in hand, the glow of a burning fire bathing the room in soft light and warmth. Such a picture, however, does not equate with the reality of women's lives in Nauvoo. Finding a private corner in a crowded household, a free moment in a day in which work began before dawn, or a spare piece of paper, not to mention pen and ink, challenged the most assiduous Nauvoo diarist.

Yet they wrote. The need to record their Nauvoo experience as they were living it drove women to become "secret sharers," stealing minutes and private places to put their thoughts on paper. For them, the urge to write, to distill their experiences through the prism of their own words, was too imperative to restrain. "There always seems to be so much to write about, . . . thoughts that come crowding up in throngs," lifelong diarist Emmeline B. Wells once wrote, that "we write to be quit of them, and not let the crowd increase." Certainly Nauvoo gave even the most casual writer ample material to record.

Some women desired to speak to their posterity, to establish an intergenerational continuity and tangibly fix their place in the family line. Other Nauvoo diarists wanted to permanently encapsulate a singular time in their lives by creating a record for future readers. Still others wrote simply because they wanted to hold on to their lives, to confirm the reality and significance of their experience by mentally recreating it and preserving it in the written word. And, of course, there were those whose diaries also played the part of confidante, an alter ego silently receiving the diarist's deepest thoughts and feelings. Their diaries were instruments of self-realization and served as tangible mementos of a doubly lived life—the outer, those events that made up a day, and the inner, the diarist's reflections on and responses to those events.

Whatever their purpose, the diaries of Nauvoo women reclaim their authors' lives and confirm the truth that their lives did indeed count for something and that they were full participants in the events of their time and place.

But even more than their need to assert their identity or justify their lives, the personal narratives of these early Latter-day Saint women confirmed their faith. Their decision to "cast their lot with the Saints" and accept the consequences of that leap of faith initiated a chain of personal, economic, social, and spiritual challenges. Their diaries offered a chance not only to record but also to reflect on the meaning of those challenges in their lives at the time they encountered them.

Whatever their part was in establishing the Kingdom, it needed to be preserved in some form as a testament of the authenticity of the work in which they were engaged. The world they lived in was harsh and demanding, offering all of the exigencies of human existence, but the minds and hearts and spirits of these women were firmly focused on a better one. A sense of mission, of purpose beyond the merely temporal, permeates their writing. Conversion, especially for women, was a major act of self-assertion, and many felt an urgency to permanently inscribe how it felt and what followed that dramatic change in their lives, now viewed through the lens of the restored gospel.

The diary excerpts that follow were written by three of early Mormonism's "leading sisters." Both Eliza R. Snow and Zina D. H. Young had been members of the Church since Kirtland days and were "old-timers" compared with the newly converted Emmeline B. Harris (later Wells). Eliza had already established her role as a leading sister in Nauvoo. She was well educated and known as a teacher, a poet, and, after 1842, secretary of the Relief Society. In Nauvoo she began her lifelong temple service and leadership in the Relief Society, two of her great contributions to early Mormonism. Already evident was her charismatic appeal, which would eventually raise her to a preeminent position as "presidentess of all Mormon women." The Nauvoo portion of her diary reveals the strength of her religious conviction, the importance of her family ties, and her absorption in the life of the Prophet. Each entry is always more than the summary of a day. Both the inner and the outer life of Eliza R. Snow are clearly evident in her daily jottings. Unfortunately, the diary ends just two months before the martyrdom of Joseph Smith.

Zina Diantha Huntington Young—who became a companion wife to Eliza when both were married to Brigham Young, and was the closest of Eliza's co-workers in the Kingdom—had not yet secured her place among the female hierarchy of the Church, but she was rapidly becoming known and loved as a comforter and healer, a woman of extraordinary compassion and sensitivity. People fill her diary. She was tied closely not only to her kinship network but to neighbors, friends, and Relief Society sisters.

Emmeline Harris (Wells), on the other hand, was young and largely unknown during her two years in Nauvoo, moving there too late to join the Relief Society and being too young to exhibit the qualities that would later make her a leader among Latter-day Saint women. But she already possessed the literary talents and intellectual resources that would eventually carry her to prominence in Utah, where she would use her abilities in behalf of the women of the Church. Unlike the diaries of Eliza or Zina, Emmeline's entries in her brief Nauvoo record, which begin this section, are entirely introspective. They give no evidence of what comprised her days in Nauvoo, only her tangled thoughts during a brief, intensely emotional period. Her diary served as a secret friend with whom she shared the yearnings and heartbreak that dominated her Nauvoo experience. It does not resemble the detailed account of her daily life that characterized her later diaries.

In these diaries can be heard three diverse voices speaking from widely differing perspectives of the Nauvoo experience. Distinctive in style and content, each one clearly signals a different personality drawn by their common faith to become one with the community of Saints in Nauvoo.

EMMELINE B. HARRIS WELLS

1828-1921

Few Latter-day Saint women have left a larger literary legacy than Emmeline B. Harris Wells. A diarist from early youth, she also wrote several letters nearly every day of her adult life, compiled a volume of her poetry, wrote numerous short stories, kept the minutes of the Relief Society general board for twenty years, and served as editor of the *Woman's Exponent* for thirty-seven years, contributing editorials, articles, stories, and poems to its semi-monthly issues. From them all, one can trace the life and thought of a remarkable Latter-day Saint woman.

Emmeline B. Harris Wells

Emmeline began her writing as a young girl in her native Massachusetts when, going through some papers in the attic of her home, she discovered that "women sometimes put their thoughts upon paper." She began writing simple verses, which convinced her widowed mother to provide her the schooling she needed to develop her latent talents. Privileged to study at the New Salem Academy near her hometown, Emmeline followed her training there with a stint of school teaching before joining the Church in 1842. The next year, at age fifteen, she married James Harris, the son of the New Salem branch president, and the following spring she moved with James and his parents to Nauvoo. Within the next six months Emmeline's world crumbled around her. The Prophet Joseph and his brother Hyrum were murdered, the Harrises abandoned Nauvoo and the Church,

Emmeline's newborn son died, and James went downriver to find work but instead chose the life of a seaman. Emmeline never saw him again.

Not knowing his whereabouts and desperately hoping for his return, Emmeline wrote the following passages, which constitute her entire Nauvoo diary. They are the anguished outpourings of a broken teenage heart, a young woman bereft of husband and child with neither family nor friends near at hand. The death of the Prophet occasioned more than the loss of a leader to Emmeline. It robbed her of her lifeline.

The entries begin four days before she was married to Newel K. Whitney as a plural wife, only a few months after James's departure. The marriage seems only to have intensified her grief and longing. In time, however, her relationship to the Whitneys proved to be her salvation, and Elizabeth Ann Whitney, Newel's first wife, became a cherished mentor and friend as well as a companion wife. Emmeline cared for Elizabeth Ann's crippled infant, born in Winter Quarters, on their journey to Utah.

Emmeline was to suffer another blow with the death of Newel in 1850, but two years later she married Daniel H. Wells in what proved to be a more enduring marriage. Five daughters were born to Emmeline in these two unions. As her children reached maturity, she took her literary talents into the public realm, first contributing to and then editing the *Woman's Exponent,* an LDS women's publication lasting from 1872 to 1914. She also became active in general Relief Society leadership, serving as corresponding and then general secretary from 1888 until her call as general president in 1910, when she was eighty-two. She served in that position for eleven years.

Besides journalism and poetry, Emmeline was interested in women's affairs, becoming an active suffragist and an enthusiastic representative to the National and International Councils of Women. She organized literary clubs to promote the writings of Utah women and throughout her life attempted to bridge the misunderstandings and differences between LDS and non-LDS women, both in Utah and throughout the country. Her efforts were recognized posthumously in the form of a marble bust, placed in the rotunda of the Utah State

Capitol by the women of Utah, inscribed simply "A Fine Soul Who Served Us."

The focus of the following diary entries is entirely personal and could have been written in any setting. Emmeline's expressive words embrace the reader in her overwhelming grief and loneliness. Even at sixteen, she seemed aware that her life would not follow a conventional path but would indeed become "a romance."

NAUVOO DIARY OF EMMELINE B. HARRIS (WELLS)*

Feb 20 1845: When will sorrow leave my bosom all my days have I experienced it oppression has been my lot when O when shall I escape the bondage is not my life a romance indeed it is a novel strange and marvellous here am I brought to this great city by one to whom I ever expected to look for protection and left dependent on the mercy and friendship of strangers Merciful Providence wilt thou long suffer this must I forever be unhappy wilt the time never come when happiness and enjoyment will be the lot of this lump of clay when thralldom and oppression will be cast off my life has been one continual round of troubles and afflictions it seems sometimes as if death would be a comfort & then again when I think of the Gospel I feel resigned to the lot God has assigned me but what has life ever been to me from the day of my childhood almost ever since I left my mothers arms I have been afflicted and troubled yes in school I had enjoyment to be sure but how often was I crossed were not some of the scholars persecuting me because Susa [?] and I were friends and as soon as Mormonism began to flourish were they not harassing me on every side did they not tear me from my beloved home and the arms of a tender parent to keep me from Mormonism and then the

---

*Original is in Special Collections, Harold B. Lee Library, Brigham Young University, Provo, Utah.

Aaron Johnson home (foreground), one-time residence of Emmeline B. Harris Wells

Good Spirit interposed and provided a way for me to be released from the hands of a cruel guardian who pretended so much respect for me that he did not wish me to associate with my own mother and sister because they were Saints of the Most High God or as he called them Mormons I adopted this method of escape not merely for escape but he with whom I was to be connected was my lover in truth I loved him and I believed his professions to be true[2] Then I thought all danger would be past but alas misery presses me heavier and more heavy can I go farther O God my Heavenly Father assist me do not let it always be thus thou hast promised me days of joy and gladness and O Lord send not more affliction than I can bear before it O Lord impart thy spirit I grow sick at heart in vain does the sun shine bright my heart is faint my soul longs. . . .

Feb. 24, 1845: This day like all others is full of trouble sorrow and affliction are my attendants O *my God* how long will Thou suffer this once I could have filled this book with expressions of happiness but Alas sorrow is my portion I behold those around me enjoying the society of their dearest friends while I am cut short and why is it is it because of my sin and wickedness or is it a trial of my patience Heavenly Parent in the name of thy Holy Son Jesus do I beseech thee to pity and send comfort and consolation to an afflicted soul have mercy and forgive and grant me the desire of my heart and I will forever praise thee O that I had a mother or sister to advise me but I was cut short of all these blessings I have friends dare I unbosom my heart to them no no I know them not but those I have tried and proved I am not afraid to trust Great Father of mercies be pleased to grant me the request of my heart.

Feb. 28, 1845: Last night there came a steamboat up the river O how my youthful heart fluttered with hope with anxiety my limbs were affected to that degree I was obliged to lay aside my work I rely upon the promises he has made me and not all that has yet been said can shake my confidence in the only man I ever loved but to return hope revived in my bosom I watched the boat I looked out at the door I walked a few steps out of the yard I saw a person approaching my heart beat with fond anticipation it walked like James I came nearer and just as I was about to speak his name he spoke and I found I was deceived by the darkness last night I dreamed he came home O that it were reality Heavenly Father again bring us together. Today I am alone and I have time for reflection memory brings the past before me in all its joyous light life seems like a dream am I awake would that this were a dream and that I could awake and find myself at the side of him my h----- Boats are coming two have past today and where is James can he have forgot all his promises all his vows no never they must sting him to the very soul and I pray God that they may and that remorse of conscience will bring him back to the path of duty had I been treacherous I might have expected as much but God knows I have ever been true to him and if he would be as true to me I could not complain O God grant that he may soon return for my heart is braking for him and O God if he is situated so that he cannot return allow him to write to me that I can know something about his whereabouts

March 24, 1845: O God I bless thee that in Thy mercy Thou hast this day permitted me to hear news from a distant shore and that thou art kind and tender O God forgive my unbelief and save him from the wave give him dreams and visions of the night that he may know Thy will O Lord and do it and grant that he may return to me and not forget his firstlove.[3]

June 6th, 1845: Again have my friends in a distant country at the home of my child hood remembered me and him whom I love they know not he is far away on the stormy ocean perhaps sleeping in the bottom of the sea and perhaps tossed on his vessel by the furious winds that blow across the sea this though is almost to much for human nature to bear my heart aches my brain is dizzy at the idea It brings the past before me in all its various lights and shades with all its labyrinths and in some places I see happiness pictured in its most vivid colors in others I see joy and sorrow intermingled and in others I see dark places where I could hardly distinguish the Hand of Providence where I could barely cope with life where sorrow got a foot hold in my bosom which can never be driven away save by one whose power over my mind has ever been sufficient to soothe me in affliction to calm me in distress to make me happy in his society and I hope soon very soon (May God grant it) to see him and hear words of love and affection wilt Thou O God forever seperate me from one to whom I gave my whole and undivided affection in all the honesty and truthfulness of my heart and with all the simplicity and virtue of a youthful girl I knew nothing of the world then and I know but little now but I find it full of deceit and wickedness when those we consider our best friends deceive us what are we to expect from others? no mercy is the answer I feel it daily the world looks upon me perhaps as though I had driven him away by my cruelty but never no never can he rise up and say I neglected him or reproached him no even now when he has left me to the mercy of a cold unfeeling world am I ready to receive him to my heart again whenever he returns and I want O how much I desire to have him come O James where art thou O that thou couldst hear my voice and thou wouldst return O come to her who gave and forsook all others for thee My heart is wrung with sorrow And I cannot retaliate or . . . Once more My very soul is tried Beyond the limits nature has assigned

Love

And what is love
I know not
and let me bend
the knee and kiss the rod
As every Christian in
affliction should
Come Holy Spirit
heal my wounded heart
And help me that I may
Thy spirit keep
It['s] all the comfort we poor mortals
have   O comfort me and
teach me while I sleep
O cruel wrong most bitter
to endure
Today has pierced me
to my inmost soul
And must I suffer
and be patient still
Because I have no
power these burdens to control
Will there come a day when
I shall meet
One lost and gone who will
my cause defend
He loved me and his friend
ship was most true
Will he not in vision
be my friend
Teach me O Lord the wisest
course to take
Though I should suffer
let it be for good

ELIZA ROXCY SNOW

She was eulogized as the "mother of all mothers in Israel," this childless woman, Eliza Roxcy Snow, who, though nurtured in familial unity and married to two prophets, seemed strangely unbound to traditional family circles and identities. This is not to say she did not experience close personal relationships. She loved her parents, though regretted their disengagement from the Church, enjoyed the companionship of her sisters Leonora and Amanda, adored her brother Lorenzo, revered her first husband, Joseph Smith, and respected her second, Brigham Young. She developed close kinship ties with her companion wives and Relief Society co-workers. But she was free from those familial and domestic claims that often bound women closely to home and children and upon which they often depended for their own identity and station in life. Mormonism was her cause, Mormon women her family, and Mormondom the boundaries of her world.

Eliza Roxcy Snow

Intellectual, talented, capable, and almost zealously devoted to the Church, Eliza R. Snow occupied a unique place in Latter-day Saint history. It took her five years to commit to baptism, but when she did, she pledged—and gave—her all to the building of the Kingdom.

From the organization of the Relief Society in Nauvoo, of which she was secretary and keeper of the record, until her death in 1887,

Eliza R. Snow used the society as her vehicle to serve the women of the Church. Preeminent among the "leading sisters," she not only headed the Relief Society in Utah for twenty years, but she also helped organize and direct the Primary and Young Ladies' Mutual Improvement Association until her death. She set and answered questions of policy and procedure, demonstrated leadership, and expounded doctrine with authority and insight, her directives and sermons to the women of the Church serving as procedural guides for decades after her death. In her time there were those who characterized her as bearing the mien and stature of "a Hebrew prophetess," and indeed her prophetic blessings and devoted temple service earned her the appellations "prophetess" and "priestess."

Long before she rose to be "head of all the women of Zion," Eliza found poetry a satisfying medium to express her religious fervor. Of all her hymn texts that have been set to music, "O My Father" has made Eliza R. Snow a household name. She was an occasional diary writer. She kept a partial account of her life in Nauvoo and a record of her journey west. To these she added a brief history of her life.

In the following extracts from her Nauvoo diary, Eliza's literary skills are evident as she expresses both daily happenings and her reflections on the extraordinary events taking place about her. The diary is firmly anchored to the activities of Joseph Smith, whom she could observe firsthand when she lived with the Smiths. His travails with the law run as an undercurrent throughout her whole Nauvoo account. Her own nomadic pattern, taking up a new residence five times in the space of two years, served to broaden her circle of intimate friends, which came to include most of the leading families of the city. Even in these brief excerpts, one can see the steady layering of her commitment to the Church, her steadfast acceptance of its principles, and her unwavering fidelity to its leaders.

THE NAUVOO DIARY OF ELIZA R. SNOW (1842–1844)*

City of Nauvoo, June 29th 1842.

This is a day of much interest to my feelings.[4] Reflecting on past occurrences, a variety of thoughts have presented themselves to my mind with regard to events which have chas'd each other in rapid succession in the scenery of human life.

As an individual, I have not passed altogether unnoticed by Change, in reference to present circumstances and future prospects. Two weeks and two days have pass'd since an intimation was presented of my duty and privilege of remaining in the City of the saints in case of the removal of my father's family: one week and two days have transpired since the family left, and though I rejoice in the blessing of the society of the saints, and the approbation of God; a lonely feeling will steal over me before I am aware, while I am contemplating the present state of society—the powers of darkness, and the prejudices of the human mind which stand array'd like an impregnable barrier against the work of God. While these thoughts were revolving in my mind, the heavens became shadowed with clouds and a heavy shower of rain and hail ensued, and I exclaim'd "O God, is it not enough that we have the prepossessions of mankind—their prejudices and their hatred to contend with; but must we also stand amid the rage of elements?" I concluded within myself that the period might not be far distant, that will require faith to do so; but the grace of God is sufficient, therefore I will not fear. I will put my trust in Him who is mighty to save; rejoicing in his goodness and determin'd to live by every word that proceedeth out of his mouth.

Thursday [Friday?] July 29th [1842].

Just returned from Quincy, where I visited the Governor

---

*The following excerpts are taken from the Nauvoo Diary of Eliza R. Snow, edited by Maureen Ursenbach Beecher and published under "Eliza R. Snow's Nauvoo Journal" in *BYU Studies* 15 (Summer 1975): 391–416. Photocopy of original diary is in the LDS Church Archives.

[Thomas Carlin] in company with Mrs. Emma Smith who presented him a Petition from the Female Relief Society. The Gov. received us with cordiality, and as much affability and politeness as his Excellency is master of, assuring us of his protection, by saying that the laws and Constitution of our country shall be his polar star in case of any difficulty. He manifested much friendship, and it remains for time and circumstance to prove the sincerity of his professions.[5]

Wednesday, August 3 [1842].

Day before yesterday I rode to the burial of bishop Knights [Vinson Knight]—from there to Prest. Smith's house, from which place I have just returned to my excellent friend, Mrs. b.

Tuesday, 9th [August 1842].

Prest. S[mith] and P[orter] R[ockwell] taken for the attempt to assassinate [Missouri ex-Governor Lilburn] Boggs. Prest. S. left in the care of the City Marshal while those who took him return to Quincy to ascertain whither they must submit him to a City trial. . . .

Sunday 1[4]th [August 1842].

Yesterday Mrs. [Emma] Smith sent for me, having previously given me the offer of a home in her house, by Miss [Elvira] A[nnie] Coles [Cowles], who call'd on me, on the 12th. Mrs. [Sarah] Cleveland having come to the determination of moving on to her lot; my former expectations were frustrated, but the Lord has opened the path to my feet, and I feel dispos'd to acknowledge his hand in all things. This sudden, unexpected change in my location, I trust is for good; it seem'd to come in answer to my petitions to God to direct me in the path of duty according to his will. . . .

Thursday 18th [August 1842].

Monday evening I return'd to my former residence [with Sarah Cleveland] in order to adjust my things for a removal, and return'd with them last evening to Prest. Smith's. . . .

Monday, 22 [August 1842].

Last night, six men came in, suppos'd to have a new Writ [for Joseph Smith's arrest].

Yesterday Prest. [Sidney] Rigdon spoke on the stand in the grove; giving a narration of Eliza's [Elizabeth Rigdon] sickness and the very singular manner in which she address'd the family after having been as he express'd it dead three times. He declar'd his confidence in the work of God—said it had been reported of him that he had call'd Prest. S. a fallen prophet—but he denied having said it, &c. How it would rejoice my heart to see him once more standing firmly in the dignity of his station and strengthening the hands of those who are struggling against every kind of opposition for the cause of God!

Thur. 25th [August 1842].

It has been satisfactorily ascertained that those men who came sunday evening, were not authorized to take Prest. S. but that there is a new Writ issued and on its way. Esqr. Powers called today.

This evening Prest S. said he had some good news, viz. that George W. Robinson had declar'd his determination to forsake his evil deeds and return to the church. If he *does* return, I hope it may be for his soul's salvation: not to act the part of [George M.] Hinkle and betray the innocent, in the time of danger.[6]

I had a rich treat yesterday in perusing the Book of the Lord—was much gratified with the spirit breathed in the letters of Maj. Gen. [Wilson] L[aw]—felt myself rather reprov'd for having distrusted his integrity and devotion to the cause. In such critical times, much is depending on the fidelity of those who fill the higher offices.

Sunday, 28th [August 1842].

Last evening Prest. S. was at home and met in the large drawing room with a respectable number of those considered trustworthy—counsel'd them to go out forthwith to proclaim the principles of truth. I was busied the forepart of this day in needlework to prepare br. [Erastus H.] Derby for his mission.

Sunday Sept 4th [1842].

Surely we know not what a day may bring forth. The little season of quietude with which we have been bless'd for a few days, has gone by, and our City is again infested with some eighteen or twenty men, who are lying in wait, for the blood of the innocent!

Yesterday Pitman from Quincy and Ford from Mo. with another stranger arrived about one o'clock at the house of Prest. Smith, who having a moment's notice, left the dinner table, where he was seated and made his escape. Pitman enquired for him and ask'd permission to search the house. Mrs. S[mith] said she had no objection if he had the proper authority. Pitman said he had *no authority* but with her consent he proceeded to search, preceeded by John Boynton and D[imick] Huntington, whom Mrs. S. requested to show them into the rooms.

After sundown, [Thomas] King, the Deputy Sheriff and his associate came in. King seem'd in an unpleasant humor—after enquiring for Prest. Smith spoke about searching the house, Mrs. S. mention'd authority—He said he had authority at any rate he said his *will was good enough.* Mrs. S. said she thought he could have no objections to telling what he wanted Mr. S. for. He said in a surly tone that it would be time enough to tell *that* afterwards.

Sunday Sep. 11th [1842].

Returned from Lima, where I had a very pleasant visit with Sister L[eonora].[7] After a short time at the Conference on sat. evening, where Elders G[eorge A.] Smith & A[masa] Lyman, who rode down in our carriage—met Prest. [Brigham] Young, already started on his mission.

Sun. 18th [September 1842].

Went to meeting in the forenoon & heard elder G[eorge] J. Adams, who arriv'd here last monday, deliver an eloquent discourse from the 15th of 1st Cor. commencing with the 12th verse, "Now if Christ be preached that he rose from the dead" (&c, on the subject of the resurrection of the dead). . . .

Friday 23d [September 1842].

Last evening spent at sister Knights—On my way, call'd at the Post-Office, and found a letter from Eli & Amanda, announcing their expectation of moving to this country.[8] Their intention of settling near father & mother is a subject of much gratification to my feelings, hoping it may add much to the comfort of the aged; in this age of disappointment and sacrifice. But the mind must be fix'd on God, that the cheering influence of his spirit may elevate our hopes above the power of changing circumstance; then will the aged rejoice, and the young be encouraged, even amid scenes of difficulty and peril....

Sunday October 9th [1842].

Last night Prest S. left home in consequence of intelligence that King & Pitman were on the way in search for him. It was a sorrowful time. Sister Emma had been sick eleven days,—still confined to her bed—but he must go or be expos'd to the fury of the merciless! Gov. [Thomas] Carlin has offered [$]200, and [Thomas] Reynolds [$]300, for his apprehension.

Wed. 12th [October 1842].

Having heard of the safe arrival of Prest. S. at the place of his destination, I wrote as follows and sent to him

> Prest Smith
>
> Sir, for your consolation permit me to tell
> That your Emma is *better*—she soon will be well;
> Mrs. Durfee stands by her, night & day like a friend
> And is prompt every call—every wish to attend;
> Then pray for your Emma, but indulge not a fear
> For the God of our forefathers, smiles on us here.
>
> Thou hast found a seclusion—a lone solitude
> Where thy foes cannot find thee—where friends
>   can't intrude;
> In its beauty and wildness, by nature design'd
> As a retreat from the tumult of all humankind,
> And estrang'd from society: How do you fare?
> May the God of our forefathers, comfort you there.
>
> It is hard to be exil'd! but be of good cheer
> Thou art destin'd to triumph: then like a chas'd deer

Hide yourself in the ravine, secure from the blast
Awhile, till the storm of their fury is past;
For your foes are pursuing and hunting you still—
May the God of our forefathers screen you from ill. . . .

Dec. 12th [1842].

This day commenced school-teaching in the Masonic Hall—the weather very cold and I shall never forget the kindness of Bishop [Newel K.] Whitney, who opened the school by prayer after having assisted in preparing the room.

In undertaking the arduous business with my delicate constitution, at this inclement season of the year, I was entirely governed by the wishes of Prest. and Mrs. Smith; trusting in God for strength to fulfill, and acknowledging his hand in this as well as in every other circumstance of my life; I believe he has a purpose to accomplish which will be for my good ultimately, inasmuch as I desire and aim to be submissive to the requirements of those whom he has plac'd in authority over me.[9]

Feb. 11th 1843.

Took board and had my lodging removed to the residence of br. J[onathan H.] Holmes. . . .

March 17th 1843.

This day clos'd my school much to my *own* satisfaction; having the pleasure of the presence of Prest. J. Smith, his lady—Mrs. Allred, Mrs. Durfee and others. After reading in the hearing of the school several beautiful parting pieces, addressed to myself by the scholars, I read a farewell address which I had prepared for the occasion. . . . Prest. S. closed the school by prayer. . . .

Sunday April 9th, [1843].

Conference closed yesterday—it has been a very interesting season to those present, but from ill health I have been deprived attending except one half day. With mingled emotions of pain and pleasure I perused a letter written by P[arley] P. Pratt, with which I was this evening favored by the politeness of elder Woodruff. The joyful intelligence of the arrival of my brother [Lorenzo] with a company of 230, in St. Louis was accompanied with the announcement of the death of br. L[orenzo D.] Barnes, the first elder in the church of Latter-day Saints, who has laid his bones upon a foreign soil. . . .

Wednesday 12th [April 1843].

This day I have the inexpressible happiness of once again embracing a brother who had been absent nearly three years. I cannot describe the feelings which fill'd my bosom when I saw the steam-boat Amaranth moving majestically up the Mississippi, and thought perhaps Lorenzo was on board: my heart overflowed with gratitude when, after the landing of the boat, I heard Prest. Hiram Smith say to me "your brother has actually arrived." It is a time of mutual rejoicing which I never shall forget.

Sat. 15th [April 1843].

Spent a very interesting and agreeable afternoon at Mr. Lyon's present L[orenzo], Mrs. Scovill, Miss Geroot, &c.

Tues, May 9th [1843].

Had a delightful excursion up the river to Burlington.

Thurs. May 11th [1843].

Accompanied L[orenzo] to Lima—very pleasant ride.

Monday 15th [May 1843].

Returned to Nauvoo after a very pleasant visit and an interesting Conference at which present Prest. J. Smith, W. Woodruff & George A S[mith].

Friday [19 May 1843].

Visited at Prest. [William] Marks in company with Sophie Robinson, O[live Grey] Frost, Miss Mitchell &c. Sat. visited at Mr. Harris'.

Tues. 23d [May 1843].

Last night L[orenzo] and myself staid at New Lancaster & this evening arrived at our father's residence in Walnut Grove; where we

Old Nauvoo burial ground

found sister A[manda], and all in tolerable health and pleasantly
situated in a beautiful country; for which I feel very thankful; The
care and anxiety which I have experienced for the difficulties to
which my parents have been subject since our expulsion from our
home in Mo. have been a source of much bitterness of feeling; and
that bitterness has been aggravated by the reflection that they did not
in their trials draw out from the springs of consolation which the
gospel presents that support which was their privilege, and which
would have enabled them to rejoice in the midst of tribulation &
disappointment.

Thurs. June 1st [1843].

My brother & I returned again to our beloved City after visiting
my aunt & cousins at Spring-Creek 12 miles south-east from
LaHarpe. A severe storm occur'd this day week—much injury done
in Monmouth.

Sun. 4th [June 1843].

Yesterday & last night I spent alone except L[orenzo]'s company for a few hours; the people having gone on a pleasure excursion to Quincy.

Friday 9th [June 1843].

The melancholy news of the sudden death of Elias Higbee Esqr. who died yesterday morning has spread a feeling of deep sorrow over the City. How truly it may be said that "in the midst of life we are in death." It is to us a mysterious providence at this time, when every talent and exertion are peculiarly needed for the erection of the Temple; that one of the Committee should be so suddenly call'd from time to eternity.

Today Lorenzo leaves for Ohio—may the Lord prosper his way and return him soon to my society.

Tues. 13th [June 1843].

Last sunday I had the privilege of attending meeting and in the forenoon listening to a very interesting discourse by Prest. J. Smith. He took for his subject the words of the Savior to wit. "O Jerusalem thou that killest the prophets and stonest them that are sent unto you! How oft would I have gathered you as a hen gathereth her chickens under her wings and you would not!" He beautifully and in a most powerful manner, illustrated the necessity of the *gathering* and the building of the Temple that those ordinances may be administered which are necessary preparations for the world to come: he exhorted the people in impressive terms to be diligent—to be up and doing lest the tabernacle pass over to another people and we lose the blessings.

Sunday 18th [June 1843].

Last tues. Prest. S. & family started for a visit to her [Emma's] relatives.[10] Friday spent the night very pleasantly at bishop Whitney's after attending a very interesting meeting of the Relief Society in the afternoon. This morning sister Mills left us for the eternal world. I spent the day at home—wrote a letter for Mother [Lucy Mack] Smith. Several brothers and sisters call'd on me in the evening— inform'd me that brother L[orenzo] did not leave at the time we expected—probably did not go till monday morning.

Tues. 20th [June 1843].

Last evening heard the unpleasant intelligence that the Gov. of Missouri has issued another Writ for the arrest of Prest. Smith. How long will the hand of persecution retain its iron nerve! How long must the innocent be harrass'd and perplexed! Heard that a messenger arrived from Springfield, sent by Judge [James] Adams, saturday night to apprize Prest. S. of the expected arrival of the officers. Visited at elder [John] Taylor's.

Friday 23d [June 1843].

Judge Adams arrived this morning from Springfield. I call'd to see him—he confirm'd previous intelligence respecting the Writ being issued, but nothing as yet is heard of the officers. Yesterday I was presented with the following lines, which had been sent to press without my knowledge, & of which I had retain'd no copy.

From the Wasp.

To *who needs Consolation.*

O can a gen'rous spirit brook
    With feelings of content
To see an age, distrustful look
    On *thee* with *dark intent*!

I feel thy woes—my bosom shares
    Thy spirit's agony:—
How can I love a heart that dares
    Suspect *thy* purity?

I'll smile on all that smile on *thee*
As angels do above—
    All who in pure sincerity
Will love *thee*, I will love.

Believe me, thou hast noble friends
    Who feel and share thy grief;
And many a fervent pray'r ascends
    To heav'n, for thy relief.[11]

Sunday June 25th [1843].

This afternoon, while the people were assembled for service in the grove, Br. [William] Clayton who had been sent with br. [Stephen] Markham to Lee Co. to notify Prest. Smith of the issue of the Writ for his arrest, returned which occasioned considerable excitement. He announced the capture of Prest. S. with his request that a number of the Militia should be sent to his assistance if needed. It was truly gratifying to see the spirit manifested on the occasion, not only by brethren but also by many persons not members of the church. All seem'd desirous of proving their patriotism in the cause of the persecuted prophet. The City literally swarmed with men who ran together from every quarter to volunteer their services. A selection of about eighty horsemen started about dusk, while fifty others were chosen to go by water, who went on board the "Maid of Iowa" to go down the Mississippi and up the Illinois to Ottawa, expecting that Prest. S. would be taken there for trial.

Tues. 27th [June 1843].

Mrs. S. [Emma Smith] arrived—I went to see her, and learned more particulars concerning the the manner in which her husband was taken by J[oseph] H. Reynolds, Sheriff of Jackson Co. Mo. and Willson [Harmon T. Wilson] a constable of Hancock Co. Ill. who came to Dixon on Rock river professing to be Mormon elders & enquired for Joseph Smith who they were informed was 12 miles distant at a place called Palestine Grove. They proceeded there & took him in a savage manner & brought him to Dixon, intending the same evening which was friday the 23d, to take him into Mo. but thro' the providential interference of the patriotic citizens of the place he was rescued & reserved for a more lawful proceeding.

Thurs. 29th [June 1843].

Took a ride to br. Lot's[12] in company with Mrs. Whitney, Mrs. Durfee & Mrs. Holmes. Before we returned, it was announced that a messenger had arrived bringing the joyful intelligence that the prophet would arrive in a few hours.

Sat. 30th [June 1843].

A very interesting day. A military Escort accompanied by the Band and a number of ladies on horseback & a vast multitude of citizens, in carriages left the City at 11 o'clock A.M. and returned at 2, to the house of Prest. S. with the Prest. where I witness'd a scene of mingled joy & sorrow, which language cannot describe; for who can paint the emotions of the heart—the burst of parental and filial affection amid scenes of deepest anguish and the highest joy? The affectionate manner in which he introduced his family to those worse than savage officers, and the very hospitable treatment they received, was a lesson that should have made an impression on every heart, not to be eradicated. . . .

July 20th [1843].

Sister [*blank in original*] call'd to see me. Her appearance very plainly manifested the perturbation of her mind. How strangely is the human countenance changed when the powers of darkness reign over the empire of the heart! Scarcely, if ever, in my life had I come in contact with such forbidding and angry looks; yet I felt as calm as the summer eve, and received her as smilingly as the playful infant; and my heart as sweetly reposed upon the bosom of conscious innocence, as infancy reposes in the arms of paternal tenderness & love. It is better to suffer than do wrong, and it is sometimes better to submit to injustice rather than contend; it is certainly better to wait the retribution of Jehovah than to contend where effort will be unavailable [useless].

July 21st [1843].

In company with br. Allen left Nauvoo for the residence of sister [Leonora] Leavitt in the Morley Settlement. We rode most of the way in the night in consequence of the annoyance of the Prairie flies. It was the season for contemplation, and while gazing on the glittering expanse above, which splendidly contrasted with the shades that surrounded me; my mind, as if touched by the spirit of inspiration, retraced the *past* and glanced at the *future*, serving me a mental treat spiced with the variety of changes subsequent to the present state of mutable existence.

The likeness and unlikeness of disposition & character with which we come in contact, is a fruitful theme of thought; and the *very few*, who have strength of mind, reason & stability; to act from *principle*; is truly astonishing, and yet *only such*, are persons *worthy of trust....*

Aug. 28th [1843].

This afternoon had the innexpressible happiness of greeting Lorenzo, just return'd from Ohio.

Sept. 1st [1843].

Br. L[orenzo] left this morning which leaves a great void in our association—it seems like forcing a wide breach in our family circle. The more endearing the reciprocation of friendship—the more implicit the confidence; the more painful is the separation. This we realize in the present instance....

Oct 10th [1843].

Yesterday returned from Nauvoo. The trial of Prest. Rigdon occupied that portion of the Conference which I attended. Some circumstances of very peculiar interest occur'd during my visit to the City. Every thing connected with our *affections* is engraven on the heart, and needs not the perpetuating touch of the sculptor....

Dec. 6th [1843].

Spent the day at Mr. Lindsay's in cutting clothes.

[Dec.] 9th [1843].

Lorenzo left for Nauvoo.

Dec. 19th [1843].

Tuesday evening L. having return'd, we had the pleasure of the company of Father [Isaac] & Mother [Lucy] Morley: it was an interesting season, in the order of a blessing meeting, father Morley officiating. The following is a copy of the blessing confer'd on me, as a Patriarchal Blessing.

"Sister Eliza, In the name of Jesus Christ I lay my hands upon thy head, and I confirm all thy former blessings together with the blessings of a Patriarch upon thee. Let thy thoughts, thy mind and thy affections be stay'd upon the mighty God of Jacob.

"Thou hast the blessing and gift to know in whom thou has put thy trust—he is thy friend and thy great Benefactor. He has been mindful of thee and has given thee an intellect capable of receiving & understanding all things necessary, pertaining to thy present and everlasting welfare; and thou hast & shall have the blessing to improve upon every talent and gift that the God of nature has bestow'd upon thee. The powers of thy mind are fix'd as firmly as the pillars of heaven, to comply with the requisitions of thy Creator, and thou shalt never be disappointed in the cause thou hast espous'd. The Lord thy Savior loves thee and has been bountiful in pouring his blessings upon thee, and thou shalt have the blessing to be admired & honor'd by all good men. Thou hast the blessing to speak in wisdom & to counsel in prudence, and thou shalt have the blessing to be honor'd by those who have spoken reproachfully of thee; and thou shalt yet stand in high & holy places, to be honr'd and admired for the integrity of thy heart. Thy fidelity has reach'd the heavens, and thy name is honor'd & admir'd by the heav'nly hosts. Thy steps shall be trac'd in prudence—thy examples are worthy of imitation, and thou mayest ever confide in the friend of thy bosom. Thou mayest open thy mind to thy Creator and thy requests shall be granted because thou hast an advocate even Jesus, & in his name thou art invited to pay thy devotions to the Most High, and in and thro' his name thou mayest ever rejoice in the New & everlasting covenants; Ask, and thou shall be given an additional blessing to thee; and thou shalt have influence & power over all those who have sought to injure thee, to do good unto them; and to cause them to become a blessing to thee. Thy influence shall be great—thy examples shall not be excel'd. Thou hast a heart to be enlarg'd and a mind capable of expansion; and for thy comfort remember in thy retired walks, that yonder sun is typical of a crown of glory that shall be sealed upon thy head: The stars that twinkle in yonder sky shall show to thy mind the workmanship of thy Creator, and by those glories thou shalt read the destinies of man, and be capable with thy pen to communicate, to thy fellow man the blessings & glories of futurity: and thy blessing shall roll and continue to thee until time is lost in eternity: and thy name shall be handed down to posterity from generation to generation: and many songs shall be heard that were dictated by thy pen and from the principles of thy mind, even until the choirs from on high and the earth below, shall join in one universal song of praise to God and the Lamb.—These blessings, together with Eternal life I seal upon thy head in the name of thy Redeemer, Amen." . . . [Recorded in book E. Page 67. A L Morley]

Thurs. [Tues.?] 20th [February 1844].

Spent last evening much to my satisfaction, entertainment and instruction, at a Blessing meeting at br. Beeby's in Lima. It was quite a treat to my mind—one of the bright spots on the page of my life, never to be forgotten.

April 14th [1844].

On the fifth I came to the City to attend the Conference. Spent the time very pleasantly in the affectionate family of Bishop Whitney in company with my sister. Having received counsel to remain in the City, after spending a few days at elder Sherwood's & br. Joshua Smith's; I took up my residence at the house of Col. S[tephen] Markham being invited to do so; and I feel truly thankful that I am again permitted to enjoy society which is dear to me as life. I find Sister M. an agreeable, noble, independent minded woman; willing to sacrifice for the truth.[13]

ZINA DIANTHA HUNTINGTON JACOBS YOUNG

"A saintly face and a great mother-heart."[14] These characteristics, noted by a friend, made Zina D. H. Young one of the best-loved women in early Mormondom. "Aunt Zina"—the term rings with loving kinship—also acquired the honored title "Mother in Israel" for her devotion to the gospel, her ministrations to the sick, and her lifelong service to the Church. "As mother, foster-mother, nurse, counselor or friend," one admirer wrote, "she was equal to every need."[15]

Zina Diantha Huntington Jacobs Young

Zina Huntington was born in Watertown, New York, just sixty miles from Palmyra, to a family devoted to prayer and scripture reading. Thus, the gospel message, brought to them in 1835 by Hyrum Smith, fell easily on listening ears and believing hearts, and all but the oldest son became Latter-day Saints. The family emigrated to Kirtland, then to Missouri and to Nauvoo. In Nauvoo, Zina joined the Relief Society, received the temple ordinances from Emma and Joseph Smith, and began her lifetime of service as a temple worker. She married Henry Jacobs in 1841, bearing two sons in that marriage, Zebulon (Zebulun in her diary) and Chariton. She was also married to Joseph Smith for eternity and later, for time, Brigham Young, with whom she had one daughter, also named Zina.

Until her death, Zina Young divided her time between temple

service and the Relief Society. In both these callings she joined Eliza R. Snow, her companion wife of Brigham Young and a devoted friend. She served as Eliza's counselor and successor in the general Relief Society presidency and also as "presidentess" of female temple workers. Sister wives in marriage, sisters in the gospel, Eliza and Zina were also sisters in spirit, their commitment to building the Kingdom binding them together more strongly than kinship ties. The "strength and beauty" of their relationship was as remarkable as that of David and Jonathan, observed one contemporary.

Zina was early granted the gift of tongues and interpretation, which she was counseled never to suppress, since the gift was a manifestation of the presence of the Spirit. She was also granted the gift of healing, and hundreds of women were the beneficiaries of this spiritual endowment. Only months before her death, though frail and weak herself, she interrupted a visit from a friend when she was called to the bedside of a young woman in need of "blessing and comfort."

As a bride of Henry Jacobs in her early twenties, Zina kept a journal of her experiences in Nauvoo, beginning shortly before the death of the Prophet Joseph. The terse diary entries recounting her daily rounds contrast vividly with the dramatic events taking shape around her. Through her diary she serves as both a participant and an observer, creating a historical record of her life and her times. Her diary is populated with family, friends, and neighbors, many of whom she served as midwife and healer, and many others for whom she was just a good neighbor.

The vigor of her religious commitment allowed Zina to be relentlessly hopeful and composed despite the ominous foreshadowings of the fate of the Mormons in Nauvoo during the period of her writing. Her exultant bursts of psalm-like praise and thanksgiving reveal her joy in the gospel and her earnestness in striving to live its teachings. Her marginally correct grammar and spelling never deflect the impact of her poetic imagery and religious ardor.

In the brief excerpts that follow is evidence of the qualities that came to characterize her throughout her life: her deep-seated faith, her love of the gospel, her desire to be a "saint," her watch-care of others, and her happy, hopeful nature. Besides the chronicling of a rich and active life, her diary is a spiritual account book, full of exultations in praise of God's goodness and repeated pledges of fidelity to the work of the latter days.

DIARY OF ZINA DIANTHA HUNTINGTON JACOBS (YOUNG)*

June 1844

17. The Bretheren are halving to prepare to defend them selves again.

18. I went to the Masonic hall with the sisters.

19. Tra[i]ning. 3 companes arived, to [two] from over the river. O God save thy people.

20. Stayed at Wm [William Huntington's] all knight. The bretheren are still in town tra[i]ning.

21. Had a letter from the Governor, to Joseph. He is at Carthage, that is the Gov[ernor].

22. Saturday knight about midnight the g[u]ard came in, also about 40 men of the other party or from Carthage. The Goviner deman[d]s Joseph.[16]

23. Joseph and the bretheren are in councel supplicating the throne of grace for His divine direction. Elder [George] Adams spoke at the stand. Henry and I went. It was an interesting sermon. He also related the tale of his being at sea, the Maraclous [miraculous] hand of God being with him in visions, &c. He is soon to start on an important mission to the east. May God bless him.

24. A day long to be remembered. This Day Joseph, Hiram, John P. Green, Dimick [Huntington] and others started for Carthage to be met at the Mound.[17] Returned about noon acconipned [accompanied] by a number by the Goviners orders. Took the

---

*The excerpts that follow are taken from the complete Nauvoo diary of Zina Jacobs (Young), which was published under the title "'All Things Move in Order in the City': The Nauvoo Diary of Zina Diantha Jacobs," ed. Maureen Ursenbach Beecher, in *BYU Studies* 19 (Spring 1979): 285–320. Original is in LDS Church Archives.

cannons and all the U.S. arms also the before mentioned prisoners and left this place late in the after noon. O God save thy servents, save them for Jesus Sake.

This night after the brethren left here for Carthage the Hevens gathered blackness, the thunder and lightning was dreadful, the storm arose in the west.

25. Joseph and Hiram ware exhibeted to the mob by the Govinor. The anger of the Mob still increased. The Govinor Pledged his sacred word and honor also the faith of the State of Ill[inois] that they should be protected, especially Joseph and Hiram. This was done before they left there [their] Homes.

26. Joseph['s] Lawyers endeverd to make them secure. Done all in there power for there safety, especially Lawyer [H. T. Read].

O the ever to be r[em]embered awful day of the 27 of June 1844. The men of Carthage drove off some of the Bretheren at the point of the bayonet and swore they would kill Joseph. The Goviner knew of it yet he left them in the gale [jail] (with a light g[u]ard), took a number of men, came out here. About the time they arrived here in Nauvoo the awful s[c]ene took place. About 100 or 100[?] men with painted Faces burst open the gale [jail] dore. Shot in. (No man entered the room.) Joseph discharged three of the barrels of a six shooter. Hirum was shot first in the head or under the left eye. Shod [shot] Joseph through. He leaped from the upper window of a 2 story bilding. Br[other Willard] Richards started to Follow him but seed [seeing] that he must fall uppon the enemes bayotel [bayonet?], desisted. Brother Talor [John Taylor] is wounded. By the meraculous hand of God br. Richards was not hurt, for the bullets flew like hail in A violent storm. They ware both shot twice. Thus in one day about 3 or 4. oclock fell the Prophet and Patr[i]arch of the Church of the Lat[t]erday Saints, the kind husbands, the affectionate Father, the venerable statesman, the Friends of man kinde, by the hand of a ruthless Mob mixed with desenters. O God how long before thou wilt avenge the innosent blood that has be[e]n shed? How long must widdows mourn and orp[h]ans cry before thou wilt avenge the Earth and cause wickness to seace [cease]. Wilt thou hasten the day, O Lord, in thine own way. Wilt thou Prepare me and to stand all things and come of[f] conqerrer through him who hath Loved us, and give me a seat in thy selestial Kingdom with the Sancitified. I ask these favors for thy son Jesus sake, amen.

28. This after noon the Bod[i]es of the Marters arived in town. I went herd the speeches m[a]de by our bretheren and Friends. They stood where Joseph last stood and addresse[d] the bretheren, or he called them sons. Went into his house for the first time and there saw the lifeless speechless Bod[i]es of the towo [two] Marters for the testimony which they held. Little did my heart ever think that mine eyes should witness this awful seen [scene].

29. The People of the City went to see there beloved Prophet and Patriarch who had laid down there lives for the cause and there Bretheren. The night after the bretheren ware buried we had an awful thunder storm and lightning, so the mob did not come as they intended.

30. It is Sunday, a lonely h[e]art-sorrowful day. Also it rains.

July 1st, 1844. I washed, they Joseph and Hirams cloth[e]s. . . .

4. Spent the day at Sister Jonese's, Carlos Smiths Widdow [Agnes Coolbrith Smith], the girls that resides with her, Louisa Bemon [Beaman], and Sister Marcum [Hannah Markham]. Very plesent to day, but ah what drearryness and sorrow pervades evry bosom. The once noble banner of liberty is fallen, the bo[a]sted land of fre[e]dom is now sta[i]ned with innocent blood. O God wilt thou save us. . . .

8. I again commence my sc[h]ool but mournfully.

9, 10, 11, 12, 13, 14. At[t]ended at the Stand. Parl[e]y [P.] Prat preached in the power of the speret [spirit]. It was truly comforting, for truly did we need it.

15. The brethren are a going afishing like unto the days of old when Jesus was slain.

16,17,18. The Church had a day of fasting and Prayer. I attended the meeting, payed my 10 c[en]ts tithing to the Temple. A violent thunder Storm. I was alone in the night but God preserved me. . . .

31. I closed my school to day.

August 1, 1844, Samuel Smith died.[18] O God have mercy on thy People, comfort those that mourn.

2. I went to sister [Elvira Cowles?] Holmes.

3. President [Sidney] Rigdon arived here.

4. I herd him preach. He spoke of Josephs halving a Kingdom built up unto him; also of the father Son and Holy G[h]ost.

5. Some of the [Quorum of the] 12 arived. . . .

8 of August, 1844. I went to meeting in the afternoon, Thanks be to Him who reigns on high, the majority of the Twelve are her[e]. Brigham Youngs spoke and the Church voted that the 12 should act in the office of there calling next to Joseph or the three first presidents. . . .

18. Went to meeting. B[righam] Youngs Spoke concerning the unity of the church and the danger of dividing. In the after noon Heber Kimble [Kimball] and O. Hide [Orson Hyde] spoke. It was an excelent meeting About as the Sun was setting Father, Henry, and Oliver [her brother] arived from Lima. O[liver] is very Sick. Stood his journey beyond expectations. I feel to thank the Lord that I have seen him alive.

19. P Edmons had a chill here. I washed. Took a voilent cold.

20. Henry had a chill.

21, 22, 23, 24, 25. H[enry] and Zebulun [her son] quite sick with the ague.

26, 27. H[enry] has his ague. . . .

September 1844.

3. We went to Dimicks [her brother], stayed all knight at Fathers. The Twelve labored with S Rigdon most of the night and demanded his lisence, but he refused.

4. S R is reported in the [Nauvoo] Neighbor with others, to appear at the stand next sabath.

5. The Twelve preached at the stand, very well.

6. Viseted at Sister [Patty] Sessions.

7. A lowry [dull?] day.

8. We went to meeting. Sidney Rigdon was cut off from the church with others.

9. The Rigdon followers had a meeting in the evening.

10. I was at Mother [Patty] Sessiones.

11. Sold our improvements [on their land] to Br Wetherby.

12. I went to Prayer meting Parley Prat spoke of the welfare of the Church, the necesity of building the Temple, our endewment, &c.

13. Dimick and Wife and Julia ware here. Watched with Br Bells Child. It died about 12 oclock. . . .

21, 22. We went to Meeting. B Young spoke uppon the power of the Priesthood, when Joseph was ordained, &c.

23. I was at Sister Crosbes [Caroline Barnes Crosby?].

24. We moved to Wm Huntingtons house to stop until Henry can build a house uppon a piece of land he bought of Wm size 2[?] in front and 100 back.

25. Some of the Goviners troops arived within 2 miles of town.

26. To a Thursday prayer meeting at brother Tidwells.

27. The Goviner with [two aides] past through the City of Nauvoo and re protecting against the wolf hunt [harassment] that has ben in agitation by the citizen[s] of this state and said to wish the detection of the assasins of our Prophet and Patriarch. O Lord wilt thou soften there hearts towards the Saints and permit us to do all things thou hast Commanded and make our calling and election sure and thy name Shall have all the glory.

28. The Legion came out. The Goviner and his men saw them, said they done well. The Govner still holds there arms [the Nauvoo Legion's]. In a fals alarm there was a man kil[l]ed, shot through the body.

29. The Goviner and men left for Warsaw.

30. October the 1st. 1844, 2 Caroline and I sowed at Dimocks. . . .

October 1844.

20. Some Bretheren arived from th[e] East of Henres and Olivers acquaintance. Also Father and Mother Huntington ware here. What a blessed privilige to have the Sosiety of on[e]s friends. I feel truly grateful for the privilige I enjoy.

21. About 200 brethren went to Carthage some few ware bound over for trial last Summer. The day of trial has now arived; it arose

from burning the press [which published the *Nauvoo Expositor*]. O God protect thy saints.

Oct. 22nd, 1844. No fresh news from Carthage. Mother Liman [Lyman?] was here, an old friend.

23. Wm returned from Carthage. The fendesh dsenters [fiendish dissenters] are mostly gathered at Carthage. No trouble yet.

24. The bretheren mostly returned home to Nauvoo. Some ware indited but there trials put of[f] until the next setting of co[u]rt. . . .

November 1844.

5. All well. I assisted Sister Car[r]ington in quilting. Went to prayer Meeting, had a very good season in wa[i]ting before the Lord. Some new ideas to me. I feel grateful to My Heavenly Father for all these priviliges and blessings. . . .

17. My Father Spent some time with me to day. In the evening Hasiel Clark and I went to hear Or[s]on Hide. He spoke concerning our guardian Angels that attended each Saint, and woud until the Sperit became grieved. Then they take there departure and the Person is left to hardness of hart and blindness of mind. I Pray thee, O Heavenly Father to send by whom thou wilt. Let the angel of thy Peace attend me and never Forsake me, but may I ever have grace to listen to the Spirit of truth forever more, and for Jesus sake, may I have the gift of eternal life. He also spok concerning the judgements or those that had not kept the commandments but had grieved the Sperit. The Saints would not know the[i]r's, therefore they would be left or looked uppon as they had looked uppon others. Also concerning the roling forth the Kingdom, and the necesity of being prepared for the Judgement day, the Law being bound up and the Testimony being Sealed, and the dreadful dilemma of those that ware not prepared, and the necesity of the Temples being built that we might prepare ourselves and be ready and claimed the blessings that had ben promised to us as a people by Joseph, A Man of God, and I believe after God's own hart.

This day long to be remembered, Sunday the 17 of November 1844. Em[m]a Smith, the Wife of Joseph Smith the Martyr, had a Son born, in the morning. O may the Choisest of Heavens blessings attend the Child. May it grow into manhood, and may it walk in the way of its Father, be A comfort to its Friends and be the means of performing a Mighty work to the Glory of God and Prince Forever. . . .

22. Sister Lions [probably Sylvia Lyons] was here Lucretia Fulton stayed here. Went and saw the Mummies and records.[19]

23. A day of fasting. O father wilt thou forgive my sins, enlarge my understanding, strangthen my memory, increase my Faith, and mercifully grant that I might be acceptable unto Thee, and be prepared for all things.

24. Eliza Partridge and Caroline P[artridge] ware here and took Dinner with us. Also Cornelia Levet [Leavitt] was here. . . .

December 1844

8. Cold, but pleasent. Pased the day in reading and committing to memory a few precious words of Joseph Smiths of keeping the commandments of God.

9, 10, 11. A day of fasting to me alone.

12. Had most an exelent meeting in the evening. . . .

21. Little Daved Hiram Smith grows fin[e]. O Lord wilt thou bless the Child from on high. . . .

27. Henry and I went to the dedication of the Seventes Hall. Heber C. Kimble [Kimball] spoke in the fore noon. Had exelent musick. At recess Brother Eldridge and Levi Hancock Danced being filled with the Holy G[h]ost. It is the first time mine eyes ever beheld this. O God bless the Saints until thy will shall be done on Earth as it is in Heaven.

28, 29. Stayed at home and took care of Sister Limans [Lyman's] Caringtons Children for them to go to Meeting. In the evening we went to hear Lorenzo Snow preach. It was an interesting meeting to me. Help me to prophet [profit] thereby.

30. Sister Julia Parks was here. Had a good viset.

31. Washed and Ironed, and in the evenin[g] Sister Ripshier and Daughter, Dimick, Wm and Wife ware here. Conversed uppon President B Youngs sermon. It was the greatest that has ever ben Given to the Church, uppon Priesthood, the Godhed, the dutes of Male & Female, there exaltations &c. O Father wilt thou enlarge my

minde. Help me to hear and do thy will in all things as shall be agreeable to thy will. O Fa[t]her who ar[t] in heven I ask it in the Name of Jesus. . . .

January 1845

2. Zebulun is 3 years old to day and in good health for which I feel truly Grateful. Also Isaac Jacobs and Wife ware here on a viset. H[enry] commenced his house.

3. Margret McDugle came here. . . .

7. Viseted at Sister Hatfields an old playmate or an acquaintance.

8. Saw Sister Empy at her house with sister Carrington. Br. C[arrington] brought us home. . . .

10. Eliza Partridge was here. Had a good viset.

11. Mother was here. The theves begin to Stur up strife and desturbances making trouble for the Saints. O Lord wilt thou have mercy uppon thy People.

12. Herd Lorenzo Snow preach. Sister Scovill carried me in her buggy to see Henrys sister Am... Edmons. Saw sister [Nancy] Nowel. She conversed most excelent.

13. Caroline, Wms wife, was here. Had a good viset.

14. Sister Grant was here. The bretheren met at the stand. Quite a number to be sent out to preach to this state. . . .

18. Sister Fulton was here from the other side of the river. Sister Margret McDugle stayed here all night. She let Me take a cloke to ware. . . .

22. I went to see Old sister Liman [Lyman], a woman that my own Mother was familiar with.

23. I went to Prayer meeting with sister Ripshier. Br Hause took the Lead of the meeting. Had a good meeting. . . .

31. Went over to my Br Wms. Stayed all night. Dreamed of seeing Joseph Smith. I Did not think this was my birthday. This pleasent day I am 24 years old. . . .

February 1845

19. A beautiful day, but in the evening a thunder storm. Nancy Nowel stayed all night with me. Wm Linza [Lindsay] and Julia Parks

ware married at Dimicks. O may her heart be comforted in the Lord. Learning to brade [braid] palmleef hats at Mothers. . . .

21. Making Me a bleue dress. I knit mittings [mittens] for at 2 bits a pare [pair]. . . .

28. I went to see Sister [Elvira] Ho[l]mes in the morning, and went up mane [Main] Street. Made several calls. Saw mother [Patty] Sessions and Sister Lions [Sylvia Lyons]. Left Zebulun at Wm. Caroline, Wm Wife, had 18 fals teeth put in on plates and springs to them done by Hue Patrick. They look very nice. Harriet came home with me and stayed all night. A good viset. It is also Wm birth day. He is 27 years old. O may he be blest forever and ever, amen. . . .

March 1845

4. Went to br Frees and to the Concert Hall in the evening accompaned by Emiline and Eliza Free. Wonderful to tell.

5. Assisted sister Ripsher to dress for the Concert. . . .

10. The Church is in prosperous circumstances for there appears to be the most union that has ever ben. The faithful are determined to keep the law of God. O Father binde us as a People to gether in the bonds of love that we neve[r] shall sepperate. The Temple prospers O Father backen the powers of our enemies, that we as a people may accomplish thy works, that our sole may be saved. . . .

14. Sister Hancock and Emiline Free ware here, Father Huntington and Caroline in the evening and gave me a table cloth. Mother Huntington took supper with us. Business moves rappidly, all things in union among the Saints. Some are leaving that do not feel to felloship the present authorities of the [Church], but God knows and the Saints know. We are in the sure way. If we continue to persevere to the end we shall rest with the Propheets, yea the sanctified ones. O Lord help this people and all thy covenant People for thy sons sake. Wm Marks and family left one day this week, went up the river on the Madison Ferry boat, I expect[,] to unite withe others that have gone out from us because they ware not of us and love Darkness more than light. . . .

20. Attended a funeral at Bro Frees, a daughter. Went to the place

of interment. Called at Lidea [Lydia] Stewarts, also to see Mother
Thorn at Sister Pecks. Returning home I also called at Sister Browns. . . .

24. Emiline and Eliza Free ware here. Had a very good viset.
Making soap. Good time. Br Lewes was here. . . .

Apr. the 1st, 1845. Went to Br Brewers to see Mother Brewer, the
first time I have ben there. Father Huntington came in in the
evening. He spake in tong[ue]s. Henry also Sung in tungs. It was
very good. I interpreted the talk by the help of the speret of God.
Had an agreeable viset.

2. I am not very well. Mother Liman was in. I call her Mother
because of her age and her being an acquaintance of my own
Mothers when we were living in the state of Ohio. She is one of the
worthy women of the Earth. Allen, H. is sick.

3. Through the mercy of My Redeemer I [am] injoying
Comforable Health to day. Henry, Father and Oliver admistered to
me for my health and through the mercy of God I am healed. Sister
Brewer and Sister Lennord [Leonard] and her daughter [*unfinished*]. . . .

9. Sister Eliza Partrage called and had a good viset. I am not very
well. The 70tes met on the Meting ground. . . .

15, Tuesday. Wm. moved back to his house. I was no beter. Sister
Eliza Free came to assist me. I trust that she and her Sister Emiline
may ever be blest and ever finde Friends to assist them and there
Children in time of need for there kindness to me in my Sickness.
Also Mother Liman, Mother Huntington, and Lee Girls, Fanny, Julia,
Sister Brewer, Sanders, Meric, and others. Also Amacy Limans wife.
I feel grateful to God and my friends.

16. My face still worse. Anny Magin, Caroline went to Quincy.

17, 18. Sleepless nights almost.

19. The sun about three quarter of an hour high, My Face broke
about half way between my chin and ear rather nearer the chin.
Discharged wonderfully. O living mortality, how soon thou canst
decay. O may I be prepared at the Great and last change. Eliza and
Emilie Partrage came over and made my bed and prepared me some
supper. All these kindnesses I never shall forget, and the oft times

Mother has sent me milk and things for my comfort. (Fanny Merick came to help me.). . . .

Saturday 26. The Temple moves rappidly. O God wilt thou speed thy work, give us as a People union. . . .

May 1845

11. Herd Wm Smith Preach. He returned last week on Sunday. It brought Peculiar feelings to hear the last one of the family that are living of the Males speak to the saints. O may he be preserved in honour to the name of Isreals God. His Wifes health is very poor. . . .

15. A day of Fasting and Prayer, each family carrying there day's Provision to the Bishop for the Poor Saints. May the blessings of Heaven attend his people. O hear thou the Prayers of this People this day, that the Season may crown us with Plenty and in espesial manner Protect us from our enemes. Let them eat the bread that they prepare for us, O Lord. Lord has ben merciful, the [*incomplete*]

16. Peace and Prosperity reignes in the City, good order and br[otherly] love.

17. My minde is solemn these days. O help me ever to do right, O Lord.

Sunday, 18. Elder Sherwood arrived from the South with 3 can[n]ons that he obtained from a merchant, and 10 kegs of powder, when all [*incomplete*]

19. Herd that George P. Dikes was very sick at Ioway. He is sent to perchase glass for the Temple. Monday the brethren have gone to Carthage to attend the court for trial. . . . [20]

24, Saturday. This memorible day the Sun arose clear in the east. The morning was serene and silent. The Sun and Moon ware at about equel hith [height] in the horizen, as if to rejoice wit[h] the Saints in Praises to the most high. The Saints repared (all that knew it) to the Temple at 6 in the morning. The 12ve and the workmen, some brethren, the Band with the banner of liberty floting in the gentle brese, the last stone was lade [laid] on the Temple with shouts of Hosanah to God and the Lamb, amen, &c. Joy filled every bosom and thanks to our God that had preserved us. Pres B Youngs made some remarks very appropriate. This is the Seveth day even on which

God rested from all his works and the Jews still keep it. O may Isreal in these last day keep all thy statutes. O Praise the Lord for all his goodness, y[e]a his mercies endureth forever. Exalt his holy name for he hath no end. He hath established his work uppon the Earth no more to be throne down. He will r[em]ember all his covenants to fulfil them in there times. O praise the Lord Forever more, Amen. . . .

June 1845

8, Sunday. I stayed at home and took care of Sister Browers children. She has oft done the same for me. The Earth needs rain.

9. A beautiful Shower the Lord hath again blessed the Earth that she may bring forth in her streangth, for which the Saints feel to praise Him. . . .

16. Joseph Youngs brought us a pan of flour and 7 eggs. May He be blest an hundred fold. A friend in need is a friend in deed.

17. I went to Sister [Patty] Sessions. She is quite sick with the Clery Mobus [cholera morbus].[21] I pray that she be quick restored to health, for her labors are very much needed in the Church. In the afternoon we went to my brother Wms. He has been sick but is beter. It is the first time H[enry] has ben out since he was sick. We took supper with them. Sister Balis [or Boles or Bales] was there. We returned home some what tired. Mother Huntington came in with some milk. Mother has visited Sister Brower to day. Behold how lovely it is for Friends to dwell together in unity. O God ever let union Prevail. After we ware in bed Pres J[oseph] Youngs brought us another pan of flour. I Pray God to bless him, and his forever, for I believe his alms will come in remberence before God. O may we r[em]ember his example and if God ever blesses us with means, may we go and do like wise. There was frost on the night of the 16 [June] up the river that killed trees, and some of there vegitables. No frost here. . . .

19. The rafters are on the Temple. All things move rappidly and in order about it.

20. Steady rain Sutch as we need. Praise ye the Lord for His merces endureth forever. Evry thing in the City looks promissing.

21, 22. A lowery Sabath to day. Wm Smith is Marr[i]ed to Miss

Robens. Br Mikesel[l] and wife came here in the evening and brought us a pan of flour and some string beans. He brought us some beans and dride [dried] pumpkin last week. I hope they may be blest for all there kindnesses. When we ware sick Hiram Mikesel[l] administered to us. . . .

24. One Year ago to day Joseph and Hirum Smith left for Carthage, a day never to be forgotten in the anels [annals] of History, ne[i]ther in the bosoms of the saints. A foundation of sorrow was then laid. . . .

27. One year ago to day did My Mortal Eyes behold the slain Marters for of our God for the cause of truth. Behold they rest in peace. The Work of which these men by the assisting Grace of God succeeded in laying the foundation moves with rappidity. We can see the hand dealings of God in mercy from day to day. The roof of the Temple is now about ready for the shingles. But Joseph and Hirum are not here. Yet we belive they are doing a great work in our favour behind the Vale [veil]. We feel that when the cause of truth advances we are blest whether in the body or out. It is a lowry day, our hearts are filled with meditation. Presendy Buell [Zina's sister] and Caroline Huntington ware here to day.

28, Saturday. All in good health. Reparing my silk dress that my Parents got for me in the state of N[ew] Y[ork] 10 years ago. Presendia and I took Supper with Father and Mother. Surely we are blesed.

29. Attended Meeting at the Grove on the Temple block at the same spot whare oft I have seen the Prophet Stand and Patrearch with there countenences beaming with inocence. May I say the index of there heart, the words of eternal life flowing from there Lips filling the hearts of the Saints with Wisdom and jolly Days and Hours have past uppon this concecrated spot will never be forgotten throughout all Eternity. O May I have wisdom to prffet [profit] with all and be accepted before the throne of Grace at the morn of the First resurrection to come forth with the Sanctified and be crowned with the Just for Jesus sake. . . .

July the 1st, 1845. Julia assisted me in sewing. Mother Brower was here. The Twelve and the old Poliece Had a Din[n]er or Feast at the Masonic Hall, a day of recreation, also Music. I am grateful that those who have stood by the Authorates B[e]aring the Burden both night and day can have A time of rejoicing.

2. Sister Robins and Caroline took supper with us. Henry brought home 13 yards of carpetting from the weavers which is the works of my own hands.

3. At the Thursday Prayer meeting Father John Smith made some exelent remarks concerning the Priesthood, Prayer, Endewment, &c.

4. A day long to be remembered. O liberty how ha[s]t thou falen O Lord wilt thou restore thy People to trew [true] liberty, even to keeping thy selestial Law. Forgive me all my sins that I may be free indeed. Show unto me my self that I may be wise. Give unto me Thy speret that I may ever desern [discern] the trew Speret and be a [blotted] thereby and Thy name shall have the Glory, Amen. I feel to thank thee for food, for raiment, for causing vedgitition to come forth as thou hast this year. O may thy blessings continue with thy People forever worlds without end. I Also thank thee for health and the innumerable Blessings that this People enjoy. Help us O Lord ever to be grateful and Humble. These are a few of my desires. Pen is inadiquate to numerate thy mercies. O ever let my minde dwell with wisdom and comprehend thy laws to thy glory.

5. Sister Eliza Partrage and I took dinner together. Sister Nowel made me a viset this afternoon. Nanc[y]s name was spoke of for good. Mother Thorn stayed here all night.

6, Sunday. I took care of Sister Brower children this after noon. I am alone. O that my time and thoughts might ever be guided in wisdom. Yesterday, it being Saturday, the 5th of July, 1845, Father Huntington locked up his chest of tools at the Temple. He has Labored 3 years mostly. He has done 818 days works. Now in good health, Aged 61 the 28 of Last March. . . .

13, Sunday. 14, 15, 16. I called to see Sister Eliza Snow. She has ben confined to her be[d] 5 weeks, but O the patience. She is worthy of imitation. She is at E[l]der S Marcums [Stephen Markham], a fine family. I went with sister [Patty] Sessions to br Geens Funeral. Pres B Youngs spoke. May I never forget the words that fell from his lips. He spake of the power the Saints would have over disease, The fall of the Earth, its redemption, also all those that ware destined to this planet or world. . . .

21, Monday. I and my little Son are still in Lima at my sisters.[22] Her company is sweet but at lovely Nauvoo or City of Joseph how dear is the sosiety of the Saints. . . .

29. A time of Peace in this City. . . .

30. I commenced spinning for Presendia. Sister Liman was here and Sister Nowell took sup[p]er with us.

31. Thursday. No prayer meeting to day. Warm and plesent. Bisness moves rappidly. Great advancements made on the Temple daily. Let it hasten.

July [August] the 1, 1845

Mother Brower was here. O may I have trew wisdom and knowledge.

2. Zebulun was taken to day with the Scarlet fever. . . .

8. To day is a day of fasting and Prayer with me. Mother Brower and I set over the feeble body of my little son. He is very sick. Caroline and Lydia Partrage set up with us. Father Jacobs administered to Zebulun after sun set. Sayed he thought he would live. May it be so.

9. Z[ebulun] is some beter than he was last night. May the prospect continue to bri[gh]ten. Walter Davis set up with Henry. H[enry] Baptized him in the state of N Y. He, Davis, is or has ben a Salor. He now assists in pulling up timber on the Temple. He that Sings thus in the wisdom of God, the Gospel net has caught all and the building is fitly framed.

10. Mother Huntington spent part of the day with me and time of conversing uppon the resurrection of the ded, &c. Zebulun is a little beter. If it is the will of Heven may he soon recover to perfect soundness and God shall have the Glory.

11, Sunday. Wm W Felps [Phelps] addrest the Church to day from the stand. In the afternoon the differen quorums Met.

12. Another Election to day. Zebulun cannot walk a step. A colored woman washed for us to day. O God help me to humble my

self before thee in that thou will own and bless me for I feel Poor and needy rember me in mercy, O Lord, even the God of my Sperit that I may praise Thee fo[r]ever worlds without end and O that I may be an honour to thy Church.

13. Eliza P and Sister Liman ware here.

14. Cleaning house. Nancy was here, also Br Rephser and his wife. The Last shingle was lade on the Temple. Prase the Lord.

15. A general fast for the whole Church. Although I am at home with my sick son I feel that the Speret of God is with the people at the meeting ground to bless the Meek. O let me be one of that number for I desire it with all my heart, for I feel to renew my covenant with Thee O God my Heavenly Father, desiring to lay hold on Faith and obediance unt[o] Salvation that I may be saved with a fulness of joy among those of the hi[gh]est Glory. Wilt thou prepare me for this and may I be an honour to those with whom I am concerned. O wilt Thou give me grace in the eyes of the trew saints and thy Name shall have the honour, worlds with out end, amen and Amen. Wm called and had a chat.

16, 17. Zebulun is some beter, on the amend.

18, [17]. Sunday. Wm Smith Spoke to the People. Elder Talor [John Taylor] made an appropriate reply. It was needed. And God wilt thou be merciful to Thy People for thou art acquainted with all there needs. Give us wisdom.[23]

19. I am bra[i]ding Palmleef.

20. Washing. A beautiful day, and may my heart be clean. . . .

23. Henry worked on Joseph Youngs house. [I] spun 34 [k]nots of warp.

24. Attended Meeting at the Stand. Joseph Youngs spoke. It is the 3d time that he has spoken publickly to this People and has ben a resident of this place 6 years. He is first, of the 7 Pres of all the Seventes. He spoke uppon the resurrection some. Pres B Youngs spoke after him uppon what was wisdom for us to preserve our healths &c. Very good. A bisness meeting in the P M for all the Males of the Church.

25. Took sup[p]er at Wm. They had company and sent for me. A fine repast of ripe Peaches and melons. I feel truly grateful that my

life has ben spared uppon the Earth to partake of the bountes therof. Praise Ye the Lord for his merces endureth forever. O may all these things lead us to faithfulness, to humility and diligence in keeping all the commands of God.

26. A very warm day. I am laboring at the [spinning] wheel to procure an honest living. O Lord wilt thou give me streangth for I fee[l] the flesh is weak. Let not my minde be to[o] much plased uppon the things of this world, but may I labor with my might for the things of a beter and finde acceptance with my Redeemer.

27. Viseted the sick, and washed. Quite warm. Dimicks Child is very sick, the babe.

28. All in good health for which I am truly grateful. Henry was on the prairie. I stayed at Fathers all night.

29 [30]. The small boys have there tra[i]ning every Saturday. It looks very nice. May they be blest I pray.

30 [31]. Parl[e]y P Prat[t] returned from N Y City, arived last week, has ben absent 9 months. He spoke uppon his mission. The World, being ripe [for] the fulfilment of Prophecy, the Spread of the Gospel. Said in 18 or 20 months there would not be an Island but what the saving gospel should be in evry place. So may it be, O Lord. Stated had he arived in Dec he would have ben astonished to see things advan[c]ed as far as they are especially the Temple and Nauvoo House.

Sept. the 1, 1845. A pleasent day of meditation uppon the work of God in thes last days.

2. Spinning. Spun 22 [k]nots. When the body is weary the mind is also.

3. Very warm yesterday and to day. Between 5 and 6 in the evening a violent thunderstorm arose accompaned with hail and wind. Most of the Glass in the city on the north side of the buildings ware broken. The longest hail storm that I ever saw. Vines ware ruined. I would think upon the Last days.

4. Quite Cool. The Air is more pure and comfortable, for which I feel thankful. I feel to acknoledge the hand of God in all things. . . .

11. Lewes Damp, a Lamanite, gave me a money purse that his

step Daughter Nancy sent to me from the Mo Territory. She has ben here and was baptized some years ago. When she left me or this plac[e] for the far west, I took a ring from my finger and gave it to her. She was a fine appearended girl. The purse is velvet, beautifully ornamented with beads or her own hands work.

12. Herd again from Lima. The mob has burnt 7 buildings.

13. Herd from Lima [that] the mob are raging, burning buildings, grain, driving all before.

14. Went to meeting Pres Young, Heber C K[imball] Amacy [Amasa Lyman] spoke, told us the necessity of hearing to councel, mentioned the enemy, told us not to fear, put our trust in God. At Father Jacobs in the P M. He is very sick.

15. The enemy still continues to burn and drive in the Bretheren, not even giving time to save all there furniture. O God, all flesh is in thy hands. Thou canst turn there hearts even as the rivers of water are turned. In Thee do I put my trust in all things.

16. They, the Mob, burnt a brothers hous 4 miles this side of Carthage last night, and 400 bushels of grane [grain]. To day Porter Rockwell Shot [*blank*] as they ware pursuing Mr. Backenstos on the parrarie near the rail road.[24] Ther was about 30, this one was at the hed. He helped to concoct the plan to slay Joseph and Hirum; he was at the Jail at the murder.

17. The Bretheren are all at the stand armed and equiped. (To day I went to see about getting some weving. Done when I was gone—o my!) Henry went with Br. Marcum's [Markham's] Company in the region of Bare Creek [at] 2 P M. Just as the sun was setting a Company returned from the region towards Warsaw, all well.

18. When I cast mine eyes out, what do I behold, evry brother armed, his gun uppon his shoulder to protect his family and Bretheren from the violence of the furious Mob who are now burning all that falls into their way round about the Country. Ah Liberty, thou art fled. When the wicked rule the People mourn.

19th, Friday. This morning at about 7 oclock 2 cannons ware fired near the Temple which signified for all to be on the ground. As I am alone I have not learned the particulars yet. Clear and pleasant.

20. The first thing I saw as I looked toward the Temple just as the sun was risen, a white flag, a signature to gather. A company is called for to assist a company that is out to execute the Laws of the Land to put down the mob.

21. All things move in order in the City.

NOTES

1. Judy Nolte Lensink, "Expanding the Boundaries of Criticism: The Diary as Female Autobiography," *Women's Studies* 14 (1987): 41. Much has been written about diaries as both literary texts and historical sources. See, for example, Donna C. Stanton, ed., *The Female Autograph, Theory and Practice of Autobiography from the Tenth to the Twentieth Century* (Chicago and London: The University of Chicago Press, 1987); Harriet Blodgett, *Centuries of Female Days: Englishwomen's Private Diaries* (New Brunswick, New Jersey: Rutgers University Press, 1988); Elizabeth Hampsten, *Read This Only to Yourself: The Private Writings of Midwestern Women, 1880-1910* (Bloomington: Indiana University Press, 1981); Phyllis Rose, *Writing of Women: Essays in a Renaissance* (Middletown, Connecticut: Wesleyan University Press, 1985); Carolyn G. Heilbrun, *Writing a Woman's Life* (New York: Ballantine Books, 1988); Leonore Hoffmann and Margo Culley, eds., *Women's Personal Narratives: Essays in Criticism and Pedagogy* (New York: The Modern Language Association of America, 1985).

2. This is a reference to her arranged marriage to James Harris.

3. External evidence suggests that Emmeline learned indirectly that James had gone to sea, though she received no letters from him.

4. The day was Eliza's wedding day, when she was married as a plural wife to Joseph Smith.

5. In her "Sketch of My Life" (microfilm of holograph, LDS Church Archives), Eliza wrote, "But alas! soon after our return, we learned that at the time of our visit, and while making protestations of friendship, the wily Governor was secretly conniving with the basest of men to destroy our leaders."

6. Hinkle had earlier persuaded Church leaders to negotiate with Missouri officials who, instead of negotiating, imprisoned them.

7. Eliza's older sister Leonora, married to but separated from Enoch Virgil Leavitt, lived in Morley Settlement, about thirty miles south of Nauvoo.

8. Eliza's sister Amanda Percy Snow married Eli McConoughey shortly before the Snows left Ohio.

9. The Smiths had a special interest in the school, since four of their children attended.

10. The visit resulted in Joseph's capture at Dixon, Lee County, Illinois. See *History of the Church* 5:431-75, 481-88.

11. The poem, published in the *Wasp*, a Nauvoo newspaper, on September 16, 1842, is clearly addressed to Joseph Smith.

12. Possibly to Joseph Smith's farm, where Cornelius Lott was foreman.

13. Eliza maintained her residence with the Markhams throughout the rest of her time in Nauvoo, staying with them until they reached Winter Quarters after the exodus.

14. From a poem, "Zina D. H. Young," by Emmeline B. Wells, *Young Women's Journal* 12 (June 1901): 254.

15. May Booth Talmage, "Past Three Score Years and Ten," *Young Women's Journal* 12 (June 1901): 257.

16. The threat at this time resulted from the destruction of the *Nauvoo Expositor*, an anti-Mormon publication, which ultimately led to Joseph Smith's arrest later in the month.

17. The Mound was a small hill east of Nauvoo where a branch of the Church was located. Joseph Smith's farm was near that area.

18. His death left only one surviving brother of Joseph's: William.

19. The scrolls from which the Book of Abraham was translated were found with the mummies and purchased by the Church from Michael Chandler. These were in the keeping of Lucy Mack Smith, who showed them to visitors, sometimes for a fee.

20. She is referring to the trial of the five men accused of murdering Joseph and Hyrum Smith.

21. *Cholera morbus* was the usual term describing acute gastroenteritis, marked by severe cramps, diarrhea, and vomiting. Patty Sessions was a midwife; hence "her labors are very much needed."

22. Zina occasionally visited her sister Prescindia Buell in Lima, a settlement thirty miles south of Nauvoo.

23. Hosea Stout describes the meeting thus: "W. Smith [spoke on] what he called the first chapter of the Epistle to St. William and was followed by Elder John Taylor to which William showed considerable feelings" (Stout, *Diary*, pp. 57–58). William Smith lost his position as apostle at the following October conference, and on October 12, 1845, he was excommunicated.

24. Sheriff Backenstos, though a non-Mormon, was solicitous of the welfare of the Mormons.

LETTERS

❧

"Yours, in the Bands
of the Covenant"

"YOURS, IN THE BANDS OF THE COVENANT"

"I do not intend to relate particulars and senes I have been called to pass through," wrote Mary Ives to her parents in 1840 from Nauvoo; "it would require types instead of a pen. I shall only mention verry few." Mary was true to her word. But in her brief letter she was able to convey the trials of leaving Missouri, the misery of trudging over and sleeping on frozen ground, the heartbreak in watching her husband die of dysentery, and her efforts to earn enough money to support her children by herself.

Nauvoo letter writers discovered that much could be conveyed in few words. With little time and fewer materials, they found ways to write their impressions and convey the enormity of the changes in their lives since they had become Mormons. The strength of their conversion, the difficulties of Kirtland and Missouri or the voyage across an ocean, and the challenges of Nauvoo all had to be explained, or at least described, to absent loved ones.

As they struggled to make their readers understand, the letter writers did not fall into a self-pitying mode. Their compelling need was to convey the truth of their experience, both their trials and their triumphs, to communicate the commonplace, which their readers would quickly understand, and explain the extraordinary, which they might not. As readers from a later generation, we are as dependent on their written accounts for understanding as were those in their own time who were geographically distanced.

But sending a letter was not an easy process in the nineteenth century. Pen, ink, and paper were usually in short supply. As a result, some writers wrote both vertically and horizontally across the sheet, crisscrossing the paper like a multi-lined "tic-tac-toe."[1] Moreover, postage was expensive, the amount determined by the weight of the paper used and the distance the letter was to travel. If the sender didn't pay the postage, the receiver had to in order to retrieve the letter. Thus, mail was often sent along with missionaries or other travelers. Someone could usually be found who was traveling in the same direction as the letter. Correspondents often found their letter writing extending over several weeks while they waited for a missionary to leave. Sometimes they hastily jotted down only a few sentiments in order to catch an unexpected departure. Despite the long weeks and even months that passed between letters, they are surprisingly intimate, immediate, and conversational. Unlike most other personal writings, they were tailored to fit a specific reader.

The letters that follow not only convey the immediate thoughts and experiences of individual women, but also offer each woman's response to the times and circumstances that gave her life context. They range in style from the highly polished, like Charlotte Haven's and Mary Fielding Smith's, which were eventually published, to the expressive but untutored efforts of Mary Ann Young and Bathsheba Smith. Like most personal narratives, they are unstructured and flow almost haphazardly from the writer's pen, guided only by the author's random thoughts, the dramatic moments merging with the commonplace. "I have no news to write," Susan Jolly informed her son in 1845, adding as if in an afterthought, "accept [sic] we have been surrounded by mobs for three or four weeks just what the result will be God only knows."[2] After an impassioned, "O Mother I often think of you and although we are separated from each other you are not forgotten by me," Eliza Cheney perfunctorily continued, "I have a girl spinning for me, we shall make about fifty yards of flannel this fall. Please give my respects to all inquiring friends."[3] This seemingly desultory style did not signify a leveling of experience or feeling. It simply reflected the writer's mind, flooded with images and thoughts allowed to escape in the indiscriminate order in which they occurred.

While the Nauvoo letters expressed the conventions of letter writing—reports of the weather, state of health, family data, social activities—they were created against an extraordinary historical backdrop.

How to convey such historical and spiritual drama, especially to unbelievers? Nothing short of their personal witness would suffice.

Ellen Douglas (Parker) expressed gratitude for receiving the gift of the gospel: "I for one feel to rejoice and to praise my God that he ever sent the Elders of Israel to England and that he ever gave me a heart to believe them."[4] Eliza Cheney reconfirmed her decision to convert: "I did not embrace this work hastily," she reassured her parents. "I came into it understandingly, I weighed the subject, I counted the cost, I know the consequences of every step I took. I have not been disappointed in the least."[5] And even while suffering the terrible effects of the Missouri expulsion, Mary Fielding Smith affirmed to her brother Joseph Fielding her joy that she "was ever made acquainted with the everlasting covenant!"[6]

Uncommon people in an uncommon cause. Life for them was an experience of the soul as well as the body. Their letters expressed not only the challenges of their world but also the awakening of their spirits.

Eight of the letters that follow were written by women to member relatives and friends and reflect the intimacy of shared conviction and understanding. The four letters written to nonmember families exhibit the urgency of their writers to reaffirm commitment to the gospel and their momentous decision to gather with the Saints. Charlotte Haven, a non-Mormon resident of Nauvoo, adds an outsider's perspective, admiring but sometimes mocking. And, finally, one collective letter, a petition to Governor Carlin signed by a thousand women, demonstrates the Relief Society's support of its president, Emma Smith, by adding their voices to her numerous appeals to the governor in behalf of the Prophet.

Though each letter tells the tale of one writer, together they create a story of Nauvoo that institutional records alone cannot relate. The reader will discover that these personal, intimate missives are not mere ornaments to the official histories. They are the flesh and blood of those histories, the vitalizing element that gives them life.

MARY FIELDING SMITH

When Mary Fielding followed her brother and sister from England to Eastern Canada in 1834, she hardly anticipated the dramatic events that would mark her life during the next eighteen years. She had left England only to assist her sister during a prolonged illness, but neither Mary nor her siblings would make England their home again.

Two years after Mary's arrival in Canada, the Fieldings accepted

Mary Fielding Smith

the gospel at the hands of Parley P. Pratt and joined the Church in company with John Taylor, Leonora Cannon, and other British emigrants living in the vicinity of Toronto and upper York. The next year the Fieldings migrated to Kirtland, where, in December 1837, Mary Fielding married Hyrum Smith, instantly becoming a mother to the six children left motherless by the death of Hyrum's first wife, Jerusha Barden. One of the great experiences of Mary's life was her witness of numerous manifestations of the Spirit during the dedication of the Kirtland Temple. She joyfully described in a letter the love and unity expressed by "some of the sisters while engaged in conversing in tongues, their countenances beaming with joy," as they "clasped each other's hands . . . in the most affectionate manner."[7]

Moving with the body of Saints to Missouri, Mary learned just how precarious her life as Hyrum Smith's wife would be. She gave birth to her first child, Joseph F. Smith, in November 1838, just twelve days after her husband was arrested and incarcerated with the Prophet Joseph in Liberty jail. Mary saw her husband only once before leaving Missouri, when she accompanied Emma Smith on a short visit to the jail, though Mary was nearly bedridden. After she moved to Nauvoo and was reunited with her husband, her anxieties about him only intensified, with good cause. She experienced all of the uncertainties and fears that Emma knew in connection with Joseph, since their husbands' lives were tightly entwined. Yet she was not the Prophet's wife, and history has not always recognized how deeply she shared with Emma the trauma of the last years in Nauvoo. The martyrdom heaped just as tragic a burden on Mary Smith and her children as on Emma and hers.

Their shared sorrows and common experiences did not bind their futures together, however. While Emma elected to remain in Nauvoo among familiar, if unhappy, memories, Mary, with her sister Mercy and brother Joseph, chose to follow Brigham Young to the Great Salt Lake Valley.

With Mercy's help, Mary took on the task of directing the westward move of her own little band of pioneers, consisting of eight children, including Mercy's young daughter, and several elderly adults. Destined to move every time she called a place home, Mary hoped the valley would be an exception. Indeed it was. Only four years after arriving there, Mary Fielding Smith died at the age of fifty-one. Salt Lake City was her final resting place.

From the day of their conversion in Canada, the Fieldings were steadfast in their faithfulness to the Church, always hoping their relatives in England would join them in accepting the gospel. Mary wrote the letter that follows to her brother Joseph, who was one of the first missionaries to introduce the gospel in the British Isles. Their brother James opened his church to the missionaries' preaching but quickly became hostile when many of his congregation were baptized. When Mary wrote this letter to her missionary brother, she had just arrived in Nauvoo after fleeing the mobs in Missouri.

MARY FIELDING SMITH TO JOSEPH FIELDING*

Commerce, Ill., North America
June 1839

My very Dear Brother:

As the elders are expecting shortly to take their leave of us again to preach the gospel in my native land, I feel as though I would not let the opportunity of writing you pass unimproved. I believe it will give you pleasure to hear from us by our own hand; notwithstanding you will see the brethren face to face, and have an opportunity of hearing all particulars respecting us and our families.

As it respects myself, it is now so long since I wrote to you, and so many important things have transpired, and so great have been my affliction, etc., that I know not where to begin; but I can say, hitherto has the Lord preserved me, and I am still among the living to praise him, as I do today. I have, to be sure, been called to drink deep of the bitter cup; but you know, my beloved brother, this makes the sweet sweeter.

You have, I suppose, heard of the imprisonment of my dear husband, with his brother Joseph, Elder Rigdon, and others, who were kept from us nearly six months; and I suppose no one felt the painful effects of their confinement more than myself. I was left in a way that called for the exercise of all the courage and grace I possessed. My husband was taken from me by an armed force, at a time when I needed, in a particular manner, the kindest care and attention of such a friend, instead of which, the care of a large family was suddenly and unexpectedly left upon myself, and, in a few days after, my dear little Joseph F. was added to the number. Shortly after his birth I took a severe cold, which brought on chills and fever; this, together with the anxiety of mind I had to endure, threatened to bring me to the gates of death. I was at least four months entirely unable to take any care either of myself or child; but the Lord was merciful in so ordering things that my dear sister could be with me.

---

*Edward W. Tullidge, *The Women of Mormondom* (New York, 1877), 255–58.

Her child was five months old when mine was born; so she had strength given her to nurse them both.

You will also have heard of our being driven, as a people, from the State, and from our homes; this happened during my sickness, and I had to be removed more than two hundred miles, chiefly on my bed. I suffered much on my journey; but in three or four weeks after we arrived in Illinois, I began to amend, and my health is now as good as ever. It is now little more than a month since the Lord, in his marvelous power, returned my dear husband, with the rest of the brethren, to their families, in tolerable health. We are now living in Commerce, on the bank of the great Mississippi river. The situation is very pleasant; you would be much pleased to see it. How long we may be permitted to enjoy it I know not; but the Lord knows what is best for us. I feel but little concerned about where I am, if I can keep my mind staid upon God; for, you know in this there is perfect peace. I believe the Lord is overruling all things for our good. I suppose our enemies look upon us with astonishment and disappointment.

I greatly desire to see you, and I think you would be pleased to see our little ones; will you pray for us, that we may have grace to train them up in the way they should go, so that they may be a blessing to us and the world? I have a hope that our brothers and sisters will also embrace the fullness of the gospel, and come into the new and everlasting covenant; I trust their prejudices will give way to the power of truth. I would gladly have them with us here, even though they might have to endure all kind of tribulation and affliction with us and the rest of the children of God, in these last days, so that they might share in the glories of the celestial kingdom. As to myself, I can truly say, that I would not give up the prospect of the latter-day glory for all that glitters in this world. O, my dear brother, I must tell you, for your comfort, that my hope is full, and it is a glorious hope; and though I have been left for near six months in widowhood, in the time of great affliction, and was called to take, joyfully or otherwise, the spoiling of almost all our goods, in the absence of my husband, and all unlawfully, just for the gospel's sake (for the judge himself declared that he was kept in prison for no other reason than because he was a friend to his brother), yet I do not feel in the least discouraged; no, though my sister and I are here together in a strange land, we have been enabled to rejoice, in the midst of our privations and persecutions, that we were counted worthy to suffer these things, so that we may, with the ancient saints who suffered in like manner, inherit the same glorious reward. If it had not been for this hope, I should have sunk before this; but, blessed be the God and rock of my salvation, here I am, and am perfectly satisfied and happy, having not the smallest desire to go one step backward.

Your last letter to Elder Kimball gave us great pleasure; we thank you for your expression of kindness, and pray God to bless you according to your desires for us.

The more I see of the dealings of our Heavenly Father with us as a people, the more I am constrained to rejoice that I was ever made acquainted with the everlasting covenant. O may the Lord keep me faithful till my change comes! O, my dear brother, why is it that our friends should stand out against the truth, and look on those that would show it to them as enemies? The work here is prospering much; several men of respectability and intelligence, who have been acquainted with all our difficulties, are coming into the work.

My husband joins me in love to you. I remain, my dear brother and sister, your affectionate sister,

Mary Smith

LEONORA CANNON TAYLOR

Leonora Cannon, a native of the Isle of Man, emigrated to Toronto, Ontario, Canada, to be the household companion of the wife of the newly appointed private secretary to the Governor General of Canada. Soon after arriving she met John Taylor, also a British emigrant, and the two were married in 1833. The Taylors, with Joseph Fielding and his sisters, also from England and living near them in Canada, found their lives dramatically changed when they heard the gospel preached by Parley P. Pratt and accepted baptism in 1836. John and Leonora traveled to Kirtland, Ohio, to be with the Church and followed it to Missouri and then to Nauvoo.

Leonora Cannon Taylor

After the flight from Missouri, Leonora Taylor settled with her three children—George, five; Mary Ann, three; and Joseph, one—in a single room of an abandoned barracks building in Montrose, Iowa, while her husband served as a missionary in England. The ordeal was long and difficult, and on her husband's return she confessed, "I had gone through all but death during his absence. [I] lived in an old barrack room twenty feet square with one small window the back door . . . of the hinges and walls so open that a skunk came in every Night one Winter."[8]

In Nauvoo Leonora joined the Relief Society, and later, she and her husband received their endowments from Joseph Smith in the upper room of his store before the Nauvoo Temple was completed. The Taylors left Nauvoo in 1846. After settling in the Salt Lake Valley, Leonora devoted herself to her family, accepting the many personal and domestic disruptions to which her membership in the Church and her husband's callings subjected her. The gospel had fulfilled her religious yearnings, but at a high personal cost. "The Lord often led me by a way that I knew not," she wrote in her diary, "and in a path that I naturally did not wish to go, every sweet has had its bitter . . . to whom shall I go or look for succor but unto thee my Father and only Friend."[9] Leonora lived quietly in Salt Lake City, never seeking a public role or prominence. She died of pneumonia in 1868.

More than four years separate the two letters that follow. The first, one of several she wrote to her husband while living in Montrose, describes her own and the Church's circumstances after John's departure for England several months earlier. It also expresses the depth of her conviction of the work in which he was so fully engaged. The other letter, written from Nauvoo under more pleasant circumstances to her friend Phebe Woodruff, shows a lighthearted, more comfortably situated Leonora, sharing news about Phebe's son.

LEONORA CANNON TAYLOR TO JOHN TAYLOR*

Montrose
2 January 1840

I wish my John a Happy New Year and many of them. I have just come from meeting in Brother Cathrens. This is the first Prayer Meeting in this place. After this they are to be regular once a week and preaching on *[undecipherable]*. I must write so as to tell you all the news in a few words. I hope my dear you are well in your body as

---

*Leonora Cannon Taylor to John Taylor, January 2, 1840, Leonora Cannon Taylor Papers, LDS Church Archives.

you seem in yours of the 19th. of Nov. to be in your mind. I so pray the Lord to continue to bless and comfort you. I do praise Him for what He has done for you all ready. I wish you could see George and Mary Ann, as fat and rosy as ever they were. Joseph is better and can run alone again, but teeth are still coming and I have to nurse him a great deal. I feel better able than I was when I last wrote. I have been *sick* but am better; he is still to be the baby.[10] The Lord knows what is best for us. I live in Sister [Phebe] Woodruff's house. Brother Pratt has gone over the river to live. He is well. Sister Woodruff has gone to live to [undecipherable] is well and so is Sarah [Phebe Woodruff's daughter]. She got two letters and a paper from New York lately. Brother Joseph is likely to get a hearing. I heard a letter read from him—very incouraging indeed. He wants all to pray for him.[11] He sent Brother Manholm over hear some time since with papers relative to the lots on the other side. He came to me and said you had bespoke and I must sign the papers for you. I thought them very dear. He said that he could sell it for you and perhaps get 25 dollars more for it. He died suddenly soon after poor man. Edward Lawrence is dead. Brother Daniels is also dead; heard the school masters wife and many others also and some families are still sick. Many are well. I have cause to be thankfull. I have suffered little compared with others. I am well supplied with fire wood by Dr. Patten. That has been some trouble to me since you left me. But I hope the worst is past. Sister Young and family are well and expect to leave this for Kirtland as soon as the boats come along, with Father Granger who is here still. I went across to see him after I got you[r] letter. He was away from home. I told his daughter my business and next day wrote the letter you wished to Brother [Hiram] Kimball and enclosed it open to Bro Granger telling him what you said. (I have seen Bro Granger who says he will do all in his power for you he is going as soon as the River opens)[12] I asked him to send Bro Humphry his Letter. I have heard nothing from him since but shall go over the River if all is well very soon it is frosen over now very hard. People walk over.

Bro Law and Family are on the other side.[13] I have not seen them yet he sent me four Dollars at Christmas by Brother Ripley—I wish you would write to him as soon as you have anny thing interesting to write and thank him for me I do want to know how you got Money to pay your way at the Tavern and to travel—if you should go to England or anny where else write as soon as possible and tell me where to direct. we have got a House Boat on the River and a House [?] Mill on each side the River—I have not heard anny thing from your Father's People lately I wrote to them but have had no answer— there is a conference out in Father Hauley's neibourhood to day where he us'd to live rather he has removed to Quincy

I spent new Years day in Brother Rosers with some Friends in the Evining I had three Indian Women a papuce and an Elderly Man all very clean to supper with me the[y] sat around the Fire and talked away quite comfortable little Joseph kisst the little papuce and was delighted with it the Children all send there love and a hundred kisses to Father Joseph gives me one evry day for you and points to your Old Hat when shall we see dear Father again is my cry and the Childrens, but I do not want to hinder the work of the Lord my comfort is not to be compard with the worth of one Soul and I do pray that many may hear & believe the truth with whome we shall yet rejoice in the presence of the Lord.

My dear John, Br Law has been to see me His Brother & Br Snider walked over the River. He is a kind man askd if I wanted anny thing (I said no) and to remember I had a Friend over the River whenever I did I got your Letter of the 17th Dec & two papers I fear you will feel disappointed on receiving this you know my dear what you have often said to me that every thing is ordered for the best. *I fully believe so in this instance.* Joseph is the most affectionate little thing if I look serious he holds up his mouth to kiss he dont speak anny yet to signify. George and Mary Anne go to Sunday School to Mrs. Booth I teach them evry day at home. Geo & M. Ann often dream of father as well as poor Mother. Sister Young Amelia Rodgers, and I walkd over the River the way we had to walk was three Miles (there were a great number of our bretherin Lamanites going before us amongst them was Black Hawks Son and two Sons in law his Son can speak english if I had not been alone I should have likd them to have come in one day the[y] stood outside the Door to have some thing to eat the[y] were drest very fine, Bells on there legs

Feathers on there heads, we went to take a Letter to J.O. Prat who lives now with Sister Patten that was [when] we saw Sister [Vilate ?] Kimball and Sister [Frances] Turley the[y] were all well Brother Snider went with us and returnd to Springfield the next day, he intends to move here in Summer. Br Laws new Store is open—there has been so many reports about how our bussiness got on at Washington that I have been waiting to have some certainty for you. Brother Joseph, the last acount we have had was in Philadelphia with Br Higby [Higbee] visiting the Church and left Pre'nt Rigdon at Washington who is to send for them when they are wanted Br Joseph wrote to new York to say all that had not saild of the twelve were to go to Washington to his assistance many belive nothing favourable will be done you had just saild when the Letter went I want to hear from you very much my Health is not good I pray the Lord to spare me to see you once more I feel thankfull to the Lord that I am able to do what is needfull for my dear Children I bought them warm and Wollen frocks and had long wollen stockings knit for myself and them and all had new Shoes on at Xmas I have made my Bed wide G and M. sleep at one end and Joseph and I at the other, the House is so cold never been plastered we have had steady cold weather I have a Screen round the Fire and burn plenty of wood and shall have to pay for it *[undecipherable]* D[octor] Patten began to find it at Christmas & he agreed to bring it in from the country half the time I had to beg it and cary it home the week before Xmas it stormd and Snowd. I had no wood for five days but what I beggd and caryed home in my arms B Ripley came I told him I felt discouraged and could not stand it long he then ingaged my wood of Doctor Patten.

You must excuse my bad writing, I have a bad pen and no *Father* to mend it.[14] I hope my dear that you had a good passage; if favorably you were there before I got your letter. Sister Woodruff is well and comfortable. Elder Curtis in New York wrote to Brother Mace that you had sailed and that there are nearly fifty members in Philadelphia, in New York and vicinity nearly five hundred. The work is going on. I hope that you found my friends well and favorable to the truth. Give my love to them all, write soon and often, I don't know how to wait for a letter from you now but hope for the best. The children and I send our love and kisses to a loving Father. Sisters Smith and Thompson are well. Give my best wishes to Brother and Sister Fielding. If you should go to the Isle of Man be sure to stop at Mister Higgins in Peel and try to lead him into the truth. Give my love to all that ask after me in the Isle of Man. May the Lord bless my dear John and bring him safe back is the prayer of your affectionate wife,

Leonora Taylor
Montrose, Feb. 2, 1840

LEONORA CANNON TAYLOR TO PHEBE CARTER WOODRUFF*

Sunday

My Dear Sister Woodruff

we are all well I just returned from meeting there was a Sherif there from Springfield with a few *writs* for the Bretherin as usual Wm Taylor spoke and gave them and all mobs, there *blessing*, the Peoples *Amen* made the *[undecipherable] ring* we should get used to persecution and think nothing about it like the Womans *[undecipherable]* by and by, the Sisters and there Familys are well generally I long to see you and yours Sister Benbow is poorly.[15] I went there with Mr T and stayed a few days, little Willy [Phebe's five-year-old son] is one of the best boys ever was content and happy he heard a Song and remembered one verse /twas there my *Sisters* play'd, my *Mother* kis'd me there, my *Father* shook my hand, forgive this foolish Tear, but let that Old Oak *stand*: it made an impression on him he

---

*This letter, with several others, was appended to a letter written by George A. Smith to Wilford Woodruff, April 13, 1845. Wilford Woodruff was then serving with his wife Phebe in the British Mission. They had left their five-year-old son, Willy, in Nauvoo. The original is in the Wilford Woodruff Papers, LDS Church Archives.

often repeats it, another he sang for us was I am a happy farmers boy and live upon my Farm I work all day and sleep all night and so keep free from harm. Miss [Hannah] Ells lives there I shall go out again shortly please give my love to all that will accept of it in the Church and I should like my Sister to know I got her letter and I want a long one from her and you if you have time very soon may the Lord bless and keep you and yours forever in great haste L. T. if not too much trouble I should like to have some Drawing Paper and pencils for George when you send S[ister Bathsheba] Smiths the[y] cannot be got *here* ever yours L. Taylor

ELLEN BRIGGS DOUGLAS (PARKER)

One of the earliest British converts, Ellen Briggs Douglas, was baptized by Heber C. Kimball on March 28, 1838, in her native village in Lancashire, England. Ellen and her husband, George Douglas, also a member, emigrated to Nauvoo in the spring of 1842 with their three sons and four daughters. With a healthy husband and three sons to support the family, Ellen envisioned a comfortable life in Nauvoo.

However, the sudden death of her husband a few months after they arrived changed her prospects, which were further compromised when family members contracted malaria and suffered the privations experienced by many other immigrants.

Ellen turned to her fellow British converts for support. Many of them lived in a British enclave on the eastern edge of Nauvoo, assisting one another to make the adjustment to life in an American frontier community. The Relief Society also became a lifeline to Ellen during those stressful weeks.

Ellen Briggs Douglas (Parker)

Ellen's letters answered the curiosity of her relatives in England, keeping them informed of the current status of their British friends in Nauvoo as well as her own experiences in the Church and a new land. She similarly asked for news about friends and the family members she had left behind. Her long-held hope that all her family could share the experiences conversion had brought to her infused her letters with professions of conviction and assurance that neither hardship nor tragedy seemed to diminish.

After her husband's death, Ellen remained a widow for four years before marrying, in 1846, "old Brother [John] Parker," a British friend whom she mentioned several times in her letters. His wife died about the same time as her husband, George. Ellen and her new husband, John, left Nauvoo in May 1846, about three months after the body of the Church, traveling south to St. Louis, where they remained until 1852, when they had acquired sufficient means to transport all of their family to Salt Lake City. They lived there until 1862, when Brigham Young called them to help settle Southern Utah. They made their home in Virgin City, where John Parker served as bishop for many years. Ellen died there on February 25, 1888.

Ellen's letters to family members in England were lively and detailed. Pervasive throughout was her strong desire to share the blessings of the gospel with those she left behind.

ELLEN BRIGGS DOUGLAS TO PARENTS*

Nauvoo, June 2, 1842

Dear Fathers & Mothers:

I now take up my pen for the third time to address you, hoping these lines will find you in good health, as it leaves us at present. I sent one letter from New Orleans, with an Englishman, which I expect you will get soon. He was not getting off for Eng. until the beginning of May. I also sent another with one of our brethren who was coming to Eng. to warn them for another time to prepare for the coming of Jesus Christ, which we believe is drawing nigh, & I expect

---

*Photocopies of original letters in possession of author. Originals are in private possession. Transcript copies are in the LDS Church Archives. Some letters are also published in Kate B. Carter, ed., *Our Pioneer Heritage* (Salt Lake City: Daughters of Utah Pioneers, 1960), 154–61.

that you will get this the first. I sent the other about a month since &
I am going to send this by Amos Fielding. He has come over from
Eng. with some of the saints & he is returning to Liverpool, so I send
this letter by him so that you will have less to pay.

Dear Father and Mother, I am at a loss what I can say to you. I
feel so thankful for what the Lord has done for me & my family, for
truly all things has worked together for our good. You will see in our
former letters how all things did work, for which I feel to praise my
Heavenly Father but I will now say something about our situation.
We rented a house at 5 shillings a month and we have fire wood on at
that, and a good garden, about an half an acre. It lies on the side of a
hill close before our door. Our house is not such a fine one, but there
are many that are much worse, and I prayed that we might have one
to ourselves for there is 3 or 4 families in one room, and many have
to pitch their tents in the woods or anywhere where they can for it is
impossible for all to get houses when they come in for they are
coming in daily. Scores of houses have been built since we have come
here and they still continue building & it is 8 weeks this night since
we came in.

We have got our garden plowed and planted. All our seeds have
come up & looks very well. We have planted corn, potatoes, beans,
peas, onions, punkins, melons, cucumbers & a many other thing too
numerous to mention, and we have also got a pig. A man come one
day & wanted one of our boys to go & clear him off a piece of ground
before he ploughed it, & he would give him a pig, so he went about
one day & got it. In Eng. it would have cost 15 or 16 shillings at least.
It was Ralph that got it.

We also have got a flock of chickens. We have 13 & I have bought
11 besides, so you have account of all our property, & I think we are
far better here than in old England.

We wish all our fathers & mothers & brothers & sisters & all our
friends were here, for there is plenty of work & plenty of meat and we
can afford to play a day or two anytime when we please & not get
into debt. Butter is 5 pence a pound. Sugar the same. We have not
had much fresh meat, but we have had plenty of good bacon and
ham. I wish the people in Eng. could get as much as we can. As to

prices of other goods I need not mention because you have heard before. I sent you word in my last letter what we all were doing but I will mention it again.

George & Ralph is working at the Nauvoo house & Richard has been working at a farm-house close by & Isabell[a] at the same place. Richard is now going to work for another man & I expect he will receive for wages 5 dollars a month besides his board, but we have not exactly agreed till we see how both sides likes. George is walling when he is at the Nauvoo house, but they are now waiting for some wood work, so he is ditching until they want him again. They love their work at the Nauvoo House very well. I forgot to tell you what Richard was going to work at, but he is going to plow & break up prairie. It has been his work ever since he came here.

James Smith[i]es and his family are all in good health. Ann got another child on the 31st day of May. I have been over to see her & she is doing very well. I also mention Hannah Thornber & her family. Henry is in good health at present. Jane has been sick, but she is mending very nicely. Hannah has been a little sick, but she is beginning to mend. Ellen and her husband are well. Old John and Ellen Parker are both in good health & spirits and are expecting their daughter Mary every day. Give their kind love to all enquiring friends. Joe Spencer, Jo Elison [Ellison] & Alis Cotam [Alice Cottam] & Ann and Jo Rushton and Wm. & Betty Moss are all in good health and spirits. Wm. Moss is building him a house not far from where we live.

There is now in this city a Female Charity Society of which I am a member. Jos. Smith's wife is the head of our society & we meet on a Thursday at 1 o'clock where we receive instructions both temporary [temporally] & spiritually. I must say something about the Prophet the Lord has raised up in these last day[s]. I feel to rejoice that I have been permitted to hear his voice, for I know that this is the work of the Lord & all the powers of earth or hell can not gainsay it. The time is not far hence when all will know that this is the work of the Lord & not of man. The time is near at hand whan all proud & they that do wickedly shall be as stubble & the day that cometh shall burn them saith the Lord of Hosts. I pray that the Lord may remove all darkness from your minds so that you may see clearly the way which you should go, that at last you may enter in at the gates into the city.

Give our kind love to all enquiring friends & to all our brothers & sisters. Tell Jo[hn] Thornber that Henry will write soon and we will send some particular word in his letter.

I could [would] like you to send me a letter the first opportunity & let me know how you are going on & how my sister Mary is & all her family.

Tell all the saints that come here to bring all these necessary things with them such as pots & pans & tubs & all your necessary things. Tell John Thornber to bring plenty of print & check, light prints & a little patren & fust[i]an[16] of anything he pleas.

We remain,

Your affectionate son & daughter,
George & Ellen Douglas
Direct Nauvoo, Hancock Co. Ill.
North America

ELLEN BRIGGS DOUGLAS TO HER FAMILY

Nauvoo, Feb. 1, 1843

My dear fathers, Mothers, Bros. & Sisters:—

I take the present opportunity of sending a few lines unto you, hoping they will find you in good health as they leave us at present. I know not whether [you] will have heard or not of the great & unremedied loss that I have sustained in the death of my husband, my children of the loss of the kindest, most affectionate father & you my fathers & mothers of a son & brother and sisters of a beloved brother. What shall I say, my heart is too full to dwell on this subject by looking on the melancholy loss, as it were, from him being took from us. I should have informed you by letter before now but Bro. Thos. Cottam sent a letter to his friends & mentioned about George and all about us, but as to whether the man that brought it arrived safe or not we cannot tell. George had been working at the Nauvoo House & they was not so busy at harvest time, so a neighbor was going about 25 miles to harvest & he was to take a man with him, so George thought he could like to go, so he took Richard with him. This was on the 5th of July when he left us. He took sick on the 12th about noon & died in about 6 hours, the man that he went with took a horse & came to tell us. When I got there he was in the coffin, it being night [when] he got to us, so I startad in the morning early, so I brought him to Nauvoo to inter.

I will tell you that when he left us he was in perfect good health & quite cheerful, felt to be quite pleased as he was going. A thot struck me as he was going that if we should never seen him again alive what a thing it would be but if I had known that it would have been so he should not have gone, for I have thought that if he had not gone he would not have died then. You will perhaps want to know what he died on. I think he felt to be unwell, but did not give up working until it was to late, but he did not complain before he did give up. He felt to rejoice that he had got here & was firm in the faith, so I do not mourn as those that have no hope, for I trust that on the morn of the resurrection of the just I shall there behold him amongst the sanctified & have the privelege of enjoying with him in those things that remains for the people of God. Now my dear fathers, mothers[,] brothers & sisters I would say do not mourn for him neither for me nor the children but mourn for yourselves for the judgments that are coming upon the inhabitations of the earth unless they repent of their sins & do those things He requires at their hands & by those that have authority from God to execute his laws, for we know that this is the work of God and unless we be obedient to those things which he requires at their hands the judgment of God will fall upon them as it did in the days of Noah, of Lot and many more I might mention, for I declare unto you & to all that hear this letter that this is the work of God & that Joseph Smith is a Prophet of the Most High God.

As respect[s] a living. We can get our living without troubling anyone if we have our health & we have enjoyed good health as ever we did in Eng. Ralph can earn as much as will maintain us. I have all my family at home & have had all through the winter. The last work that Richard did he earned 15 hundred brick toward building us a house & since then I have had him at home. I can have an acre lot of land if I will without paying anything for it if I will, but I do not know whether I shall have it or not (belonging to the Church) We have had plenty of beef, best kind at 1 1/2 c & some at a penny per lb. & pork at a penny or 2 c per pound, as good as any in Eng. We had 20 bushels of potatoes besides wheat we grew ourselves. Potatoes is 2 bits or a shilling a bushel. Ann and Isabella was living of[f] the most of the Summer.

Isabella came home sick. She was sick about three weeks & now is very well. Ralph is a very good boy & does the best he can to get us a living & so is Richard. Henry Thornber got a letter from John on the 25th of last month. I am glad to hear as they are all well. He sends his best respects to George, but is sorry he is not here to receive it but we are & desire to be remembered to him.

Henry & his mother & Jane all well. Ellen got a son on the 30th & is doing well. Abraham and Margaret Shaw is well. James Smith[i]es and family is well. He received a letter from Durham & am sorry to hear of sister Mary's misfortune. Wm. Moss & Betty, Thos. & Ann Cottam, John Rushton, John Ellison & wife, all from Waddington is well. I would mention that John Rushton has made me a present of 7 bushel of wheat. Give my respets to Thos. & Betty Wilkinson of Liverpool & Alice & James at Accrington, Thos & Nancy Sharp of Burnley, & John & Nancy Dusbury of Harwood & I want you to let them know that George is dead & I pray that the Lord may inspire their hearts to do his will & be obedient to his commandments, that they may have a right to the tree of Life & enter in through the gates into the city. I will now give you a few lines of the feelings of my mind:

> 1st   Farewell all earthly honors, I bid you all adieu;
> Farewell all earthly pleasures, I want no more of you.
> I want my union grounded in thy eternal soil,

Beyond the powers of satan, where sin can ne'er
   defile.

2nd   All earthly tribulation is but a moment here
And then, if I prove faithful, a righteous crown I'll
   wear
I shall be counted holy & feed on angels food
Rejoicing in bright glory among the sons of God.

To my sister Mary I would say a few words. I am sorry to hear of
her daughter Elizabeth being poorly & likewise of Henry having his
leg cut off but I hope the time as these few lines reaches you they will
be got well and as God hath appointed means whereby those that
had not the privilege of obeying the Gospel not having heard it, it is
the privilege of me to be baptized for my friends, I shall then be
baptized for her husband, so that she can please herself about
preparing to meet him for as Paul says,
   "Why are they then baptised for the dead, if the dead rise not at
all." 1st Cor, 15 C & 29 verse. I send my kind love to her & all the
family & hope you will either send her this letter or a copy of it, &
hope they will be wise & do those things that God commands them
to do & as there is but one way, one Lord, one faith, one baptism &
one God & Father of all, so I hope she and all of you will seek where
the authority and be obedient so that we may all meet together in the
Kingdom of God with those we love as is gone before.
   I remain your affectionate daughter & sister,

Ellen Douglas

Give my respects to all the Saints & let them read this letter, & I
desire an interest in the prayers of the Saints that I may train my
children in the way they should go. Ralph & Richard send their best
respects to grandfather & grandmother & to all the saints in
Downham & Clitheroe.
   We have sent three or four letters since we came to America. I
should like to know if you have received them and want you to write
and let us know how you all are. And send by direct to me, Ellen
Douglas, Nauvoo, Hancock Co. Illinois. North America.

ELLEN BRIGGS DOUGLAS TO FAMILY

Nauvoo, Apr. 14, 1844

Dear Fathers, & Mothers & Sister and Brothers.

I now take my pen to write a few lines to you to let you know that we received your kind letter dated the No 19th hoping to find us all well in health. We received your letter on the 9th day of Mar. How it came here we know not. We are all in good state of health & spirits at present, for which I feel thankful. We have had some sickness in our family since we wrote last. Ralph & his uncle went up the river about 10 miles to work on a brick yard. They hired each for one month. They came home every week & Ralph when he had done his time came home in good health, but the next day was taken very ill. This was about the middle of Aug. He was very ill the first 9 days, not able to sit up while I made his bed. After that he began to have the ague & fever which is a common complaint in this land. He was about 10 weeks before he could work much & before he got well I was taken very ill with the same complaint but a great deal worse. I was four or five weeks very ill: indeed not [able] to do any thing. Ralph gave me some medicine to throw it off & I began to get a little better so that I would try to wash a few clothes, & it just brought me down again. I was just 13 weeks & never washed but that one time. Sometimes I thot I should die and then I thot of my poor children. I prayed for their sakes that I might live. I didn't pray alone, but many of my brothers & sisters prayed likewise & our prayers were answered & I now am living in a good state of health at present for which I feel to praise my Heavenly Father.

Richard has been very healthy ever since we came to this land & he looks as well as ever you saw him. Ann & all the rest of the children but Isabella have had very good health. Isabella has been ill two or three times, two or three weeks at a time. She looks about the same as she did when we left you. After I begun to get well I went down into the city on a visit to where Ann lived & staid to nights & I had a horse to ride home on. The woman where Ann lived would have me make application to the female Relief Society for some clothing which I needed for myself & family. I refused to do so but she said I needed something & that I had been so long sick & if I would not do it myself she would do it for me. I agreed & we went to one of the sisters & she asked me what I needed most. I told her I needed many things. While I was sick my children were [wore] out their clothes because I could not mend them so she said she would do the best she could for me. Ann came over in a few days and they brought a wagon & fetched me such a present as I never received before from no place in the world. I suppose the things they sent me were worth as much as 30 shillings.

I wrote before and told you that I would have a house of my own before now by the assistance of the church but I have not got one yet. We was sick so long. Ralph & James got a cow up the river & we have kept her all winter without giving any milk but we expect her to have a calf every day. She has had one calf & is but three years old. She cost 9 dollars in work. She is a very pretty cow. We live where we did when we first come here & expect to do till we get a place of our own. We raised about 35 chickens. We keep them for our own use. How long do you think we might have stayed in Eng. before we could have a cow?

Ralph & James is ditching on the prairie & Richard is sawing in a saw pit close by where we live. They have all of them earned a little money this Spring. I have told you before that money was scarce. We can buy good strong cotton here now at 5 pence & 6 pence a yard, a yard wide, good print at 6 pence[,] thread and pots are the dearest of anything here.

You also want us to give you some account of Margaret Wilkinson. I expect you have heard of her death before now. She lived at a place called Happanooce. She had a very good place. She was sick about 10 days & died. James was with her when she died. It was at the time that Ralph & James was working up the river & he came down to let us know that she had died & James Spencer & me went & brought her down to Nauvoo & had her buried close by my husband. They were very nice to her & thought a great deal of her. They said she was a good girl. She came to Nauvoo on the 4th of July on a visit and stopped one week. She was a night at my house & we went the next day to Old John Parker's & Nancy Smith[i]es and Jane Hall was there also. We had a happy day all together & did not think it was the last time we should meet on earth, but you see in the midst of life we are in death. She died firm in the faith that she professed. There is a letter at James Smithies she wrote herself & wished them to send along with one of their own, but they have never had the opportunity but they will send it & then her friends will know how she ejoyed herself.

You also wanted to know something about James Spencer. He is well & he is got married about two months since & I was very glad of it because he is old and needed a home so that he could be comfortable in his old age, & I think he has acted wisely in choosing a companion. I mean near his age. She had a house & a cow[,] 2 horses & 2 mules, & she was a widow. Her husband died about the time that Isabella died. She is American, no children.

Dear parents there are many things which I could like to mention, which would do you good, but I have not room. Ralph wants William to come to Nauvoo & I say that he would do better here than in Eng. We should be glad to see any of you. I never in my life enjoyed myself better than I do now. We had conference here which begun on the 6 day of April & lasted four or 5 days. I attended it 4 days & it is supposed that there was from 15 to 20 thousand present & the teachings which we heard made our heart to rejoice. I for one feel to rejoice & to praise my God that he ever sent the Elders of Israel to Eng. & that He ever gave me a heart to believe them. I want to know whether you belive my testimony or not concerning the Prophet of the most High God, because the day will come when you will know that I have told you the truth.

I want you to send us some berry trees & a few choice plum stones. You may put them in a firkin[17] & send them the first opportunity. I will pay anyone for the trouble of them. I should also be glad of a ball of twist,[18] you may send them with Cottoms at Wadinton if the[y] come. I hope you will forgive all my mistakes.

I remain your affectionate daughter

Ellen Douglas

James Hawworth landed here on the 5th day of April and is at Cottoms. He brought Jo Boothman a letter & I read it & I found that Wm's child was dead. My very best respects to you all, fathers, mothers, sisters & brothers, Uncle & Aunts & Cousins & to Ann Wiglesworth & tell her I still mean to fulfil my promise if it lies in my power, & my very best respects to all the saints & to all enquiring friends.

Ellen Douglas

Dear Mother, my girls wishes you to send them a lock of your hair & they want some of you to send them every one of them a doll. There is no dolls to sell here. There is almost everything here now. There is 1 or 2 hundred shops in this city now & when we came here there was not more than 2 or 3. William Tomson said he would buy Vilate Ellen another when she had done her other, so now is the time. George wants his grandfather to come. While I have been writing he has asked more than a half dozen times if I had sent for him. My children all join in sending their kind love to you all. V. Ellen wants Uncle Robert.

I remain yours affectionately
Ellen Douglas.

SARAH MARIETTA CLEVELAND

A fleeting presence in the Nauvoo story is Sarah Marietta Cleveland. Her name appears only briefly but significantly in the historical record. She was born October 20, 1788, in Becket, Berkshire County, Massachusetts, which was the birthplace of her dear friend Eliza R. Snow sixteen years later. Sometime after their marriage, Sarah and her husband, Judge John Cleveland, moved west to Quincy, Illinois.

Like her biblical namesake, Sarah opened her home to strangers during the Mormon exodus from Missouri. It was in her home that Emma Smith and her four children found respite from the indignities and depredations they had suffered in Missouri. Sarah offered companionship and support during the trying months that Emma's husband, the Prophet Joseph, languished in Liberty jail. The tragedy that brought these two women together engendered deep affection between them. Though John Cleveland did not convert to the Church, Sarah became a member, and

Sarah Marietta Cleveland

the Clevelands eventually followed the Smiths to Nauvoo. One need not wonder why Emma chose Sarah Cleveland to be her counselor in the Nauvoo Relief Society.

Sarah had served with Emma only a year when her husband decided to leave Nauvoo. Her poignant farewell to her Relief Society sisters shows her respect and expectations for the organization she had so devotedly served and her joy in the strong ties that had bound the women together in so brief a time.

Joseph Smith Store, site of the organization of the
Female Relief Society of Nauvoo, March 17, 1842

SARAH M. CLEVELAND TO THE FEMALE RELIEF SOCIETY OF NAUVOO*

TO THE PRESIDENCY, AND LADIES OF THE FEMALE RELIEF SOCIETY OF NAUVOO.

Beloved sisters and friends—As I shall necessarily be absent from your pleasant society, for a season, my husband not having succeeded in business in Nauvoo as he anticipated, I could not take my leave without soliciting your kind wishes and prayers for the time being, that we find it necessary to locate ourselves elsewhere, until a more favorable door is opened, for our residence with the church.

I wish also to acknowledge my grateful sense, of the much kindness, and good feelings, which has been manifested toward me, during my visit amongst you; and in return you have my sincere prayers, that the best of heaven's blessings may rest upon you: and may the cause of *humanity, benevolence*, and *mercy*, flourish in your

---

*Printed in *Times and Seasons* 4 (May 1, 1843): 187.

midst, under the benign auspices of an approving heaven, and the smiles of the Holy one of Israel. And may the heart of the widow, the fatherless, the poor, and the destitute, for whose benefit the society was organized, be made to rejoice through the means of your benevolent exertions. And feel assured, that while this is made the grand rallying point, for the active energies of your minds, no power, however desirous it may be to vilify, and call in question your good name, will be able to tarnish the lustre of your good deeds, or pluck from your standard, the laurels which will be woven by the hand of gratitude as a shining trophy to your name, to all eternity.

With respect and affection, I am yours in the bands of the gospel,

SARAH M. CLEVELAND.

CHARLOTTE HAVEN

Charlotte Haven, a lively and perceptive writer, brought a Gentile's perspective to her observations of Nauvoo. In a series of nine letters written from January to September 1843 to her relatives in Portsmouth, New Hampshire, she described her life among the Mormons in colorful, if sometimes prejudiced, detail. The letters were published fifty years later in *The Overland*, a San Francisco publication. The following letter is from that source.

Charlotte visited Nauvoo as a guest of her brother and his wife, Elizabeth. In November 1842 her brother, always designated as "H." in her letters, moved to Nauvoo to try his hand at business in the thriving city. After securing a house, he sent to Quincy for his wife and sister, who were visiting friends there, to join him. The Havens immediately made friends with some of the resident Gentiles in Nauvoo and their associates, especially Judge Sylvester Emmons, a city councilman who became editor of the infamous *Expositor*; Onias C. Skinner, an attorney who was involved in several of Joseph Smith's litigations and also defended those accused of Joseph's and his brother's murders; Dr. Charles Higbee; and Dr. J. F. Weld. Charlotte enjoyed the frequent outings around the city and its environs with Dr. Higbee in his horse and sleigh. He was the one "most at leisure," having few patients since the Mormons, Charlotte noted, "performed wonderful cure by the laying on of hands."

The Havens were surprised to find that the John Haven family, who were also from Maine, claimed a common ancestry. Though the John Havens were Mormons and eager to convert the resistant Charlotte, she enjoyed their friendliness and the company of their daughter Maria. In colorful, conversational style, Charlotte's letters also describe various LDS meetings and other events that she attended, as well as some of the

Mormons she met. She wrote impressive descriptions of the city and the land surrounding it, in which she found much beauty and pleasure.

Just a year after their arrival, Charlotte and her family members began making plans to leave Nauvoo. Her brother hoped to sell his inventory to his friend Dr. Weld and move his family and business to St. Louis. Charlotte made arrangements to visit friends and relatives in other parts of Missouri before returning to her family in Portsmouth. Their brief Nauvoo sojourn was coming to an end.

Charlotte's letters are reminiscent of another volume of published observations of Mormon life written by Elizabeth Kane, the wife of Brigham Young's friend Thomas L. Kane. In letters to family members in the East describing her 1874 trip to Southern Utah as one of the group accompanying Brigham Young on his annual pilgrimage, Elizabeth Kane, like Charlotte Haven, presented a lively, sometimes mocking, but often admiring account of the people she met during the journey. In both Elizabeth's and Charlotte's accounts, the letters were likely edited for publication and, like other published travelers' accounts, intended to entertain as well as inform the reader. Reflecting the author's imaginative eye for detail, Charlotte's description of the Rigdon party gives an enticing glimpse of some of the social activities of Nauvoo.

CHARLOTTE HAVEN TO FAMILY*

VENUS, *alias* COMMERCE, *alias* NAUVOO.

March 5, 1843.

My dear brother and sister:

Friday I had the pleasure of receiving your very welcome letters, also letters from Mother and Isa. We have but two mails a week and twice I had come away disappointed, therefore was overjoyed when so many letters and papers were smilingly handed me by Elder Sidney Rigdon, P.M. [postmaster]. I hastened home and read them

---

*This letter is taken from "A Girl's Letters from Nauvoo," published in *The Overland Monthly*, December 1890, 616–38.

again and again,—indeed, the smaller the incident mentioned, the greater seemed the interest.

This Sunday morning Elizabeth breakfasted with us for the first time since the birth of her infant, and H. is at home for the day in a state of perfect happiness, and wishes Sunday would come twice a week. He has the boy on his knee, talking all kinds of nonsense to him and teaching him to smile and recognize his father. E. is quite well and the boy thrives, gaining one ounce a week. He is to be named for his grandfather, Samuel Cushman. I tell E. I hope he will not be a Democrat.

This winter has been extremely cold; I almost despair of sunny, warm weather in the West. We had quite a fall of snow last night, and the river has been ice-bound since the middle of November. I used to think we had high winds in New England, but I look back to them now as gentle breezes compared to the violent ones we have here. Every few days we have here a perfect hurricane, lasting for forty-eight hours. Occasionally we have had a thaw, and then—oh, the mud! it seems bottomless. The soil is a black, sticky loam, and when your foot is once in, it is almost impossible to get it out. Crossing the road one day last week, my feet went down, down, and in all probability would have reached my antipodes had it not been for the assistance of the Judge [Emmons], who helped me out; but both rubbers were left far below and there remain to be fossilized as footprints of the primeval man.

Notwithstanding cold and mud, we have passed a pleasant winter, our society being mostly confined to our little Gentile band. A few other acquaintances we have made, Hiram Kimball's family, who lived here when it was Commerce,—Mrs K's mother has become a Mormon and Mrs. K. is leaning that way,[19]—then, at the post-office, the Rigdon family. We enter a side door leading into the kitchen, and in a corner near the door is a wide shelf or table, on which against the wall is a sort of cupboard with pigeon-holes or boxes—this is the post-office. In this room, with the great cooking stove at one end, the family eat and sit. Mrs. R. when I go for the mail always invites me to stop and rest, which after a cold, long walk I am glad to do, thus opening an acquaintance with Elder Sidney Rigdon, the most learned man among the Latter Day Saints. He is past fifty and is somewhat bald and his dark hair slightly gray. He has an intelligent countenance, a courteous manner, and speaks grammatically. He talks very pleasantly about his travels in this country and Europe, but is very reticent about his religion. I have heard it stated that he was Smith's chief aid in getting up the Book of Mormon and creed. He is so far above Smith in intellect, education, and secretiveness, that there is scarcely a doubt that he is at the head in compiling it. I looked over his library—on some book-shelves in the kitchen. It was a very good student's collection,—Hebrew, Greek, and Latin lexicons and readers, stray volumes of Shakespeare, Scott, Irving's works, and a number of other valuable books. He studied for the ministry in his youth, then was employed in a newspaper office. His wife is always busy with domestic labor. They have five daughters.

The only party I have attended in this Holy City was at their house. Here is a copy of the invitation. You will observe the date was a year ago. However, we concluded it was a slight mistake, as the Judge received an invitation somehow with this year's date.

Nauvoo Feb 20 1842

The company of Mr Mrs and Miss Haven is Solicited to attend a party at the house of Mr Rigdon on Thursday the 24 inst at three oclock P M

Sarah Rigdon
Eliza Rigdon

The Judge called me, and we trudged off. We were met at the P. O. door by Miss Sarah; her mother, who was paring potatoes near the stove, came forward, the venerable Elder stood behind the cook stove (which was in full operation) dressed in his Sunday best suit, the highest and stiffest shirt collar, and a white neckerchief with ends flowing over his shoulders. By his side was a very fine, stylish gentleman with gold spectacles whom he introduced to me as Mr. Marr—"A descendant of the Earl of Mar," occurred to me. He is a

Nauvoo, from a painting by Frederick Piercy, ca. 1857

native of Portland, Me., and a last year's graduate of the Cambridge Law School.

Leaving my escort in the kitchen, I was ushered into the next room—where lo! there was a large quilting frame, around which sat eight of the belles of Nauvoo, to each of whom I was introduced, then a seat was assigned me near the head of the frame, and equipped with needle, thread, and thimble, I quilted with the rest. But not a word was said, and fearing my presence had checked hilarity, I offered a few kindly remarks, only to be answered with "Yes, Marm," or "No, Marm." It was quite embarrassing, when my next neighbor timidly whispered, "We talk in the evening."

So I was stilled and put all my energy on the quilt, which was finished and taken out of the frame by six o'clock. The door to the kitchen or living room was then thrown open and we were ushered in. The scene, how changed! Through the whole length of the room, from the post-office to the stove, a table extended, loaded with a substantial supper, turkey, chicken, beef, vegetables, pies, cake, etc. To this we did silent justice.

Leaving the family to clear away, we young people returned to the other room and placed ourselves like wall-flowers. Gentlemen soon came in in groups, and when all were assembled, Mr. Rigdon came in, shook hands with the gentlemen, then placed himself in the middle of the room, and taking a gentleman by his side, commenced introductions, "Mr. Monroe,—Miss Burnett, my daughter, Miss Marks, Miss Ives, my daughter, Miss Ivens, Miss Bemis, my daughter from La Harpe, Miss Haven, my daughter."

Mr. Monroe retires and another gentleman is called up and the ceremony repeated, until all the strangers had been introduced. Then Mr. R. says, "Is there any other gentleman who has not been introduced?" when a Mr. Ives came forward and pointing with his finger, "I have not been introduced to that lady (Miss Haven) and that (Miss Bemis)."

This ceremony over, all seemed more joyous; songs were sung, concluding with the two little girls singing several verses of the Battle of Michigan, deaconed out to them line by line by their elder sister, Miss Nancy. Then followed an original dance *without music,* commencing with marching and ending with *kissing!* Merry games were then introduced, The Miller, Grab, etc., not at all of an intellectual order; so I suggested Fox and Geese, which was in vogue with us ten years ago. It took well. Brother says he called at the office during the evening, and the Elder was urging his wife to look in upon the young people. He heard him say that he had been half over the world but never had seen anything equal to this in enjoyment. At nine o'clock we went out to a second edition of supper, and then the games were renewed with vigor. We left about ten. The Miss Rigdons, who called on us the next day, said the party did not break up till twelve.

Kiss little Louise and Sarah and baby for me, and tell them I am glad they learn so fast. I will write them a letter bye and bye. I wish they could hug and kiss their little baby cousin.

This evening with the Judge I shall go either to Mrs. H. Kimball's, or to a prayer meeting, for you must know the saints take an interest in our spiritual welfare, by sending us to read the Book of Mormon, The Voice of Warning, and the Book of Covenants, and invite us to attend prayer meetings.

We are having beautiful sunsets these days, and from our parlor window we have an extensive western view; and later on in the night the heavens are all aglow with light from the prairie fires. Between the river and the Iowa bluffs eight or ten miles west, ten to twenty fires are started burning the refuse grass and straw preparatory to putting in spring crops. Often I sit up a long time after going to my room, watching these long lines of fire as they seem to meet all along the horizon. The sun is down and darkness is fast gathering, so I must close with much love from

Your sister
Charlotte.

PETITION TO GOVERNOR CARLIN

When the Saints straggled into Quincy from Missouri, Rebecca and Thomas Carlin were among the families that offered help and relief. Carlin, the governor of Illinois, promised permanent protection for the Mormons in Illinois and supported their protest to Congress for the harsh treatment they had received in Missouri. He even joined other governors in writing letters carried to Congress and President Martin Van Buren by Joseph Smith, asking that the depredations against the Mormons in Missouri be redressed. Ere long, however, Governor Carlin's sympathy waned, and even though he had supported the Mormon claim against Missouri, he honored Missouri's request to arrest Joseph Smith and extradite him to Missouri as a fugitive from justice. Angered when the extradition order was dismissed after a hearing before Illinois Judge Stephen L. Douglas, the governor continued to press Missouri's claims

Relief Society centennial memorial plate, illustrated with painting taken from an old etching representing the organization of the Female Relief Society of Nauvoo

against the Prophet, quickly losing the trust of the Saints whom he had once befriended.

The attempted murder of Missouri Governor Lilburn W. Boggs by an unknown assailant further strengthened Governor Carlin's resolve to extradite Joseph Smith. During this stressful period Emma Smith wrote several letters of appeal to Governor Carlin in behalf of her husband. Though he respectfully responded to them, he continually asserted his duty to abide the law and return all "fugitives from justice," including her husband.

Finally, in September 1842 a thousand women, "members of the Relief Society and Ladies of Nauvoo," signed a letter to the governor, recounting their grief and misery in Missouri and pleading for his intervention in the effort to return the Prophet to Missouri. The letter was hand delivered by Emma Smith and Eliza R. Snow. Within a few months, Governor Carlin was succeeded by Thomas Ford without a resolution of the matter. Joseph Smith remained in hiding throughout these months until he was finally discharged at a hearing in Springfield in January 1843.

THE NAUVOO RELIEF SOCIETY TO GOVERNOR THOMAS CARLIN*

Nauvoo
5 September 1842

To his Excellency Thomas Carlin, Governor of the State of Illinois:—

We the undersigned members of the Nauvoo Relief Society, and Ladies of Nauvoo hearing many reports concerning mobs, threats of extermination, and other excitement, set on foot by John C. Bennett, calculated to disturb the peace, happiness and well being of this

---

*Taken from the Journal History of the Church, September 5, 1842. The Journal History is a collection of documents and newspaper articles kept by Andrew Jenson, an early Church historian.

community, have taken the liberty to petition your Excellency for protection.

It may be considered irrelevant for Ladies to petition your Excellency on the above named subject, and may be thought by you Sir, to be officious, and that it would be more becoming for our husbands, fathers, brothers, and sons to engage in this work, and in our defence. This, Sir, we will admit in ordinary cases, is right, and that it would be more consistent with the delicacy of the female character to be silent, but on occasions like the present, that our desires for the peace of society, the happiness of our friends, the desire to save the lives of our husbands, our fathers, our brothers, our children, and our own lives, will be a sufficient palliation in the estimation of your Excellency for the step we have taken in presenting this petition in support of the one already sent your Excellency by the male inhabitants of this city.

We would respectfully represent to your Excellency that we have not yet forgot the scenes of grief, misery, and woe, that we had to experience from the hands of ruthless and blood thirsty mobs in the State of Missouri—the cup of misery was prepared by lying, slander and misrepresentation, it was wrung out and filled by tyranny and oppression, and by a ruthless inhuman mob. We had to drink it to the dregs.

Your Excellency will bear with us if we remind you of the cold blooded atrocities, that we witnessed in that State, our bosoms heave with horror, our eyes are dim, our knees tremble, our hearts are faint when we think of their horrid deeds, and if the petitions of our husbands, brothers, fathers, and sons, will not answer with your Excellency, we beseech you to remember that of their wives, mothers, sisters, and daughters; let the voice of injured innocence in Missouri speak, let the blood of our fathers, our brothers, our sons and daughters speak, let the tears of the widows, the orphans, the maimed, the impoverished speak, and let the injuries sustained by fifteen thousand innocent, robbed, spoiled, persecuted and injured people speak; let the tale of our woe be told, let it be told without varnish, prejudice, or color, and we are persuaded there is no heart but will be softened, no feelings but will be affected, and no person but will flee to our relief.

Far be it from us to accuse your Excellency of obduracy, or injustice; we believe you to be a humane, feeling, benevolent and patriotic man, and therefore we appeal to you.

Concerning John C. Bennett, who is trying with other political demagogues to disturb our peace, we believe him to be an unvirtuous man, and a most consummate scoundrel, a stirrer up of sedition, and a vile wretch, unworthy the attention or notice of any virtuous man, and his published statements concerning Joseph Smith, are barefaced, unblushing falsehoods.

We would further recommend to your Excellency concerning Joseph Smith, that we have the utmost confidence in him, as being a man of virtue, integrity, honesty, truth, and patriotism, we have never either in public or private heard him teach any principles, but the principles of virtue and righteousness, and so we have knowledge, we know him to be a pure, chaste, virtuous and godly man.

Under these circumstances we would petition your Excellency to exert your privilege in an official capacity, and not to suffer him (should he be demanded) to go into the State of Missouri, for we know that if he should, it would be the delivering up the innocent to be murdered—we would represent to your Excellency that we are a law abiding people, a virtuous people, and we would respectfully refer your Excellency to the official documents of this State during our three years residence in it, in proof of this: if we transgress laws, we are willing to be tried by those laws, but we dread mobs, we dread illegal process, we dread fermentation, calumny, and lies, knowing that our difficulties in Missouri first commenced with these things.

We pray that we may not be delivered into the hands of mob or illegal proceedings of the militia, but that we may have the privilege of self defence in case of attack—without having to contend with legalized mobs as in Missouri, and we therefore appeal to the honor, philanthropy, justice, benevolence, and patriotism of your Excellency, to afford us all legal protection, and to grant us our request, and we as in duty bound will ever pray.

PHEBE CARTER WOODRUFF

Phebe Carter joined the Church in 1834, the only member of her family to do so at that time. Her mother was grief-stricken when her daughter decided to leave her home in Scarboro, Maine, and join the Saints in Kirtland, Ohio. She was assuaged only by Phebe's promise to return if she lost faith in Mormonism. Phebe traveled with a small band of converts to Kirtland, where she met and married Wilford Woodruff in 1836. They became the parents of nine children. Three of the first four were living at the time she wrote the letter that follows: Wilford, Jr., four; Phebe, two; and Susan, eleven months.

In Nauvoo, Phebe joined the Relief Society. Later she accompanied her husband on two missions before they settled in Utah, where she served as one of the presidents of the Co-operative Retrenchment Society and on the executive board of the Deseret Hospital. She was considered one of the "leading sisters of the Church" and remembered as "one of the wisest

Phebe Carter Woodruff

women in the knowledge of the Scriptures and in her counsels among her sisters in the Church."[20] To her joy, both of her parents were eventually baptized by her husband. Phebe died in Salt Lake City on November 10, 1885. Her husband, forced into hiding during the federal raids against polygamists at that time, watched the funeral procession from the Historian's Office, unable to attend the service.

In the following brief letter to her husband, then in Boston with several other apostles to forward the candidacy of Joseph Smith for United States President, Phebe describes the conditions existing in Nauvoo shortly before the murder of the Prophet Joseph and his brother Hyrum. She concludes by recounting the details of a dream of Joseph Smith's relating to the Law brotl ers, formerly faithful Church members, who were responsible for publishing the *Nauvoo Expositor*, an anti-Mormon newspaper whose press was ordered "demolished" by the Nauvoo city council. Phebe gives no other hint in her letter that she anticipates the events about to unfold.

PHEBE CARTER WOODRUFF TO WILFORD WOODRUFF*

Nauvoo
16 June 1844

Dear Wi[l]ford

I have come down to sister [Bathsheba] Smith before I milk my cow lest her letter should be gone to the office to tell you that we are all comfortably well at present the[crossed out] we have all had very bad colds Susan & Phebe [their daughters] have been quite sick Sister Eunice health is a little better. I received 5 dolls. from you from *Newark[?]* bought about 4 dolls. worth of lumber paid Balis one & now brother Webster is at work on the house the other front room and will go to keeping house by themselves when it is done, we have not yet got the flooring—O you do not know how much you are wanted to see about things here, Sister Smith says tell him to come home when Mr. Smith comes, I suppose she has written all the news there is much talk of a mob here but I have not had the first anxious

---

*This letter was included in a letter from Bathsheba to George A. Smith, then in Boston, June 15, 1844; original in George A. Smith Papers, LDS Church Archives.

though[t] about it yet the authorities here demolished the press precisely according to law so they have left us (the Law party)[21] they tried to land in Madison when the[y] left here but the inhabitants would not have them there so they went fa[r]ther on up the river they tried to get some printing done but the editors there told them that they would not do it for their press was in good repute now. Joseph has had a dream about the Laws he thought they bound him and cast him and [crossed out] into a pit or well like Joseph of old but he made a struggle and got to the top of the well so to look out and he saw a little distance from him one of them in the grasp of a tiger the other a snake and they were calling to him to help them he told them they had tied him and he could not help them a brother soon came along and took brother Joseph out. Our garden does very well brother A Alexander is not going out this season—brother [John] Taylor is waiting for Joseph to say go to him, but there is much excitement here at present and he thinks he had better wait. A messenger has been sent to the governor has gone now. I want to see you much but had quite as lives you would be away now untill this fuss is over. I received 2 letters from home by Arthur Milliken saying that Luther would not come untill Sept. and I think sister Foss not at all I cannot say much to her on mothers account as she tells me she thinks mother would die almost or quite if she should leave. If you go to Maine I want you to buy 2 yds dark brown ribbon 1 inch 1/4 wide and give to mother for me with a kiss and tell her she has not got a child in the world that loves her better or will do more for her than her wandering Phebe, give my love to them all and

    ecept [accept] much love yourself   P. W[hittemore] W.

VILATE MURRAY KIMBALL

Vilate Murray Kimball, though married to one of Mormonism's most colorful and influential leaders in the early days of the Church, was unassuming, reserved, and seldom "on stage." But she was well known as an example of quiet strength and endurance.

Vilate Murray was born in upstate New York and married Heber C. Kimball in 1822 at age sixteen, settling with him in Mendon, New York. Seeking religion, the Kimballs concluded to join the Baptist church. Three weeks later, however, a Mormon missionary brought the message of the restored gospel to Mendon. It was a fortuitous event, bringing not only the Kimballs into the Church but also ten members of the Brigham Young family residing in Mendon. The Kimballs moved to Kirtland in 1832 and subsequently followed the Church to Missouri and then to Nauvoo. From the continual disruption of her life, the prolonged absences of her husband, who

Vilate Murray Kimball

had become an apostle in 1835, the loss of some of her children, and the introduction of plural marriage, Vilate developed a strong stoicism that demonstrated itself in steadfast and uncomplaining loyalty to her husband and the Church.

Among her Nauvoo friends were some of the "English sisters" whom Heber had baptized. On their first visit to Vilate, they "acted as glad to see me," she wrote Heber, "as though we had always been acquainted." Their regard for her husband was soon apparent. They all remarked on young David's resemblance to his father and "wept like children" when they saw Heber's picture.[22]

In 1843 Vilate and Heber received their endowments from Joseph Smith, and after completion of the Nauvoo Temple, Vilate was one of the first women to have the ordinances bestowed in a temple. She became a devoted temple officiator with her friends Eliza R. Snow, Mary Ann Young, and Elizabeth Ann Whitney, during the winter of 1845 and 1846.

In 1867 Vilate died at the age of sixty-one in Salt Lake City, preceding her husband by only eight months. The letter that follows is one of several extant letters from Vilate to Heber, who was then in the East campaigning for Joseph Smith's presidential candidacy. It expresses concern for her husband's safety and a desire to join him in order to escape the confusion and fears that engulfed Nauvoo following the martyrdom.

VILATE KIMBALL TO HEBER C. KIMBALL*

Nauvoo
30 June 1844

My Dear Dear Companion

Never before, did I take up my pen to address you under so trying circumstances as we are now placed, but as Br [George] Adams the bearer of this can tell you more than I can write I shall not attempt to discribe the scene that we have passed through. God forbid that I should ever witness another like unto it. I saw the lifeless corpes of our beloved brethren when they were brought to their almost distracted families. Yea I witnessed their tears, and groans, which was enough to rend the heart of an adamant. every brother and sister that witnessed the scene fe[lt] deeply to simpathyse with them. yea, every heart is filled with sorrow, and the very streets of Nauvoo seam to morn. whare it will end the Lord only knows.

---

*Vilate Kimball to Heber C. Kimball, June 30, 1844, photocopy of original letter, Vilate Kimball Papers, LDS Church Archives.

we are kept awake night after night by the alarm of mobs. these apostates say, their damnation is sealed, their die is cast, their doom is fixed and they are determined to do all in their power to have revenge. Law says he wants nine more, that was in his quorum [of the Twelve]. Some time I am afraid he will get them. I have no doubt but you are on[e]. what makes me feer, is from a circumstance that took place when the legeon was first called out to defend the city. there was several drums found with blood on, no one could account for it. they examened to see how many there was, they found tenn, and while they were exam[in]ing the eleventh there came a large drop on that. Wm has seen them; he says with all the drums have ben used the blood is yet plain to be seen. he has got two if he gets the nine more it will make eleven.[23] but I try to submit all things into the hands of God.

I have felt aposed to their sending for you to come home at present and didnot know as they would untill brother Adams called here a few moments ago, and told me he should start in about too hours, if I wanted to write I must send it to the mantion house within that time. so I have not time to say much, neither is it nesaceray as he can tell you all, my helth is geting better, the children are all well. I mailed a letter to you last monday directed to Baltimore. the letters you sent from Washington all came to gather last wedensday, and a paper, the mail has not ben in before for fore weeks. the letter you sent from Pitsburg I have never got. when I red your pressing invitation for me to meet you, and that you had got a witness that I should do so. I again took courage that some door would open that I should yet go. but Alass my hopes are all blasted. my constent prayer now is, for the Lord to presurve us all to meet again. I have no doubt but your life will be sought. but may the Lord give you wisdom, to escape their hands. my time is up to send this, so you must excuse me for I have writen in a great hurry and with a bad pen the children all remember you in love. now fare you well my love till we meet, which may the lord grant for his sons sake Amen.

Vilate Kimball

MARY ANN ANGELL YOUNG

With her friend Vilate Kimball, Mary Ann Angell Young shared the anxieties and hardships occasioned by the long absences of their apostle/missionary husbands, Heber C. Kimball and Brigham Young, who were themselves devoted friends. Like Vilate's life, Mary Ann's was one of quiet support—of her husband and his calling, of her family, and of the demanding tasks required to establish the restored Church of Christ. Though her choice to become a Latter-day Saint subjected her to many physical and emotional struggles, she accepted them as a necessary consequence of being committed to building the Kingdom.

A deeply religious woman, well acquainted with the scriptures, Mary Ann became interested in the Book of Mormon when she first heard of it in 1830 in Providence, Rhode Island. Two years later, after listening to the message of the missionaries, she was baptized. She moved to Kirtland, arriving in the spring of 1833. There she met Brigham Young, a thirty-two-year-old widower with two young daughters. Mary Ann, who was thirty, had waited, she said, "for a man of God to be her life companion." They were married in 1834.

Mary Ann Angell Young

She bore six children of her own, but through the years her mothering extended to all of her husband's many children, who fondly called her "Mother Young."

Mary Ann Young was one of the first temple ordinance workers, beginning that service in the Nauvoo Temple and continuing, when her health permitted, during her life in Utah. She was also an intuitive nurse, relieving pain and restoring the health of many family members and neighbors. She lived quietly and simply in the "White House on the hill," the home that Brigham Young built for her in Salt Lake City, shunning public activity for pleasant "retirement in her own home." Though she was the senior wife of the president of the Church, "there was no assumption of power in her manner," a quality noted by all who knew her.[24]

Beyond some letters to her husband, few of Mary Ann's personal writings are extant. Despite the fear and apprehension under which the following letter was written, she demonstrates calm resignation to whatever lay ahead. The poignant yet pragmatic closing sentence reflects the quiet submission to God's will that sustained her in the wake of the martyrdom.

MARY ANN ANGELL YOUNG TO BRIGHAM YOUNG*

Nauvoo
30 June 1844

My Dear Companion

I set down to communicate a few lines to you at this time My heart is full I know not what to write to comfort you at this time we have had great afflictions in this place since you left home. I expect you will have the particulars with this letter.

I wrote a letter to send to you. it was in the house three weeks without eny chance to send it. the male has been stoped from the East it is said by the mob. it has not been in but once for three or four

*From the Brigham Young Papers, LDS Church Archives.

weeks. I wrote a adition to [*page torn*] letter sent it out by P[hineas]
H Young a few days sin[ce] I hope you will get it. You have now been
gone allmost six weeks I have not had a line from you since you left
home I have not time to write much now. we are in great affliction at
this time—our Dear Br Joseph Smith and Hiram has fell victiams to
a verocious [ferocious] mob the great God of the creation only
knows whithe[r] the rest shall be preserved in safety or not we are in
tolable [tolerable] good health at presant I have been Blessed to keep
my feeling quite calm through all the storm I hope you will be careful
on your way home and not expose yourself to those that will
endanger your Life Yours in hast[e]. if we meet no more in this world
may we meet where parting is no more Farewell

Mary A Young to B Young

BATHSHEBA WILSON BIGLER SMITH

Throughout her long and eventful life, Bathsheba Wilson Bigler Smith used every opportunity to testify of the prophetic calling of Joseph Smith. Having received the temple ordinances from him in Nauvoo, she frequently expressed her gratitude for the privilege of being instructed by a prophet of God. "I know him for what he professed to be," she wrote, "a true prophet of God, and the Lord through him restored the everlasting gospel and every ordinance and endowment that will lead us into the celestial kingdom."[25]

Bathsheba Wilson Bigler Smith

Bathsheba Bigler became a member of the Church with most of her family in 1837 in the town of Shinnsten, West Virginia, the place of her birth fifteen years earlier. At the baptism was a young missionary, George A. Smith, who developed an immediate fondness for the young girl. This attraction bloomed into love and eventually led to their marriage in Nauvoo in 1841. Their early married years were marked by many separations while George, a member of the Council of the Twelve, served several missions. Their deep affection and respect for each other found indelible expression in the numerous letters they exchanged.

With all of the public responsibilities that came to her as a member of the Church, Bathsheba was at heart a homemaker who found

much satisfaction in creating a warm, hospitable environment wherever she was. Her love of beauty and artistic expression found an out-
let in painting. On the journey to the Salt Lake Valley, she carefully
protected the portraits she had painted of her husband, her parents,
and Joseph and Hyrum Smith.

When the Relief Society was organized in Nauvoo in 1842,
Bathsheba was the youngest of the twenty women who attended the
initial meeting. From that day, the Relief Society became a significant
force in her life, and she served in several ward and stake organizations
in Salt Lake City, her service culminating in her call as general president in 1901. But the temple was probably her first love. One of the
first women to receive her endowments, she officiated in the Nauvoo
Temple, in the Endowment House in Salt Lake City, in the St. George
Temple, and became "presidentess" of the female workers in the Salt
Lake Temple. Presiding simultaneously over both the Relief Society
and the women temple workers, she symbolized the interrelationship
of these two institutions whose shared intent was to save souls, a purpose added by Joseph Smith in Nauvoo to the charitable function of
the Relief Society.

Bathsheba appended the following note to Phebe Woodruff to a
letter written by her husband to Phebe's husband, Wilford Woodruff,
then serving a mission with Phebe in England. The letter is light-
hearted and free from the strain of earlier years in Nauvoo, partly
because Bathsheba's husband was at home and partly because Nauvoo
itself at that time was relatively peaceful.

LETTERS

BATHSHEBA W. SMITH TO PHEBE CARTER WOODRUFF*
~

Nauvoo April 13 Sunday Morning 1845

Sister Woodruff as my husband has given me the privelage of writing a few lines unto to you in his letter I improve it I hardley know what to say to you but if you ware here I am sure I could find enoughf we all have our healths vary well & enjoy our selves vary well if mobbers howl on evry side, *I have been to as many as 15 or twenty parties* this winter the most of them ware splendid ones to Brother Page live where[crossed out] in your house but it is not you I will be pleased to see you again I hope I shall I am agoing to school to Br Thayer a Portrait painter from London lirning to draw I am getting along pretty well I want some drawing paper & pencils. I wish Brother Woodruff could send me some, I calculate to send you a scetch of Joseph when I can draw a little better my penn is so vary bad I can hardly write their is not one knife about the hous to mend my penn with, *Father Smith has got a house built on the east end of ours & are liveing here we have two rooms under way one on the west & the other on the north.* I hope we shall have them done in a few [blank].

I cannot think of any thing to [write] that is of ipportance My brother will tell you all the news I presume give my love to Brother Woodruff my children tease me so I cant write so I must close by saying may the Lord bless you all & bring you safe home in pease as ever you[r] Sister in the bands of the covenant

Bathsheba W Smith

---

*This letter is appended to a letter written by George A. Smith to Wilford Woodruff, then serving a mission in England with his wife, Phebe. Original is in LDS Church Archives.

ANN HUGHLINGS PITCHFORTH

Ann Hughlings Pitchforth and her family arrived in Nauvoo from the British Isles in 1845, nearly a year after the Prophet's martyrdom, during the brief period of quiescence when Nauvoo had the appearance of a permanent city, and social and cultural events were in full swing. Converted by John Taylor in 1840, while living on the Isle of Man, she was welcomed to Nauvoo by Elder Taylor and his wife, along with two former residents of the Isle of Man who had emigrated earlier. Ann spent a happy year in Nauvoo living among the Saints before she and her family were forced to leave the city during the Mormon exodus. The letter that follows depicts a happy, contented woman anticipating a bright future as a new member of the Church.

Ann gave up a comfortable, secure life when she left England. She was born in Grantham, Lincolnshire, England, the fourth child of John and Ann Williams. Her father was a wealthy wool manufacturer and collector of the king's revenues. When she was nine, Ann was given a piano and instruction, and in time she became an accomplished pianist, performing frequently in public gatherings. She married Solomon Pitchforth, and they became the parents of five children, including two boys who died at birth. The Pitchforths moved several times before settling on the Isle of Man. "In spite of my Jewish unbelieving heart," she wrote, "I could not deny Baptism and at the same time believe in the New Testament." Her conversion ruptured her marriage.

Ann immigrated to Nauvoo with her children while Solomon left England to make his home in Australia. With a piano and the allowance her father regularly sent, Ann lived comfortably during her brief time in Nauvoo. Her musical talents were appreciated, and she was soon engaged to teach piano to many of the Nauvoo residents.

Ann's happiness was short-lived. On the difficult journey to Winter Quarters, the piano became the first casualty when her wagon overturned and it was crushed. Ann became the second. She took sick just before reaching Winter Quarters, and on October 26, 1846, with her children around her, she died in a small dugout with the rain leaking through the roof. She was forty-five years old. "I have followed no cunning devised fable," she testified just months before her death. "Facts are stubborn things, they cannot be beat down nor be annihilated by clamor. . . . I dare to not barter my eternal peace for man's opinion. . . . I can rejoice in the Lord all the day long and smile at the taunts of the ignorant."[26]

ANN PITCHFORTH TO HER PARENTS*

Mr. Hughlings

> Nauvoo, (Hancock Count)
> State of Illinois
> North Ameriaca
> May 1845

My dear Father & Mother:

We feel truly thankfull to Almighty God, that we arrived here safe & well about 3 weeks ago, after a long, tedious, pleasant & expensive journey.—But we are very glad we came, & rejoice exceedingly that ever we came the extreme beauty of the place & kindness of the inhabitants, & every expectation & prospect of being happy and comfortable. We arrived here by the Steamer Packet in the middle of the night the inhabitants upon the sound of the Steam Boat's large Bells came to wellcome us, many took home their relations & friends, Mr [William] Kelly and Mr [Joseph] Caine from the Isle of Man made very much of us, took us home got us comfortable [with] Tea and [undecipherable] lent us a house till we could get one, & never charged us a farthing. We had to go 2 miles from the place of landing

*Original is in Special Collections, Harold B. Lee Library, Brigham Young University, Provo, Utah.

to Mr Kelly's so he got a conveyance for me & the children to ride. Sam & Mary [her son and daughter-in-law] walked, as we trotted along, we met a Carriage with one of the Twelve In, "The President," he stopped, & some of his attendants came up to us, with this enquiry, "Are there any left houseless & homeless, without money & without friends? If there are, we are going for them, to provide them a home[."] we said, yes there were, for many families had expended their last shilling in getting here, they rode off to meet them. Well, I thought this looks well in the heads of the people going to meet the houseless and friendless.—But universal love & kindness prevail & they are not called Brothers and Sisters for nothing.

We thought we would seek up Mr [John] Taylor next day, but Mr Taylor did not give us the chance, for he & his Lady came to see us the very next morning & invited us we went to tea & dinner, & I have since been with them to a concert in their Carriage I wish Nauvoo was bit nearer Presteign [Wales], my brother and you I am sure would be delighted with it, we only wish to see you now & then, the children are as happy as can be, little Ann is getting her cheeks as rosy as can be, & talks about "Granlardy" Ann can recollect Presteign very well.

Mr Taylor was saying how nicely I could teach Music if I had a Piano, & I was saying I wonder where there is a good Piano here, & little Ann sticks up her head & says, my Grandlardy has One Piano, we were so surprised, we did not think she could recollect, She talks about Grandlardy & "my other Mother" as she calls Mother.—We are all so very busy, after so long a journey all the cloathes wanted washing to day, Mary & I were cutting Potatoes & Sam & Mercy [her oldest daughter] plants them. Sam is gardening full drive, every body here is busy in the garden just now. Sam is sowing peas and Beans, Indian corn, and trying a few of Mr Featherstone's seeds we have given a few to Mrs [Leonora] Taylor, who says she will give us some of the Plants when raised, Sam told her we should see which was best gardener, her or him, she is very fond of a garden.

Mr Taylor has promised to take Sam into his Printing Office in a little time. Sam has a deal of joiner work to do for us, for we have neither chairs nor tables, but a neighbor came in & lent us three

New Orleans, gateway to Nauvoo, from a painting by Frederick Piercy, ca. 1857

chairs, we find the Bed Stead very usefull me & Ann & Barbara sleep on it. The Little Spinning wheel has been much admired, a man offered me 5 dollars for it the other day, I could get a guinea for it, but I will not sell, it for Mercy is going to learn to spin on it, Mr Taylor is going to Make Mrs Taylor one like it, & two men came to take a pattern of it last week.—

The journey was pleasant enough but very long & tedious, although considering the distance we came very quick, but we spent a great deal more money than we had calculated as is allways the case in travelling, we landed with 32 *[undecipherable]* and felt very grateful & thankfull you had so liberally supplyed us, which enabled [us] to get so many comforts in our long journey, and necessary things, we laid out 7 in joiners tools for Sam Bought another Feather Bed in Liverpool which proved of great use, through the various climates we had to go, sometimes hot, & sometimes cold, the children stood the journey very well, though they were ill now & then, & got well again, so were we all, we never enjoyed our tea so much in our lives, as we did when we got to Nauvoo, & were at the end of our journey & so kindly received & wellcomed, it reminded us much of comming to Presteign at the first, being the same hour of the night, & having comfortable tea made we only wanted

Grandfather with us, & I often wish Mother could have a peep at the beautiful City & comfortable people, the rich & poor meeting as one family no pride visible, Sam is continually talking of going to see you all, & has set his mind of going bye and bye, but not just yet.

Meat is cheap, 2 pence a pound the choice pieces, 1 pence a pound the others, Fowls 1 shilling the Couple Eggs 2 pence the Dozen,—but I shall allways write the truth, the whole truth, & nothing but the truth, & state the disadvantages as well as the advantages, meat is cheap, but vegetables *high*, but we hope by next year to grow *our own*. Cabbages are 21 pence a piece, Turnips as high, Potatoes high, Flour under a penny a lb, two pounds of flour for one and a third pence, not quite a penny a pound, Coffee is 5 pence a pound, Sugar 5 pence a pound. Rents are *very high* owing to the *increasing value* of *land* in the City and to go and live in the wild prairies, unless one can take a farm & stock it,—is going out of the way of all trade, business & society.—

I intend to teach music, when I get a bit settled & refreshed, but nobody, only those whom very pressing necessity compells, thinks of doing anything soon after they first come the long journey & various climates makes people feel very glad to rest awhile I intend to save money to buy a house & lot, as most people here do then I shall have no rent to pay; we have a very small house with two rooms & a shed, no upstairs, and rent is 9 pound and 10 shillings a year, now money is so exceedingly valuable here, that by paying 20 pounds down I can secure a house [and] one acre of land & leave the remainer to be paid out by 10 pounds a year till paid off, & 40 pounds will buy house & lot and all, in the City, of course there are many houses 5 times as much, but we could improve ours by little & litle as we could afford,—

I am very thankfull for Father's kind allowance which I hope will be continued; and received with a gratefull heart. Sam will not be ennabled to earn much the first year, if anything, but trifling as he has not quite learned his business, indeed, he was only a few months at it, but I consider it quite providential that he can go to the same business in Mr Taylor's establishment.

I am requested to teach Mrs Taylor Music, there are concerts and the people are very musical, but I have not seen one good piano there is one somewhere I understand, which Mr Taylor is going to take me to see. I shall get one sent from Liverpool by one of the Saint's Ships, bye & bye when I can afford it as no one can teach music on the Piano but myself in Nauvoo.

The first Sunday was the Grand Conference when we were astonished at the mighty Congregation, upwards of thirty thousand people no building could hold them here so the preaching was in the open air, It was a fine sight. In the center the 12 Apostles, then the Ladies with hundreds of parasols, & women then Gents & men, then all the Carriages & horses, the singing was good, the speeches witty; enlivening and interesting, but of this I am sure it is the right religion, & by this I know it, there is universal love among them, they are all kind one to another, & *very few houses* indeed have either locks or bolts, & all leave every thing outside their houses with the greatest safety,—There is some bad people get here now & then, but the extreme plain, honest dealing of the people dont suit their chicanery, & they soon get found out & often leave the place, then is often a good chance to buy their house & lot cheap, for they want the money to go elsewhere.

The Temple has two hundred men employed continually upon it and is truly a very fine building. I feel very glad we are all so comfortable, & shall be very glad to receive a line from you both my dear Father & Mother, we none of us forget your kindness to us, & and we found all the things very usefull, honey & preserves were very acceptable & all other things.

We are as comfortable as can be. Nauvoo is a quiet, peaceable place, & we are not in the least afraid of anything; The climate so far is beautiful & agrees with us very well, we get stronger every day, as we needed both good living and rest, so I have got nourishing things for the Children & Eggs, & Fowls, & Beef are cheap enough.—

Wood is the firing used, & is not so cheap here being brought from a distance, but it is not dear.—Milk is 2 *[undecipherable]* a quart & honey 6 pence a lb., but cheafly in the Season. Thomas can write to you all the news if he likes. We all rejoice from our hearts that ever we came here.

I must now conclude, & shall be very glad to know if you received my letter from New Orleans, & I shall so rejoice to hear from you, the children and Sam and Mary unite with me in love to you, remember me to Mr and Mrs Fevier & Mr Moore and Mr Price, and my cousin Richard Price, and all other friends & Tommy, and Miss Hutchinson.

I remain my dear Father & Mother, your affectionate Daughter,

Ann Pitchforth

Peach Trees are in abundance & cheap it is a fine country.

Direct:
Mrs. P
Nauvoo
Hancock County
State of Illinois
North America

[The following text is written sideways at the bottom of letter.]

2 hundred are employed on the temple daily & 600 men are cutting wood & Stone ready for the others; the Bishops of the Church take care of the poor it is no money system, I have not been asked for one penny & all please themselves.

[The next paragraph is written sideways in the margins and appears to have been written last.]

All buy their own stoves here we have bought one with an oven in & cooking apparatus, it cost 3 pounds but it will save much fuel, we have many little things to buy, being in an empty house we find all the Pans and Irons & Bellows & Brushes very useful being all very dear here & so is earthenware but we shift as well as we can, & are very glad we have plenty to eat & likely to have, seeds are very dear but next year we shall raise our own, we have bought a good many of this country['s] seed we came in a nice time for gardening I hope Mother will write us a long letter and say how you are & Tommy and herself is and all the news.

NOTES

1. For additional details, see George W. Givens, *In Old Nauvoo: Everyday Life in the City of Joseph* (Salt Lake City: Deseret Book, 1990), 68–77.

2. Susan Jolly to Samuel Taggart, Nauvoo, Illinois, October 1845, Albert Taggart Papers, microfilm of originals, LDS Church Archives.

3. Eliza A. Cheney to her Family, Nauvoo, Illinois, October 14, 1841, in Eliza Jane Cheney Rawson, "Historical Letters and Sketches, 1919," typescript, LDS Church Archives.

4. Ellen Douglas (Parker) to her family, Nauvoo, Illinois, April 14, 1844, typescript copy, LDS Church Archives.

5. Eliza Cheney, January 1848.

6. Mary Fielding Smith to Joseph Fielding, in Edward W. Tullidge, *The Women of Mormondom* (New York, 1877), 258.

7. Mary Fielding Smith to her sister, July 8, 1837, LDS Church Archives.

8. In Kate B. Carter, *Our Pioneer Heritage,* 20 vols. (Salt Lake City: Daughters of Utah Pioneers, 1964), 7:22.

9. Ibid.

10. In underlining the word *sick,* Leonora is likely referring to a miscarriage.

11. Joseph Smith had traveled to Washington, D.C., with Sidney Rigdon, Elias Higbee, and Orrin Porter Rockwell to enlist the aid of the federal government in redressing the Missouri losses.

12. Leonora is referring to Oliver Granger, who left Nauvoo in 1840 to return to his home in Kirtland, where he died in 1843. His daughter Sarah married Hiram Kimball, a non-Mormon from Commerce (Nauvoo), that same year in Kirtland. They made their home in Nauvoo, and Hiram was baptized in July 1843.

13. William Law was converted by John Taylor in Canada and had just brought a group of Canadian converts to Nauvoo.

14. This ends the preserved remnants of the original letter. The letter is completed from a corrected typescript and will not bear the distinctive writing characteristics evident in the first part.

15. Jane Benbow and her husband, John, were among the first converts from Herefordshire, England, where their home was used by Wilford Woodruff for preaching and their pond for baptisms. The pond is now owned by the LDS Church.

16. A coarse, sturdy cloth made of cotton and flax.

17. A small wooden barrel or keg used to store butter, cheese, or lard, equal to about one-fourth the capacity of a full barrel.

18. A length of yarn or thread, usually used to bind buttonholes.

19. Lydia Dibble Granger was baptized by the Prophet Joseph Smith on January 20, 1843. Her husband had been baptized almost a decade earlier and had moved with his family to Kirtland. Though the account is unclear, it is almost certainly a second baptism, a fairly common occurrence for health or other personal reasons. Mrs. K. is Sarah Granger Kimball, already a member of the Church by the time of this letter.

20. Augusta Joyce Crocheron, *Representative Women of Deseret* (Salt Lake City: J. C. Graham & Co., 1884), 38.

21. William and Wilson Law were excommunicated in April 1844. William had been a counselor to Joseph Smith in the First Presidency. The Laws were part of a group of anti-Mormons who published the *Nauvoo Expositor*.

22. Vilate Kimball to Heber C. Kimball, December 8, 1840, typescript copy, LDS Church Archives.

23. Writing one day later than Vilate, Sally Randall also comments on the rumors that "thare is nine more thay are determined to have, and when it will end I dont know." See Sally Randall to Family, July 1, 1844, Sally Randall Papers, LDS Church Archives.

24. "LDS Women of the Past," *Woman's Exponent* 36 (May 1908): 66.

25. "Recollections of the Prophet Joseph Smith," *The Juvenile Instructor* 27 (June 1, 1892): 344.

26. "To the Saints in the Isle of Man," *Millennial Star* 7–8 (July 15, 1846): 12–15.

IN THEIR OWN WORDS

REMINISCENCES

"For the Good and Comfort
of My Dear Children"

"FOR THE GOOD AND COMFORT OF MY DEAR CHILDREN"

~

On the Fourth of July, 1885, Sarah Pea Rich commenced writing "some of the things connected with my life" at the request of her son Benjamin. She was seventy years old and had been a member of the Church for fifty-four years. Sarah's memory reached back over her seventy years and brought to life in rich detail many of the scenes and incidents through which she had lived. All of the usual milestones in a woman's life cycle were there: her birth and early childhood, her courtship and marriage, the births of her children and grandchildren, as well as her joys and disappointments. But the spirit that animates her account comes not from her clear and lively writing style nor from the singular events of her long life. Instead, the quickening element in her personal narrative is the palpable presence of her deep religious faith. More than anything else, her personal history resonates with religious conviction. It is a revelation of her faith and serves the reader as her spiritual autobiography.[1]

Her son's request was likely not the only reason Sarah turned her memory into memoirs. There may have been a number of hidden reasons for recording her spiritual journey, including a desire to make her own personal accounting to God, to testify of the restoration of the gospel, or to satisfy her own need to write her life story.[2] The task of collecting, arranging, and describing in an ordered account all of the hundreds of incidents, decisions, and relationships that comprised her life, however, gave it cohesive unity and meaning for both her children and herself. She wrote to reassure both herself and her posterity of the reality of her life experience and the validity of the sacrifices she was called to make in committing herself to her newly embraced religion. More-over, the process of writing her life story was itself significant, for it enabled her to act alone in the recreation of her own world, a world in which her experience, her perspective, and her judgment were central.

For whatever purpose, many early Latter-day Saint women, unable for various reasons to keep a daily account, felt just as com-pelled as the diarist to trace their experiences by recollection, to leave a valedictory that not only explained but also linked their lives and times with those that followed. Their writings are reality remembered, filtered through time, experience, and self-appraisal. Their authors have in effect stepped outside their lives, connected to the events they record only by memory or sometimes by the prompting of a note or diary fragment. They have had time to evaluate, reflect on, and prior-itize their experiences.

Their narratives are more structured, more selective, and more obviously thematic than diaries. Unlike diaries, whose entries are ordered by days and years, the memoir is an unbroken narrative, a seamless story that flows smoothly along the stream of memory. Shaped by an imperfect memory and a deliberate selectivity that fits the writer's purpose in recreating her life, the past these reminiscences create is not "objective history." Neither are their accounts dispassion-ate recitals of another time, another place, nor do they wear the artifice of "literary" journals, self-conscious and stylistic autobiographies most often written for publication.[3] The selections that follow are per-sonal, individual retellings of life stories or incidents that continued to strike an emotional chord in the writer as she transformed them into words. There is little reason to suppose that these reminiscences enhance reality, since the reality they portray is so consistently cor-roborated by contemporary accounts. Moreover, some human expe-riences are so intense and life-changing that memory returns not only the event in its fullness, but also the emotions that surround it.

Conversion for early LDS women established their connection to a new religious community, wherein they found identity and secured a place for themselves.[4] It also meant relocating to that community to gather with the body of Saints, a move ranging from a few hundred to a few thousand miles. This often entailed a wrenching separation from family, friends, comfortable homes, and profitable livelihoods, as well as the loss of loved ones to the travails of disease, accident, or persecution encountered on the journey. Separation and sacrifice flow as undercurrents to the dominant theme of faith and community in the women's religious writings.

Though they express distinct experiences, most of these memoirs share common characteristics. They all reveal a strong sense of history and a desire to recapture a time when events seemed larger than life. They are not just reflections on solitary, individual spiritual journeys. They are voices united in the restoration story, witnesses to those past events irretrievable in all their exquisite detail except for these personal accounts. Conversion is their keystone, the pivotal point of the life story.

All of these women were converts, first-generation Mormons who knew they were in the vanguard of the restoration movement. This fact alone made their lives extraordinary and their testimonies worth recording. Mary Gibbs Bigelow's account of her conversion lends a clear and unwavering voice to the record. When the Mormon elders taught her the gospel, she "believed it right off and obeyed it in the spring." Jane Snyder Richards, on the other hand, put off baptism until a severe illness and a brother's prayerful ministrations opened her eyes to its necessity. "I saw as plainly as if a book was opened before me with it written in it my need of baptism," she remembered. "If Christ who was sinless needed to be baptized should I hold myself as better than He?"

If a common faith binds these accounts together, the personalities of their writers give them distinct styles and individuality. Elizabeth Heward and Drusilla Hendricks are most alike, exhibiting similar literary characteristics, but they tell different stories. Their reminiscences, written from notes or diaries, vibrate with vivid anecdotal detail and smooth narrative styles. The three writers who were children in Nauvoo, Margaret Clawson, Louisa Decker, and Eliza Margetts, remembered their childhoods in very distinct ways. Light-hearted, dramatic Margaret entertainingly recounts childhood disappointments and frustrations, while Louisa movingly relates the terrible aftermath of the Nauvoo exodus that left her an orphan. Eliza's brief, straightforward narrative focuses on the martyrdom and her visit to Carthage jail the next day, followed by her memory of the "miracle of the quails" on the way to Winter Quarters, singular events of which she felt compelled to leave her own personal witness. The distinctiveness of the accounts confirms the truth that there is no one "woman's view of Nauvoo."

Whether chronicling their family life or the broader historical events surrounding it, whether painting the retrospective with large brush strokes or sketching only a corner of the historical canvas, each writer depicts a life that asks to be taken seriously. Their experiences should not be read as footnotes to the historical record. More accurately, their histories provide a counterpoint to the better known traditional male motif, adding a distinct female theme that weaves in and around the more familiar strain. Sometimes the two themes blend into a pleasing unison, but more often they move to the pulse of their own rhythms.

However individualistic these women's accounts may be, their strong sense of community merged their individual voices into that of the larger group. They may have been writing about their own experiences, but those experiences conveyed the dynamics of the religious community that was taking shape around them. Their narratives can never be wholly understood or appreciated in isolation. Each is a part of a larger story, one voice in the whole community of faith. Nauvoo was the crucible from which they emerged spiritually strengthened, energized, and committed. It is no wonder that many of their reminiscences end at the exodus from Nauvoo or soon thereafter. They had given their witness, they had successfully met the test of true believers, and they had demonstrated their commitment to laying the foundations of the Kingdom. The rest of their lives was a denouement to that historic moment in time, a playing out of the climactic experience that had been Nauvoo.

DRUSILLA DORRIS HENDRICKS

Drusilla Dorris Hendricks was born February 8, 1810, in Sumner County, Tennessee, the youngest of ten children. With only six months of formal schooling, she formed a close literary companionship with the Bible and a hymnbook, the only reading materials available to her. The easy narrative flow of her writings reflects her early Bible reading. A severe childhood illness brought her face-to-face with the power of prayer, and she never forgot her father's plea that she be spared "to become a Mother in Israel and do much good." She survived to become an earnest religious seeker but could not find a faith that fulfilled her belief in a "continuing communication between the heavens and earth" until she heard the message of two Latter-day Saint missionaries.

After Drusilla heard them preach, the Bible, with which she had so long been familiar, became to her "an unsealed book," and she was now able to "see fields of light and intelligence in it." She wanted to be baptized immediately, but her husband, James, hesitated

Drusilla Dorris Hendricks

because of the hostility that had grown up around them toward the Church. Finally, in March 1835, they became Latter-day Saints and migrated to Missouri. They knew only momentary peace. At the battle of Crooked River, James was seriously wounded.

Though James lived many more years and served as bishop of the

Nineteenth Ward in Salt Lake City, he was essentially an invalid the rest of his life. The care of their five children and most of their livelihood depended on Drusilla. The Nauvoo portion of her reminiscence shows the self-reliance and creative management she developed in order to provide for her family. Drusilla's story is engaging and episodic, each incident providing another example of God's grace to her. She is both narrator and chief actor, taking the place of her injured husband as breadwinner and family caretaker. She skillfully relates her ingenuity as provider but with no sign of pride or self-congratulation. Despite the enormous challenges, Drusilla seemed to enjoy the discovery of self-reliance and was as thoughtful and methodical in her economic pursuits as she was in her writing. One of the charms of her remembrance is her epigrammatic style. "Hunger makes sweet, cakes without sugar," was her response to a long-awaited johnnycake, made when she finally obtained a little cornmeal.

After managing the Warm Springs bathhouse in Salt Lake City for several years, Drusilla and James and their five children eventually settled in Richmond, Cache County, where Drusilla remained with her son James after her husband's death in 1870. The following excerpt begins with the family's move from Missouri to Illinois, where a number of the brethren blessed James in order to ease some of his pain and the burden of his wounds. Thereafter, Drusilla takes charge and exerts monumental efforts to sustain her family.

REMINISCENCE OF DRUSILLA DORRIS HENDRICKS[*]

We started March 17th 1839 for Quincy, Illinois. On the first of April as soon as the brethren found we were there, [they] secured a bottle of oil, consecrated it, and came with Father Joseph Smith at their head, (seven in number) while we were camped out and got him [her husband, James] on a chair and anointed and administered

---

[*]Excerpted from "Historical Sketch of James Hendricks and Drusilla Dorris Hendricks," typescript, LDS Church Archives.

to him again, then assisted him to his feet and he walked, between two of them, some thirty yards and back.

We soon got into a room, partly underground and partly on top of the ground. The room was very close and he took sick and I had to lift him at least fifty times a day and in doing so I had to strain every nerve.

We had the cattle which had hauled us here but could not sell them, but could hire them out for a small sum to break prairie, so we hired them. We had one small heifer that the mob did not take that gave us a little milk for twice a day, but in less than two weeks there came a drove of cattle from Missouri and they drove her off with them, so we were like Job of old and my husband was as sore for his blood cankered and he broke in sores all over his body so that you could not put a pin point on him without putting it on a sore, from the crown of his head to the soles of his feet.

In two weeks we neither had bread or meat so we sent our oldest son, William, three miles out on the prairie to the man who had hired our cattle. We had one spoonful of sugar and one saucer full of corn meal so I made mush of the meal and put the sugar on it and gave it to my children. That was the last of eatables of any kind we had in the house or on the earth. We were in a strange land and among strangers. The conflict began in my mind. "Your folks told you your husband would be killed and are you not sorry you did not listen to them." I said, No I am not. I did what was right if I die I am glad I was baptized, for the remission of my sins for I have an answer of a good conscience. But after that a third person spoke, it was a still small voice this time saying hold on for the Lord will provide. I said I would for I would trust him and not grumble.

I went to work and washed everything and cleaned the house thoroughly as I said to myself, If I die I will die clean. Along in the afternoon Brother Rubin Alred came. He lived fifteen miles away. He went to the bed where my husband lay and asked him if we had any prospects for bread at all and received the answer that we had none. He asked me for a sack and then went to his wagon and brought in a sack of meal and he also made me a present of a washboard saying you had to leave everything and I felt you were out of bread so I came by the mill to get my grinding done before I came here and it made me late. I thanked him and he started home. In a few moments my son, William, came in with only fifty cents. We thought he would get three dollars as that is what was due us for the hire of our cattle. The man had lost the cattle and wanted the boy to go and find them. I made the best of what we had for I took the money and went down to the river and purchased flour 6 lbs., pork 2 1/2 lbs. and 1/2 bushel of potatoes, so I had quite a supply and we were thankful but could [not] take the honor to ourselves, so we lived sparingly for at least two weeks but when that was gone we were in the same condition again for we had nothing. I felt awful but the same voice that gave me comfort before was there to comfort me again and it said, hold on, the Lord will provide for his Saints. I said if He provided for us this time I should think He owned us for his children. I washed and cleaned as before and was just finishing the doorstep when Brother Alexander Williams came up to my back door with two bushels of meal on his shoulder. I looked up and said Brother Williams, I have just found out how the widows crust and barrell held out through the famine. He asked how. I said just as it was out someone was sent to fill it. He said he was so busy with his crop that he could hardly leave it, but the Spirit strove with him saying Brother Hendricks' family is suffering, so I dropped everything and came by and had it ground lest you would not get it soon enough. I soon baked a cake of the meal and he blessed it and we all partook of it and water. Hunger makes sweet, cakes without sugar.

He told us that he had baptized the man and his wife that he was living with. He was tending the farm and that he should come again. But when he wanted more corn, the man he was working for, whose name was Edwards, said to him, "You shall not work for me for corn and take it to the Saints who have been driven and robbed." "Tell me where you go and I will go myself." So he came just as we were out. I remarked that the Scriptures said, "In the mouth of two or three witnesses shall every word be established and the D. & C. says it is the Lord's duty to look after and provide for his Saints, which has been proven true to me to a demonstration.

My husband could turn on his elbows, turn his feet out of bed and begin to take things in one hand. I began to take in work, some sewing and washing, but mostly washing, for I could make the most at that. And I found that there was more blessing to give than to receive so I made our own living from that time on.

I paid $56.00 for house rent and got me two bedsteads, four chairs, five falling leaf tables. Kept one of the tables myself and let Bro. Lewis have one for moving us to Nauvoo, sold two to Sister Emma Smith for provisions. We moved to Nauvoo in March. I had clothing for the summer. The Brethren gave us a lot and throwed together a log house and I hired a man to cover it and build a chimney. I and Sister Melinda Lewis chinked and plastered it. I still hired the same man to plow and put in my lot and we raised a good garden. We got along until the next Spring when my husband borrowed money and sent it to the mill and bought flour and sold it, so we lived on the profits. I began to make beer and ginger bread and go out on public days, this showing that necessity is the mother of invention.

I began to take boarders and we still had one yoke of cattle so my son, William, took them and hauled rock for the Temple to pay our tithing. He also paid some for others in the same way and they paid us in something we needed. I boarded the carpenters and masons and paid them to put us up a brick house; we bought the brick and paid the money for them. We still continued to keep boarders and had flour to sell, finished our house in 1842, but we had duller times then for persecution began to rage and we had hard times again.

I paid a good deal of tithing by making gloves and mittens. I had about thirty pair on hand. I still went washing for bread or molasses for my children.

Flour was hard to get. I secured vegetables. I had cabbage and potatoes and turnips. The winter set in early in November and very hard. I had to buy my wood. I had only corn meal for bread and but very little of that and nothing to season our vegetables with and we could not eat them without salt.

I was making a pair of gloves to pay for a load of wood, it was near 10 o'clock at night. My husband asked me to lay aside my work and have prayer. I wanted to finish my gloves for I was almost done.

My youngest child asked for a piece of bread and I told him I would give him one when I was through. I was soon ready for prayer and we knelt down and my husband prayed same as usual and when he said Amen, I was so full I could not get off my knees. I began to pray and I told the Lord our situation and what had brought us to it, that I was willing to do all I could to make my family comfortable and could not do so and now if He had anything in store for us to open our way, for we had done all we could. When I was through I felt like I had poured out my whole soul to him and I knew that we should have something, I had no doubts.

My Joseph said, Mother, you said when you prayed you would give me some bread. I answered him that, He that knoweth how to give good gifts to their children, the same will give good gifts to them.

The second day after, in the afternoon there came a knock at the door and my husband said, Come in. A man came in and putting his hat under his arm said, Mr. Hendricks, you don't know me, my name is Shaw. I know you and your father and brothers and they were all honest men. I have a load of pork at the gate and I have come to sell it to you. My husband said, I have no way of making any money so I cannot take it. He said, I come to let you have it on credit for a time. My husband said he could not go in debt and would not take it. I stood in the door until he drove off. I then went upstairs and humbled myself before the Lord and asked him if he had answered my prayers and sent that man to us in the first place to hedge up his way that he could not sell a pound of his pork and send him back to us, then I would know he sent him in answer to my prayer. Then I felt better again and so went to my work. The next afternoon he came again and said when he came in, "You must take my pork for I have been all over this town and can't sell a pound of it and it is getting so sloppy I can scarce get around. I came from McComb County on purpose to sell to you. I stepped to the bedroom and called my husband to me. I told him to take the pork for the Lord had opened the way for us and if he closed it up the sin would be on him and not on my head. He went and told the man he would take it. It was the best corn fed pork, there was 1100 lbs. of it at $2.00 per

hundred, so he gave his note for $22.00 payable in twelve months. I
went to work, and cut up the pork, saved the sausage meat and
rendered up the lard. I took in boarders they got me flour and
groceries and we had vegetables so we lived well and got the money
to pay for the pork. Who could not see the hand of the Lord in this
miracle worked on natural principles.

In the year that the Prophets Joseph and Hyrum Smith were
killed, I was forced again to turn to something else as our family
needed everything and had nothing. In the Spring before the
Prophets were killed, I took a notion to go to St. Louis. I asked some
of the brethren what they thought about it and they said they
thought I had better stay at home. My family was then living on a
half bushel of meal a week and nothing else with it and we had lived
that way for eight weeks. We were destitute of clothing, so I went to
Mother Whitney for I knew she had had her endowments and told
her what I was thinking of doing and asked her her advice.[5] She told
me to go and then blessed me. I went home and began to fix to go
but I had no money to take me there. On Sunday the boat come up
the river and was to go down on Tuesday and I was to be ready. I
prayed to the Lord and asked him if it was right that I should go that
He would open the way for me to get the money necessary to take
me there. On Monday morning a Lawyer who had been owing me
for board for eighteen months, (who I thought had left the country)
came in and paid me the money, then I had money to pay my way. I
took my second daughter with me and we were gone eight weeks and
I secured clothing until we were pretty comfortable besides sending
home tea, sugar and other comforts.

The Prophets were killed on Thursday, June 27, 1844. I could
well bear witness to the feelings of the brethren, who were on
missions at that time for my feelings were such that I prayed the Lord
to take them from me for it was more than I could stand, then the
load was made lighter, according to my prayer, so that I could attend
to my business.

Sister Booth and I came home [from St. Louis] together, we
started Friday, June 28. We did not know that the Prophets were
killed only by our feelings until we got out about six miles and met

another boat. They hailed each other and then we were told who was killed, saying they had the hour and minute that he was killed. Then from the Captain to the last hand on deck came running to us with the news to see how we felt. We could not have felt worse. When we reached home everything was in mourning.

It was not long before Sidney Rigdon called a meeting in order to present his claims to the Presidency of the Church. Some of the Twelve had returned from their missions and the day the meeting was held and while it was in session, Brigham Young (President of the quorum of the Twelve Apostles) and others, slipped up to the stand and said nothing until Sidney Rigdon was through, he was standing near the center of the audience in a wagon. As the meeting was in the Boury [bowery]. Then Pres. Brigham Young began to speak. I jumped up to look and see if it was not Brother Joseph for surely it was his voice and gestures. Every Latter-day Saint could easily see upon whom the priesthood descended for Brigham Young held the keys. Sidney Rigdon led off a few, but where are they now. They have dwindled away in unbelief and have come to naught.

President Brigham Young continued the work on the Temple, gave the Saints their washings and anointings in the House of the Lord and has led them to the tops of the Mountains.

JANE SNYDER RICHARDS

In 1831, when Jane Snyder was eight years old, her family moved from New York to Camden in "Upper Canada" (Ontario), where they first heard the gospel message. Robert, Jane's brother, was the first of the family to embrace the gospel. He moved to Kirtland and spent the next five years proselyting for the Church. On one of his missionary journeys, he returned to Canada and converted and baptized all of his

Jane Snyder Richards and her husband, Franklin

family except Jane and her oldest and youngest brothers. The family had a strong desire to join the body of Saints, then in Missouri, so in 1839 they sold their belongings and began a trip that would be continually interrupted for two years before they finally caught up with the Church in Nauvoo. Though she hadn't yet been baptized, Jane went with them.

The family traveled as far as La Porte, Indiana, where they stopped because Jane's niece, Sarah Jane, was ill. While they were there, Jane suffered a debilitating illness that left her unable to speak or move. Her missionary brother Robert, while preaching in a nearby community, visited his family and, upon seeing how ill Jane was, fasted and prayed for her and repeatedly expressed his desire that she be baptized. During one of his administrations to her, she said, "light came into my mind, and I saw as plainly as if a book was opened before me with it written in it. My need of baptism." The pain and paralysis left her and she was able to voice her wish to be baptized right then, despite her weakness and the winter cold. Ice was broken in the river and Robert baptized her. "My disease was cured," she recorded, "and have I need of any one to tell me what mormonism is with such a personal experience?"

Robert visited Nauvoo in the spring, and when he returned to La Porte, he brought a message from the Prophet Joseph Smith that the Snyders were to remain in Indiana to provide housing for traveling elders passing through that area. One of those traveling elders was Franklin D. Richards, a future apostle of the Church, who was on his way to Canada. His companion became ill, so the two missionaries stayed with the Snyders through the next winter. After two years in La Porte, the Snyders finally joined the Saints in Nauvoo.[6] Jane was married to Elder Richards in 1842, and shortly before they left for the West in 1846, they entered into the practice of plural marriage.

In Utah Jane served for many years in the Relief Society. She was also active in behalf of woman suffrage and other causes related to the advancement of women.

When Franklin D. Richards was appointed probate judge of Weber County, Utah, in 1869, he and his wife Jane settled in Ogden. Two years later Jane was called to be president of her ward Relief Society. Before completion of the railroad spur linking Salt Lake City and Ogden, she felt isolated from her Salt Lake City friends, especially since there was no one living in Ogden "who had been connected with the [Relief] Society in Joseph Smith's time." But she was able to maintain some of her early friendships when Eliza R. Snow and other sisters from Salt Lake City came to Relief Society quarterly meetings in Ogden. In 1877, after a reorganization of the stakes, Jane became the first stake Relief Society president in the Church. She served in that position for thirty-one years. She was also first counselor to Zina D. H. Young in the general Relief Society presidency for thirteen of those years.

As committed suffragists, Jane Richards and her daughter-in-law Emily represented LDS women in the National Council of Women and

the National Woman Suffrage Association. They both played prominent roles in preparing the Utah exhibition for the Columbian Expo-
sition in Chicago in 1893.

The following excerpt from Jane's reminiscences, written in 1880,
is seasoned with many years of devotion to the Church, during which
her faith became firm. Her contributions to the growth and welfare of
the Church, and particularly to the women of the Church, had by that
time become numerous and well recognized.

Jane's account is less a narrative than a series of descriptive statements. More historically oriented than some of the other reminiscences, it maintains a greater emotional distance. She describes the
trying scenes of the martyrdom almost dispassionately: "I should have
spoken of the excitement and distress that prevailed in Nauvoo the
night after Brother Joseph's funeral." There is no "I" in the memory,
no recital of how she felt about the events she describes.

Her husband's ecclesiastical responsibilities claim a major portion
of her recollections. Only when she writes of plural marriage and the
young (and pretty) new wife her husband takes does Jane touch an
inner chord. Her reserved style nonetheless reveals a woman deeply
immersed in Mormonism and quietly but determinedly anxious to
show her loyalty to its principles.

REMINISCENCE OF JANE SNYDER RICHARDS*

In the fall of 1841 we started for Nauvoo 300 miles distant Mr.
Richards returning with us. He was recalled by Pres Smith on
account of ill health. We settled for a-while at Job Creek near La
Harpe Ind when my Brother died. Mr Richards and I had become
engaged but not married untill a year Later upon his return from a
mission with Phineas Young in Cincinnati. We were married on the

---

*Original is in the Jane Richards Papers in Richards Family Collection, LDS Church
Archives.

18th day of December 1842 and went on to Nauvoo and settled there.

My Fathers family came on immediately and purchased a residence near us in Nauvoo Illinois on the Miss River. The place was thinly populated and all were Mormon settlers and poor having been driven out from Caldwell Co Missouri by persecutions. The houses were cheaply built frame or brick houses, and a few log houses, a temple was in a course of building Nauvoo was divided into wards and each ward had a presiding Elder with school houses and meeting houses. In warm weather we held our meetings in the Grove as there was no place large enough to hold all the people together. If it was necessary for a large gathering in Winter it was also held there. We tried to economize and build a little two story brick house which was compleated in 1846, only three months before we were oblidged to leave it. Though we lived in it while it was building.

Nauvoo was a very beautiful place its name signifies ["]beautiful," and was named by the prophet Joseph Smith. I[t] was situated at the head of the rapids at the foot of which the town of Keokuk was situated on the opposite side of the River. The first time I ever saw Joseph Smith I recognized him from a dream I had had. He had shuch an angelic countanance as I never saw before He was then thirty Seven years of age of ordinary appearance in dress and manner. A child like appearance of innocence. His hair was of a light brown blue eyes and light complexion. His natural demeanor was quiet his character and disposition was formed by his life work. He was kind and considerate taking a personal interest in all his people. Considering every one his equal. We were regular in our attendance at the meetings. And was always anxious to hear Brother Joseph.

At this time, I met for the first time men who afterwards became so distinguished[:] Brigham Young, Heber C. Kimball, Willard Richards, John Taylor and Wilfred Woodruff, George A. Smith, Ezra T. Benson & many others.

On the 2nd of November we were blessed with a little Daughter whom we named Wealthy Corvisa. When she was three months old my Father died. When she was six months old, Mr Richards started on a Mission to England. But within four months returned to

Nauvoo, not having got beyond N.Y. State. This was in May. In June on the 27th Brother Joseph Smith was murdered by the mob at Carthage. I remember perfectly well his appearance at the Grove when he delivered his last sermon. On the morrow he was to go [to] Carthage, two miles distant to answer to a charge of treason against the Goverment.

He had previously been tried and acquited. But now he seemed impressed with the conviction that he was to meet his death and seemed at the first to shrink from going. But in this meeting he told his people that he was innocent of any charge that could be brought against him. But if he must go, He would go like a man and if he should die, He would die like a man. He was promised protection to and from Nauvoo, by the Goverment and was too confiding in their promise. Among those who accompanied him were John Taylor his Brother Hiram & Willard Richards. The remaining twelve apostles were on missionary labors in the U.S.

They were tried and acquitted of the charges, Govenor Ford being present. The people retained President Smith and his Brother on the plea that they had more charges to bring up. The Elders remained to protect and comfort them That night. Gov Ford was in Nauvoo with a company of Soldiers assuring the Mormons of the safety of the brethren, who were at that very hour in the hands of the mob. Gov Ford was of small stature. And the Mormons had a song in which were lines. (Gov Ford he was so small He had no room for a Soul at all)

The mob surrounded the jail and said that if the Law would not reach him, powder and ball should. He was shot and sprang out of the Window falling to the Ground dead. His brother was shot dead in prison. John Taylor was shot several times and the mob left him for dead Willard Richards escaped as by a miracle and was the only one to attend to the burial of his companions and the affairs of his distracted people at home. As soon as word reached Nauvoo of the terable tragedy a company was formed who went out to meet and bring back the victims the mob had dispersed at once upon accomplishing their feindish crime.

Our people felt uneasy which was the way they learned so

173

quickly about the trouble. Willard Richards undertook to send us word but as he had no sympathizers. No one would carry the intelligence Some of our people went into the place and discovered the truth.

A proclamation was published and generally circulated calling back all the Elders who were sent out on missions to return to Nauvoo, and it was in responce to this call that Elder Richards returned. There was shuch a feeling of hatred that letters directed to Nauvoo would not be delivered. And so I had heard of nothing from my husband since his departure.

Upon the return of the Apostles and Elders a meeting was called and by an unanimous vote Brigham Young was chosen President as he stood on the stand he said he felt as though he would rather sit in sack cloth and ashes for a month than appear before the people. But then loneliness seemed to require somebody to step forward and he felt constrained to do so. And we knew he was [to be president] because he had the voice and manner of Joseph at the time as hundreds can testify.

I should have spoken of the excitement and distress that prevailed in Nauvoo the night after Brother Joseph funeral. Word was brought to us from the Prairies that the mob was coming in to exterminate the whole Fraternity. all night men were on guard and woman and children prepared for flight.

Even the Dogs howled and manifested great uneasiness and hourly we thought we heard the noise of horsemen. At midnight a terrific thunder storm broke on us. So unusual in its violence that as we were afterwards told it drove the mob back. A thousand men we were told were on their way bent on our destruction. But the rain wet their amunition, and so renderded them powerless, to destroy us. The mob seemed to give up further persecution at this time. They had killed our leaders and were satisfied.

Of Hiram Smith I should have said that he was the Patriarch of the Church and one with his Younger Brother Joseph in counsel and dearly beloved by everybody in the church. Joseph Smith was the Prophet and leader.

President Young was golden haired and blue eyed [with] a full round face, beaming with inocense. He was genial and always approachable always precise and modest in his demeanor with women and in his conversation. From the moment he was placed in this position the people loved him and were grateful to him for the protection he should give them. He had before been prominent a leader of the Quorum of the Twelve apostles. Now John Taylor succeeded him in that office.

Matters went on more quietely in Nauvoo untill the fall of 1845 when the mob began to burn all about us stacks of Grain and fields and settlements and driving the families from their homes night or day. Burning their Homes, but not attempting destruction of life unless they met resistance. This was at Green plains and on the outskirts of Nauvoo, fifteen or twenty miles distant. The mob said they would drive all into Nauvoo and all Nauvoo into the Mississippi River.

Early in the winter of [18]45 it was decided by President Young that the church should move farther west the temple was still being built according to the revelation. But was not entirely finished untill spring. A portion of it was dedicated by President Young during the winter and meetings held there. Late in the spring and after Pres Young and the majority were gone it was finally dedicated. It was in Feb and March that the greater portion of the population had succeeded in crossing the Miss River crossing on the Ice in order to save ferriage. poorly fitted out and travelling but a few miles at a time. We were among the last to go. The mob harrassed and threatened and tried to arrest Brigham Young and he thought it expediant to leave.

Among my woman friends at Nauvoo I must mention Mrs. Julia Farnsworth, Mrs. Leavitt Kind and motherly always ready and helpful Whenever my husband or I was sick. Mrs Fish Mrs Bilate [Vilate] Kimball Mrs Jeannetta Richards [Willard Richards's wife] very intelligent and kind and respected by everybody. Mrs John Taylor. Mrs Phobe Woodruff and Mrs. Rockwood Mrs Jeannetta Richards died just before our start from Nauvoo.

My Husband returned to nauvoo when my baby was ten months old, about a week after Joseph Smiths death. He went to work as carpenter at once on the temple and on our house. Which as I said was completed only three months before we were oblidged to leave it. While my husband was away I spent part of my time with his parents and part of the time with my Mother. I had met Mr Richards parents for the first time this winter. They had just come to Nauvoo. Father Phineas Richards I found was a man of strong character firm in his religious convictions and consistent In Mother Richards I found a noble hearted woman. Who gave me a Daughters place in her home. and in her love. I was also very warmly attached to the Brothers and sister of my Husband.

A few months previous to Joseph smiths death he had recieved a revelation in reguard to Polygamy and Hyram Smith had talked of it in confidence with my husband who mentioned it to me, though I spoke of it to no one. It seems that Joseph Smith had taken some more wives during these months. But the revelation required that he should do it without publicity at this time, as the mob spirit was already so much excited without this having been thought of at all. It was not on this account he was persecuted as it was not known untill after his death.

The celestial marriage or sealing were not solemnized untill it could be done in the temple although with Joseph Smith it neccessarily was done elsewhare as the temple was not then ready for use. During this winter and previous to the company starting [for the West], Mr Richards took his second wife, Elizabeth McFate. Polygamy was now made known to us for the first time and while the majority of the Church were made acquainted with the doctrine it was only practically entered into by few. In my case it came at first thought as a strange thing and I was uncertain as to the result. But was satisfied that it was a sacred revelation and that my religion required its acceptance. This wife Elizabeth was young (about 17 and pretty) and amiable very considerate and kind to me Never in our associating together was there an unkind word between us. I was in delicate health and from the time she first entered my home three or four days after her marriage she seemed only concerned to relieve me of trouble and labor. She was ready to take hold and do any-thing always asking me for direction. We lived in our two story brick house she occupying the upper portion.

To those in the church who knew of the doctrine, I always spoke of her as Mrs Elizabeth Richards, but even now it was not publicly talked about. I knew of other Families at this time living in Polygamy. But as yet it was a new thing. I was sick some of the time and Elizabeth would be very attentive and kind and interested to do what she could for my little Daughter Wealthy. We lived happily together and indulged no evil or Jealous feelings towards each other. In the latter part of May we sold our house which we had built with shuch sacrifice denying ourselves in every way to save enough to build and now we sold it for the paltry consideration of two yoke of half broken cattle and an old wagon. Taking with us two cows one trunk of clothing but little Furniture and scanty provisions to last if Possible untill next spring. Principally bread stuffs no tea or sugar or luxuries of any kind A neighbor a Gentile Mr Cheesbro very considerately gave me one pound of tea which through sickness and great suffering was about all the subtenance [sustenance] I had for some time.

We left our home before we were ready to start on our journeying for the mob was so threatening that I dared not remain longer. We camped out on the other side of the River for six weeks and about July 1st started West.

ELIZABETH TERRY KIRBY HEWARD

Elizabeth Terry was born in Palmyra, New York, in 1814, and two years later her family moved to Canada. Elizabeth's sojourn in Palmyra overlapped the residence of the Joseph Smith family there by about a year. The Terrys settled in Albion, Ontario, Canada, where Elizabeth received a meager education in a Sunday School because the families throughout the area were too scattered for a daily school. When she was sixteen, Elizabeth married Francis Kirby, a tavern keeper, who turned out to be a companion she "did not wish to have for life."

Always of a religious bent, Elizabeth became a Baptist, but after she heard the message of the LDS missionaries in 1837, she was determined to become a Mormon. Only after strenuous pleadings did her husband give Elizabeth permission to be baptized. In 1838 she and her parents and siblings became members of the Church. The rest of her family then migrated to Missouri and the next year to Illinois. Elizabeth remained behind with her husband, who immediately began to harass her because of the Church. An unsuccessful trip to Nauvoo to see about working with his father-in-law intensified his opposition to the Mormons.

In 1842, keeping a promise he had made to her father, Francis allowed Elizabeth to visit her family in Nauvoo, where she hoped "to see the Prophet Joseph Smith and ask him whether [she] should go back to Kirby or not." She did not meet the Prophet but did arrange an interview with Hyrum Smith, who advised her to return to her husband. Before she reached home, however, Elizabeth learned that Francis had suddenly died. She was shocked and saddened despite the difficulties of their marriage. She closed his business affairs, sold their property, and returned to Nauvoo.

The extract that follows, taken from a longer reminiscence, begins with Elizabeth's return to Nauvoo and includes references to John Heward, a friend from Albion, whom she married in Nauvoo. Though Elizabeth is not one of the more familiar women of this period, her experiences paralleled theirs and her personal consecration to the building of the Kingdom is clearly evident in her account.

After leaving Nauvoo, Elizabeth and John Heward joined one of the first companies to reach the Salt Lake Valley. They suffered many privations during their first years in Utah. In 1855 they settled in Draperville (present-day Draper), where Elizabeth died in 1878. She and John had eight children.

Until 1859 Elizabeth kept a diary (its present whereabouts is unknown), on which she based her reminiscence. Throughout her reminiscence she often omits details since, she reminds her family, they can be found in her diary. She wrote both the reminiscence and her diary, she said, "for the benefit of my children."

After she had written so regularly for so many years, it is unfortunate that Elizabeth ended her diary so abruptly. It is possible that by 1859 her life had settled into a more stable pattern, and the need or desire to preserve it in writing seemed less imperative than during the tumultuous events that preceded the exodus to the West.

REMINISCENCE OF ELIZABETH TERRY KIRBY HEWARD*

I arrived at my father's house July ?; he was then living in Nauvoo, Hancock County, Illinois. I felt to rejoice very much and was very thankful to the Lord for his exceeding great mercy in bringing me safely to my friends and to the body of the church. On this same day Brother James Emmett's son was killed with

*This excerpt is taken from "A Sketch of the Life of Elizabeth Terry Heward," typescript copy, LDS Church Archives. It is also published in a family history, "Parshall Terry Family History," typescript, compiled by Mr. and Mrs. Terry Lund (Salt Lake City, 1956, 1963), 66–78.

lightening. Their house was not far from father's, so mother and I went to see him. It had struck him on the breast, making a brown spot about four inches in diameter. He was standing in the door when he was struck. I believe he was about nine years old. There was only the one flash of lightening during the whole shower and the thunder was not very heavy.

I am only making a brief sketch of what occured from time to time. [Elizabeth makes occasional reference to or copies directly from her diary.] August 13th I was baptized for Kirby and his mother Ann Waples, his Uncle William Kirby, his Aunt Charlotte Foster, and his sister Nicholas Kirby, all were dead, but this work all had to be done again.[7] It was [a] very sickly time, so I spent a great portion of my time working for the sick.

September 6th I was at a prayer meeting and Sister Wheeler sung in tongues and gift of interpretation was given to me and we had a joyful time indeed. I never missed a meeting when it was in my power to go. At this time I was living with Bro. Samuel Clark. They lived a short distance from father's so I went home every night for I knew if I should lie down and sleep among the sick I should be sick too. In this way I was able to take care of the sick for some time and had better health than I had in Canada. Sister Clark had a daughter born and on the 2nd of October 1843 her daughter Emma Clark died. October 9 I went out of Nauvoo a few miles on the prairie to take care of my aunt Elizabeth Terry, wife of my Uncle Timothy Terry. I stayed there until November 4, 1843. I liked to live with them for they were very agreeable and good to live with and this time passed away very pleasantly.

November 18, 1843. My father and mother and my brother Jacob and his wife and myself went to Bro. Hyrum Smith's and got our Patriarchal Blessings of which we have the copies. About this time, it was taught in our meetings that we would have to sacrifice our idols in order to be saved. I could not think of anything that would grieve me to part with in my possession, except Francis Kirby's watch. So, I gave it to help build the Nauvoo Temple and everything else that I could possibly spare and the last few dollars that I had in the world, which altogether amounted to nearly $50, I believe, but I kept no account of it, for I trusted Bro. Whithead, who kept it, for he was the clerk at that time. I here insert my Patriarchal Blessing:

A Patriarchal Blessing on the head of Elizabeth Kirby, daughter of Parshall and Hannah Terry, born at Palmyra, Wayne County, New York, November 17, 1814

Sister Elizabeth, I lay my hands upon your head in the name of Jesus of Nazareth and place and seal a blessing upon your head that shall come to pass in future, for in the future is your reward and your last days shall be your best days; for the desires of your heart and you shall have peace in your habitation and tranquility in your places of abode. And for your heart of integrity you shall be blessed in the covenant of grace, being a daughter of Abraham and of lineal descent therefore the blessing of your father shall be yours to go down with your posterity. And you shall be blessed in all your avocations of life, and in your possessions and tenements, in your basket and in your store. And [you] shall have communion with the Holy Spirit, even the spirit of inspiration where with you shall be inspired, and your footsteps directed and the hand of God shall be extended and mercy, wherein you shall have deliverance more than in days that are past where you had experience in its administerations, wherein He has put forth His finger to bless you not withstanding the tribulations, afflictions and sorrows of your heart.

Therefore, now let your heart be comforted in the witness that God has been mindful of you, and the same hand of providence shall smooth the path and make easy your way in these last days and shall bring your final possessions, principalities, and [you shall] have dominion, immortality and venerated in the lineage of your posterity from generation to generation, and as to your days and years, they are numbered and shall be many. These blessings I seal upon your head, even so, Amen.

Given by Hyrum Smith, Patriarch of the Church of Jesus Christ of Latter Day Saints, November 18, 1843.

I spent a great part of my time sewing and washing and working for the sick, but made my home at my father's house. There were a great many of the Saints that died, and it grieved me very much that

the following lines came into my mind and seemed to press on me to
write them:

> Oh, all ye Saints of Latter Days,
> I'd have you give ear,
> Unto the chosen Prophet's voice,
> In this the latter year.
>
> Oh, keep his precepts and his laws,
> For they to you are given,
> Just as received from Jesus Christ,
> In revelation given.
>
> For Joseph was ordained of God,
> Stands to you as a Savior,
> If you will obey his voice
> Confident believing,
>
> And you should hold him up by faith,
> In prayer before the father,
> In Christ the great Redeemer's name,
> For of good, he's the giver.
>
> In bands of virtue, truth, and love
> And covenant that eternal
> You'll ride triumphant over hill
> And all things that infernal.
>
> Oh, all you lovers of the truth,
> That is in meekness given,
> May you with Joseph as your head,
> Receive your crowns in heaven.

My mind had been somewhat down for sometime and on the
25th of January I was reading in the Book of Mormon where it says:
"Thy watchmen shall lift of their voices and with the voice together
shall they sing for they shall see eye to eye when the Lord shall bring
again Zion. Break forth into joy, sing together ye waste places of
Jerusalem, for the Lord hath comforted His people." [Mosiah

12:22–23.] When I read these words, my whole soul was filled with joy and hope in the great mercy and goodness of God in the redemption of the human family. I began immediately to sing in tongues and sang several verses; this was the first time I had that gift, so I truly rejoiced in the Spirit and praised the Lord. I passed a great part of my time in going to meetings, working for the poor and taking care of the sick. I wrote to Samuel Hackett and my sister, asking them to come to Nauvoo to make us a visit and to bring my things that I left at Belvidere, but they could not come. So they got John Heward, who was living a few miles from there, to come. He arrived at Nauvoo on the 11th of May.

I had been acquainted with him for several years. My parents were old and my father's health was poor, and I was afraid that I should become chargeable to them. As the first year's rent of my property in Canada had to go to pay a debt, I knew it would be sometime before I could get anything from there to help me to live, so when John Heward saw the circumstances under which I was placed, he told me if I was willing he would buy a place in Nauvoo and go back to Belvidere and sell his farm and come to Nauvoo to live. I knew that I could not obtain my blessings as I was, so thought perhaps it was the best thing that I could do. So on the 20th of May, 1844, we went to Bro. Hyrum Smith and got him to marry us.

John bought Bro. Timonth King's house and lot and his cow and on the 5th of June, John started back to settle up his affairs in Boon County, Illinois and I went to my old occupation taking care of the sick. I almost always worked for those who were very poor so that I received but very little for work besides my board. On June 16th I went and heard Bro. Joseph the Prophet preach to a very large congregation in the rain; I thought I would stay and listen as long as he would stay and preach; though it rained very hard, all of the people seemed to feel as I did.

A short time before this a filthy nuisance of printing press was destroyed in Nauvoo. Many falsehoods had been published against the Church in it. The editors raised a mob and said if they could not get Joseph Smith, they would destroy the whole city for revenge.

The first thought that came into my mind when I heard they

were after the Prophet Joseph with a writ was "Curse the man that will give him up." But for the love he had for the Church, he gave himself up to save the brethern, also his brother Hyrum and others went with him to Carthage, and on the 27th of June, 1844, our beloved brothers Joseph and Hyrum were murdered in Carthage jail. But as this is all written and well known in the Church, I will not make a full account of it here, and will only say it was a time of solemnity and the deepest mourning. I felt as though I could willing go and help avenge their blood.

On July 19, 1844, John Heward came home. He had sold his place and all that was on it to his brother William Heward, but had to wait a year for the first payment; so this kept us quite destitute. John went to work in the harvest field, for which he has never to this day (1853) received his pay, but he worked so hard in the hot weather and bad water to drink that he came home July 20th and went to Father John Smith and got his Patriarchal Blessing.

While the Prophet Joseph was alive, he was President of the Church and Hyrum Smith and Sidney Rigdon were his counselors. At the time of his death the twelve were on missions and Sidney Rigdon had gone east to try to make a better living for himself and family than he could in Nauvoo. He had already got tired of living with the Saints and suffering the persecutions that Joseph and Hyrum and the rest of the Church had to undergo, but when he heard that they were dead, he came to Nauvoo as soon as possible to set himself up as the head of the Church.

On the 4th of August 1844, Sidney preached to a large congregation and tried to win their hearts with great swelling words. He told them that as the church was fourteen years old, they must now choose a guardian. I thought, when he said this, that "I have chosen Bro. Brigham Young for my guardian sometime ago, and shall not make any other choice now". I had written a letter to him for that purpose, of which I have a copy. He told them that their whole salvation depended on the choice they would make. Everybody seemed to be in the greatest trouble to know who should be the head of the Church. Bro. Rigdon had only given them three days in which to make their choice. Bro. Parley P. Pratt had got home by this time and he told Sidney not to be in such a hurry. Brigham Young came home before the time expired and just in time to save the Church, for he knew that the Prophet Joseph had given the Twelve their endowments before they left Nauvoo and had told them that the whole responsibility of the Church would rest upon them. So on the 8th of August, there was a meeting called and the Twelve Apostles were chosen to preside over the whole church. This brought peace again to the Church, all except a few who followed Sidney Rigdon for he conspired against the Twelve and drew off all that he could. Indeed, he carried his plot to such an extreme that on the 8th of Sept. 1844, he was cut off from the Church. This was truly a time of trouble and sorrow, but the Spirit of the Lord whispered peace to the faithful.

John became a great deal worse and I was sick with ague and neither of us was able to fetch water to drink. Sometimes when I heard children playing in the street I would step out and hire them with melons and cucumbers, to bring us some water. We had little to eat besides corn meal mush and milk and this gave John diarrhea so bad that he could not walk across the room unless I helped him. I was a little better soon, so that I took some melons and traded them off for about a peck of apples. The next day I traded half of the apples for four pounds of flour. We had no team and it was very hard for us to [get] wood. John was sick a long time, but on the 19th of October he was much better so that he took a little corn on a wheelbarrow to mill, but this was too much for him and it made him worse so that I was obliged to take the wheelbarrow, which was not our own, and fetch the meal from the mill. This grieved me very much to think that we were reduced to such poverty. In this way, our time passed until January 6, 1845, when I received a check from my agent Richard Carr in Canada for $90 on the New York Bank. After some little trouble, I got it exchanged and gave $10 to help build the temple and $1.25 to the Bishop for the poor and also redeemed a small keepsake, which I had given as a pledge for money enough to get the letter out of the office.

January 18, 1845, I received under the hands of Father John Smith . . . but as I have a daily journal of my life, which my children can read at any time, I will not give but a small account of the things which transpired from day to day, and John Heward says he is going to write a history of his life, so I expect he will write many things which I do not mention.

September, 1845, the mob began to break out and burn thousands of places belonging to the brethern, also stealing their cattle and driving the Saints to Nauvoo, and doing all the mischief they could out in the branches.

December 1, 1845. My daughter Rachel was born. I did live and that was all. But could not sit up for about six weeks. On January 27, 1846 I went with John to a feast held by the 14th Quorum of Seventies. On February 9th John started for Canada on foot, a distance of 800 or 900 miles to sell my land. John got a little boy, Alma Millet, to stay with me while he was gone. Our house was open and the weather was very cold and Rachel was taken very sick on the 20th Feb. While I was sick, my breasts were so bad that she had to be weaned, so now I had to get up in the night to feed her in the cold and would set some milk for her by the bed and [it] would freeze in a few minutes. Then Alma was taken sick and he was so bad father Millet had to take him home on the 25th of Feb. Then I was left alone with my little sick child. Sometimes a little girl named Katharine Alred, daughter of Lige Alred, would come and stay with me in the daytime and was very kind to me. Rachel grew worse all the time. On the 4th of March, my brother Jacob D. Terry's wife came and stayed with me until eleven o'clock at night, and we thought the child was getting better. I attended her until four o'clock and then I fell asleep and when I awoke at six o'clock she was dead. I trembled so that I could hardly stand, but I wrapped her in a blanket and took her to my father's to ask them if she was really dead. Mother said she was dead. I could not tell what killed her unless it was inflamation of the lungs. Bro. Huntington buried her out on the prairie in the buring ground east of the Temple about three miles.

I was very lonesome until the 17th of April, 1846, when John came home. He had sold the property in Canada for $700, which was less than half what it was worth, but that was the best he could do with it, for he was a Mormon and Mr. Johnson said he had possession and talked of not giving him anything for it. But his wife said the money was hers and she would buy it and send the money as soon as I should sign the deed and send it back to her. The whole Church in Nauvoo had entered into a covenant to give all that they had to help the poor from Nauvoo. This was done at the fall conference and at this time the Twelve were all gone from Nauvoo, except Bro. Orson Hyde, so we went to him for counsel. He said everyone that had property and did not help the poor would be cursed and that we had better [place] writings into the hands of Bros. Babbitt, Haywood, and Fullmer, who were trustees for the whole church in Nauvoo. This we did, believing with all confidence, that he would do what was right with it. When it came it lacked $73 of the amount agreed upon. Bro. Babbit kept $227 to help the poor and I gave $100 to my father to help him for Nauvoo. I believed I did right with the money, but some of my friends were angry because we let the trustee have the money to help the poor instead of giving it to them. They said they were poor and had done a great deal for the church and ought to be helped. But we thought the trustees ought to know who were in need of help better than we did. On the 8th of June we started from Nauvoo and followed the Heads of the Church to the west. June 20th, we camped alone on the prairie about two miles from wood or water for we did not know where the camping places were. In the night I was sick with cholera morbus. I suffered very much and it seemed as if I should die for a drink. John laid hands on me and through mercy of the Lord I got better so that we were able to go on in the morning. On June 25th we overtook Thomas Clark and family; this was the first time we ever saw them. We traveled with them to the Bluffs. On the 25th we got to Mount Posgah. I gave Bro. Clark two sovereigns, which is nearly ten dollars, for a cow; cattle were cheap then.

On June 30th we started again on our journey. July 4th we met Bros. Brigham Young and Heber C. Kimball and Willard Richards, who were going back to Pisgah to get volunteers to go to California in the United States Army to fight the Spaniards. Yes, my heart aches while I write it. After they had burned the houses and robbed the Saints of almost all they possessed, then drove them into the wilderness at the point of a bayonnet amongst the wild savages on the western prairies and desert; yes, I repeat, after the wicked had done all this, instead of the President of the US raising up and avenging our wrongs, he sent men after us calling for five hundred of our men to go into the US service and as the Church of Jesus Christ of Latter Day Saints never had transgressed any but commanded they yield to this call, also these five hundred men left wives and children without houses or provisions to perish with cold and at mercy of the wild Indians, to go and secure their vile persecutors, who had driven them from the lands of their nativity endeared by the graves of their fathers, who had suffered and bled by the side of General Washington when he fought and obtained freedom from British oppression and formed a Constitution and pursuits of happiness with liberty to worship God according to the dictates of their own consciences. Yes, the Saints have suffered all this because they have dared to believe that the Lord has spoken from the heavens again and revealed his will concerning men on the earth and also sent a Holy Angel with the gospel and the priesthood which he conferred upon Joseph Smith without which no one could be saved.

SARAH MELISSA GRANGER KIMBALL

Sarah Melissa Granger Kimball lived a long and productive life as an energetic, innovative, and faithful member of the Church. Born in Phelps, New York, on December 29, 1818, she moved to Kirtland, Ohio, with her family in 1833, after converting to Mormonism. Her intellectual curiosity soon demonstrated itself when she began attending the School of the Prophets in Kirtland. Throughout her life she was

Sarah Melissa Granger Kimball

known as "a deep religious thinker, and reasoner, and a student of the Bible, Book of Mormon and other books of a similar kind."[8] By her own habit of study she hoped to be a model for other women in the study of church doctrine and consistently urged them to read the scriptures.

When Sarah was twenty-one she married Hiram Kimball, a friendly non-Mormon, in Kirtland, and they then settled in Nauvoo, where Hiram had previously established himself as a successful merchant. She was thus much more comfortably situated than many of the Saints during Nauvoo's early days of settlement.

In 1842 Sarah's zeal to assist the builders of the Nauvoo Temple led to the organization of the Relief Society, which she explains in the following account. She served for more than forty years as president of the Fifteenth Ward Relief Society in Salt Lake City. An innovator of uncommon talent, she was instrumental in setting the pattern for

Relief Society halls (the upstairs for art and science, the downstairs for trade and commerce) and for granaries to store Relief Society wheat. She also played a role in raising and distributing funds to support immigration, the Deseret Hospital, teacher training, temple building, the furnishing of chapels, and numerous other worthy causes. During her term as a ward Relief Society president, she also served as secretary in the Relief Society general presidency under Eliza R. Snow and as a vice president under Zina D. H. Young when the Relief Society was incorporated.

But Relief Society was only part of Sarah Kimball's lifetime interests. When her husband died in 1863, she became self-sufficient by teaching school, an experience that strengthened her conviction of the need for more employment opportunities for women. She also supported the intellectual development of women by offering Relief Society lessons on such topics as physiology, the Constitution, and the Atonement. She was known as a fervent advocate for women's rights, there being "no stronger minded woman in all Israel than Sarah Kimball," according to one contemporary biographer.[9] As an active suffragist, she presided over the Utah Territorial Woman Suffrage Association and successfully lobbied the constitutional convention delegates to include woman suffrage in the state constitution in 1895. She died a much-respected and revered woman on December 1, 1898. Her contributions to the Church and her work in behalf of women place her among the most influential of early Mormon women.

A personal economizer, she was liberal to the needy; a model homemaker, she was an advocate for women's rights; a devoted mother and foster mother, she was an innovator and entrepreneur, making the Relief Society a vehicle to increased opportunity for woman's development. Identified by one associate as "a statesman, a philanthropist, and a missionary,"[10] Sarah Kimball earned the respect shown her throughout her adult life, and she died having seen the fulfillment of many of her goals. In the document that follows, she gives her account of the origins of the Relief Society in Nauvoo, the principles on which it was established, and its relationship to the Church.

REMINISCENCE OF SARAH MELISSA GRANGER KIMBALL*

◆

March 17th 1882

Early Relief Society Reminisence

Sister Geo. Godard invited a goodly no. of brethren and sisters to their pleasant home in 14th Ward S. L. City to celebrate the 40th (fortieth) Annaversary of the organisation of the Relief Society by the Prophet Joseph Smith.

The following brief account of the origin of the Society was given by Sarah M. Kimball.

March 1, 1842 the Church of Jesus Christ of Latter day Saints was poor in worldly goods and earnest in devotion to the labors required. The Nauvoo Temple walls were about three feet high. Strong appeals were being made by the President of the Church and others for help to forward the work.

Miss Cook a maiden lady Seemstress, one day in conversation with me on the subject of a recent appeal for provisions, clothing, beding and general supplies for the workmen and their families, remarked that she would be pleased to contribute needle work if it could be made available. I proffered material for her to make up, and suggested that others might feel as we did. We then agitated the subject of organising a Sewing Society. The object of which should be to aid in the erection of the Temple.

About a dozen of the neighboring Sisters by invitation met in my parlor the following Thursday and the subject was further discused, and approved. Sister Rigden suggested that Sister E. R. Snow be invited to take part and to assist in getting up a constitution and Byelaws, the speaker was delegated to wait on Miss Snow and solicit her aid which was cheerfully and efficiently rendered. A Constitution and bye laws was prepared and submitted to President Joseph Smith. He pronounced it the best constitution that he ever read, then

---

*The original is in the Relief Society Record, 1880–1892, LDS Church Archives.

remarked this is not what the sisters want, there is something better for them. I have desired to organise the sisters in the order of the Priesthood. I now have the key by which I can do it.

The organisation of the Church of Christ was never perfect until the women were organised. He then said I want you (E. R. Snow) to tell the sisters who delegated you that their offering is accepted of the Lord and will result in blessing to them. He further said I want the adjourned meeting to meet with me and a few of the brethren in the Masonic Hall on Thursday at 1 P.M. next, and I will organise you in the Order of the Priesthood after the pattern of the Church. And I wish Emma to be nominated and elected President of the organisation in fulfilment of the revelation in the Doctrine and Covenants which Says She is an Elect Lady. An Elect Lady is one who is elected.

Sarah M. Kimball

MERCY RACHEL FIELDING THOMPSON

"A veteran Mother in Israel," as one contemporary characterized her,[11] Mercy Thompson embodied the attributes of that honored title: faith in the gospel and service in the kingdom. Born in Honidon, England, near Preston, where the gospel was first introduced to Great Britain in 1837, Mercy emigrated to Canada with her brother Joseph in 1832. They were joined by their sister Mary two years later.

In 1836 the three Fieldings accepted baptism after hearing the message of Parley P. Pratt, and immediately thereafter they moved to Kirtland. Joseph

Women temple workers. Mercy Rachel Fielding Thompson is seated third from left

Fielding was selected to be one of the first missionaries to carry the gospel to England the following year.

In Kirtland Mercy met and married Robert Thompson, who, before his untimely death in Nauvoo in 1841, served as secretary to Joseph Smith. Mercy and her infant daughter then joined the household of her sister Mary and Mary's husband, Hyrum Smith.

In 1844 Mercy received her endowments from the Prophet Joseph Smith and began her long service as a temple worker in the Nauvoo Temple. She and her young daughter resided in the temple while

Mercy either officiated in the ordinances, served as clerk, washed and ironed the clothing, or supervised the cooking for temple workers.

She migrated to Utah with her widowed sister Mary and continued her ordinance work in the Endowment House in Salt Lake City. Known for her generosity in contributing to Relief Society charities, she was treasurer of the Sixteenth Ward Relief Society for twenty-one years. A highlight of her later years was a visit to Canada in 1871, where she renewed acquaintance with friends, and a trip to England in 1872 with a group on its way to Palestine, led by George A. Smith. She remained in England with family members for nearly a year before returning to Utah. She exchanged letters with her brother James, a minister in Preston who had initially been friendly to the Mormon missionaries introduced to him by his brother Joseph when the missionaries arrived in Preston in 1837. He turned against the Church, however, when many of his flock converted to Mormonism. Throughout their long correspondence (of which only a few letters remain), Mercy and James each tried to convince the other of the truth of his or her own religious claims.

As a temple worker, Mercy hoped for the fulfillment of a long-held dream: to live to see the completion of the Salt Lake Temple. After forty years of construction, it was finally dedicated in April of 1893. Mercy died the following September.

Mercy Thompson left few written records, but the following undated account relates a remarkable dream and its significance in her own life and in the development of Latter-day Saint doctrine.

REMINISCENCE OF MERCY RACHEL FIELDING THOMPSON*

In 1843, I could not tell the Month I was sleeping with my Sister Mary Smith Brother Hyrum being absent on business when I

---

*A photocopy of the original manuscript is in possession of the author, courtesy of Carling Malouf.

dreamed that I was in a garden and my late dear Husband Robert B.
Thompson (who died August 24th 1841) came to me and the
Marriage vow was repeated by someone I cannot tell who and were
Husband and Wife I awoke in the Morning deeply impressed by this
Dream which I could not interpret.

Brother Hyrum came home in the Evening being somewhat in
rather a meditative mood he said he had had a very remarkable
Dream. he said his late Wife Jerusha Barton [Barden] and her two
Children, viz. Mary and Hyrum [all three deceased] were brought
and presented to him on his arrival at home he found a Message had
been sent from his Brother Joseph requesting him to come to his
house immediately he went and to his amazement found that a
Revelation had been given stating that Marriages contracted for time
only lasted for time and were no more one untill a new contract was
made, for All Eternity and for those who had been sepperated by
Death a Proxy would have to be obtained to Act for them of cource
no time was lost by those who had an opportunity of securing their
Companions and the first presidency and as many of the Twelve as
were [available] and the Presiding Bishop of the Church were all
invited to meet in an Upper Room in the Prophets House each Man
bringing his Wife of course Such a wedding I am quite sure never
witnessed before in this generation. Of course my case was a singular
one and had to be considered but the Prophet soon concluded that
his Brother Hyrum had the best right to act for Robert B.
Thompson. My Sister Mary Smith of course standing with Hyrum
for Jerusha Barden perhaps some may think I could envy Queen
Victoria in some of her glory. Not while my name stands first on the
list in this Dispensation of women seal[e]d to a Dead Husband
through devine Revelation.

ELIZABETH ANN SMITH WHITNEY

One of the most revered Mormon women of her time, Elizabeth Ann Smith Whitney, endearingly known as "Mother Whitney," was also called "the comforter" by those who received blessings of peace and healing at her hand.

At the first patriarchal blessing meeting held in the Kirtland Temple, she received the gift of "inspirational singing," as she called it. "Thou hast been blest of the Lord by the gift of faith in singing the songs of Zion," Isaac Morley revealed in the blessing. Joseph Smith called her "the sweet songstress of Zion" and promised her that if she remained faithful, she would never lose the gift of singing in the pure Adamic tongue. Just a year before her death, she sang for her friends, exercising that spiritual gift for the last time.

Elizabeth Ann Smith Whitney

Elizabeth Ann Smith was born the day after Christmas in 1800 in Derby, New Haven County, Connecticut, to Gibson and Polly Bradley Smith. When she was eighteen she traveled with a maiden aunt, Sarah Smith, to the Ohio frontier, an unlikely venture for two single women. There she met Newel K. Whitney, an enterprising young fur trader and businessman. In 1822 they were married, settling in Kirtland, Ohio, where Newel became a partner with Sidney Gilbert in a successful mercantile business. Newel and Elizabeth Ann were attracted to the Campbellites, a millenarian sect, but were soon disillusioned and prayed for spiritual direction. A divine manifestation prepared them for acceptance of the gospel, and they eagerly accepted the Mormon message. The Whitneys provided lodgings for Joseph and Emma Smith when the Prophet first arrived in Kirtland in 1831, and the two couples became immediate friends and close associates in the Church.

In 1838 the Whitneys left their comfortable home, Newel's thriving business, and longtime friends to follow the Church westward to Missouri. They each reluctantly left a family member in Kirtland who had been unable to accept the truths of the gospel: Elizabeth's surrogate mother, her aunt Sarah, and Newel's brother and business adviser, Samuel. There was heartache on both sides, as neither could understand the choices made by the other.

Sojourning without her husband during the winter of 1838 in Carrollton, Illinois, Elizabeth and her children were reunited with Newel in Nauvoo the next year, following a siege of the ague. But Nauvoo offered opportunity for a new beginning, and after living for a period in the Prophet's store, the Whitneys obtained a home of their own. Elizabeth was one of the founding members of the Relief Society when it was organized in 1842 and became a counselor to Emma Smith, the society's first president. In 1843 she was the second woman, after Emma, to receive the temple ordinances. Joseph Smith officiated in the rites, which were performed in the upper room of his store, since the temple was not yet completed. In January 1844 Elizabeth Ann gave birth to the first child "born heir to the Holy Priesthood in the New and Everlasting Covenant."[12] She was among the first women to perform temple ordinances in the Nauvoo Temple when it was completed in 1845, working daily during the winter of 1845–46 to enable worthy Saints to receive their endowments before leaving for the West.

In 1850, just two years after arriving in the Salt Lake Valley, Elizabeth was left a widow with nine children. Her grief was assuaged through service in the Endowment House when Brigham Young called her to take charge of the "woman's department." Only when her health failed late in life did she discontinue her ministrations there. When the first general presidency of the Relief Society in Utah was organized in 1880, Elizabeth, then eighty years old, was called to be Eliza R. Snow's counselor. She served until her death two years later.

Two floral tributes at her funeral bespeak the characteristics that made her one of the best-known women in Israel. A harp, beautifully woven with colorful flowers, epitomized her inspirational singing, and a sickle, wreathed in white flowers and a sheaf of wheat, symbolized her beloved Relief Society. Little known to a present generation, Elizabeth Ann Whitney was a stalwart of her own.

REMINISCENCE OF ELIZABETH ANN SMITH WHITNEY*

In the Fall of 1838 we left Kirtland, and with what we considered necessary for our immediate wants we commenced our journey to Far West. Our family then consisted of six children, the two youngest being very delicate in health. My eldest son was then fifteen years of age. While we were on our way, a report reached us that the Saints in Missouri were being driven, mobbed and persecuted in a most shocking and terrible manner; we were careful to investigate the matter, in order to ascertain its truth. We went on to St. Louis and waited there until we could obtain the facts in relation to the matter, which we soon learned were most startlingly true. We considered it safest to go over into Illinois to spend the winter, and decided upon Carrollton, Greene Co., Illinois. Here I remained with my children alone, while my husband returned to Kirtland to settle some business and wait further orders from the Prophet Joseph. We were informed the goods we had sent up to Missouri were thrown into the street, and the store burnt to the ground. My eldest son taught school while we remained there, and as the persecution was at that time most extreme, we kept quiet in regard to religion. We were kindly

---

*These excerpts are taken from the *Woman's Exponent* 7 (November 15, 1878): 91; 7 (December 15, 18778): 195; 7 (January 1, 1879): 115; 7 (February 15, 1879): 191.

treated, but more particularly by two families who were our near neighbors. In the Spring my husband returned, and shortly after, accompanied by my eldest son, went up to Commerce, since called Nauvoo. At that place they found that the Prophet Joseph and many others of the Saints had settled and commenced to re-organize and sustain each other and the doctrines in which they believed. Joseph then told my husband to return to his family and as quickly as practicable join the Saints there. Meantime a man named Bellows, who had formerly known my husband in Kirtland, recognized us as the Mormon Bishop's family, and determined to have us mobbed and driven from the town; but those two families who had all the time befriended us, offered to render us assistance in getting away, by crossing the river in the night. So in a neighborhood where we had been looked upon with the greatest respect, we were treated like outlaws, and compelled to flee for safety. My husband and son returned in time to cross the river with us; when we reached the opposite bank and felt comparatively safe from our immediate enemies, I shall never forget my husband's taking off his hat, wiping the perspiration from his brow, and thanking God for our deliverance. Strange how trifling incidents like these, sometimes leave indelible impressions upon the memory which can never be effaced. From there we went up the river to Quincy, Illinois, where several families of the Saints who had been driven from Missouri were living; among these was the family of Titus Billings, one of our nearest neighbors in Kirtland; his wife was the first woman baptized in Kirtland, and is still living [1878]. We found many other friends and their families. We remained in Quincy during the winter, and passed the time rather pleasantly; my eldest son was fond of music, and so were the Billings' boys, and they used to go out together to play for parties, and thus rendered some assistance in obtaining a living, for we had left our means in Kirtland.

Early in the Spring of 1840 we went up to Commerce, as the upper portion of the City of Nauvoo continued to be called. We rented a house belonging to Hiram Kimball, whose widow [Sarah M.] and children are residents of this city [Salt Lake City]. Here we were all sick with ague, chills and fever, and were only just barely able to crawl around and wait upon each other. Under these trying circumstances my ninth child was born. Joseph, upon visiting us and seeing our change of circumstances, urged us at once to come and share his accommodations. We felt the climate, the water, and the privations we were enduring could not much longer be borne; therefore we availed ourselves of this proposal and went to live in the Prophet Joseph's yard, in a small cottage; we soon recruited in health, and the children became more like themselves. My husband was employed in a store Joseph had built and fitted up with such goods as the people were in actual need of.

One day while coming out of the house into the yard the remembrance of a prophecy Joseph Smith had made to me, while living in our house in Kirtland, flashed through my mind like an electric shock; it was this: that even as we had done by him, in opening our doors to him and his family when he was without a home; even so should we in the future be received by him into his house. We afterwards moved up stairs over the brick store, as it was designated. It was during our residence in the brick store that the Relief Society was organized, March 17, 1842, and I was chosen Counselor to the President of the Society, Mrs. Emma Smith. In this work I took the greatest interest, for I realized in some degree its importance, and the need of such an organization. I was also ordained and set apart under the hand of Joseph Smith the Prophet to administer to the sick and comfort the sorrowful. Several other sisters were also ordained and set apart to administer in these holy ordinances. The Relief Society then was small compared to its numbers now, but the Prophet foretold great things concerning the future of this organization, many of which I have lived to see fulfilled; but there are many things which yet remain to be fulfilled in the future of which he prophesied, that are great and glorious; and I rejoice in the contemplation of these things daily, feeling that the promises are sure to be verified in the future as they have been in the past. I trust the sisters who are now laboring in the interest of Relief Societies in Zion realize the importance attached to the work, and comprehend that upon them a great responsibility rests as mothers in Israel. President Joseph Smith had great faith in the sisters' labors, and ever sought to encourage them in the performance of the duties which pertained to these Societies, which he said were not only for benevolent purposes and spiritual improvement, but were actually to save souls.[13] And my testimony to my sisters is that I have seen many demonstrations of the power and blessing of God through the administration of the sisters, but they should be ever humble, for through great humility comes the blessing. The Lord remembers His daughters and owns and acknowledges, in a perceptible manner, those who are striving to be faithful. I could say much to my sisters on this subject, for it is one in which I am deeply interested. I have been a living witness to the trials, sacrifices, patience and endurance of thousands of them, and my heart goes out to all those who are seeking to walk the narrow way and keep fast hold of the iron rod. The Father has great blessings in store for His daughters; fear not, my sisters, but trust in God, live your religion and teach it to your children.

It was during the time we lived at the Brick Store that Joseph received the revelation pertaining to Celestial Marriage; also concerning the ordinances of the House of the Lord. He had been strictly charged by the angel who committed these precious things into his keeping that he should only reveal them to such persons as were pure, full of integrity to the truth, and worthy to be entrusted with divine messages; that to spread them abroad would only be like casting pearls before swine, and that the most profound secresy must be maintained, until the Lord saw fit to make it known publicly through His servants. Joseph had the most implicit confidence in my husband's uprightness and integrity of character; he knew him capable of keeping a secret, and was not afraid to confide in him, as he had been a Free Mason for many years. He therefore confided to him, and a few others, the principles set forth in that revelation, and also gave him the privilege to read it and to make a copy of it, knowing it would be perfectly safe with him. It was this veritable copy, which was preserved, in the providence of God, that has since been published to the world; for Emma (Joseph's wife) afterwards becoming indignant, burned the original, thinking she had destroyed the only written document upon the subject in existence.

My husband revealed these things to me; we had always been united, and had the utmost faith and confidence in each other. We pondered upon them continually, and our prayers were unceasing that the Lord would grant us some special manifestation concerning this new and strange doctrine. The Lord was very merciful to us; He revealed unto us His power and glory. We were seemingly wrapt in a heavenly vision, a halo of light encircled us, and we were convinced in our own minds that God heard and approved our prayers and intercedings before Him. Our hearts were comforted, and our faith made so perfect that we were willing to give our eldest daughter, then only seventeen years of age, to Joseph, in the holy order of plural marriage. She had been raised in the strictest manner as regarded propriety, virtue and chastity; she was as pure in thought, in feeling and in impulse as it was possible for a young girl to be. Yet, laying aside all our traditions and former notions in regard to marriage, we gave her with our mutual consent. She was the first woman ever given in plural marriage by or with the consent of both parents. Of course these things had to be kept an inviolate secret; and as some were false to their vows and pledges, persecution arose, and caused grievous sorrow to those who had obeyed, in all purity and sincerity, the requirements of the celestial order of marriage.

The Lord commanded his servants; they themselves did not comprehend what the ultimate course of action would be, but were waiting further developments from heaven. Meantime the ordinances of the house of the Lord were given, to bless and strengthen us in our future endeavors to promulgate the principles of divine light and intelligence; but coming in contact with all pre-conceived notions and principles heretofore taught as the articles of religious faith, it was not strange that many could not receive it; others doubted, and only a few remained firm and immovable. Among that number were my husband and myself; yet although my husband believed and was firm in teaching this Celestial order of Marriage, he was slow in practice. Joseph repeatedly told him to take a wife, or wives, but he wished to be so extremely cautious not to do what would probably have to be undone, that in Joseph's day he never took a wife. When he did so, he did it to fulfill a duty due to the principles of divine revelation as he understood his duty, and believing sincerely that every man should prove his faith by his works; but he afterwards took several wives, and with one or two exceptions, they came into the same house with me, and my children; therefore, I believe I am safe in saying that I am intimately acquainted with the practical part of polygamy.

We learn to understand human nature by being brought into close connection with each other, and more especially when under trying and difficult circumstances; and we seldom think more unkindly of persons from gaining an insight into their real hearts and character. Instead of my opinion of women being unfavorable or my feelings unkindly in consequence of being intimately associated in family relationship with them, I am more favorably disposed to women as a class, learning more of the true nature of woman-kind than I ever could without this peculiar experience; and I am willing and ready to defend enthusiastically those of my sisters who have been genuine enough and who possessed sufficient sublimity of character, to practically live the principles of divine faith, which have been revealed in these the last days, in the establishing of the kingdom of God upon the earth. It has required sterling qualities indeed to battle with the opposition on every hand, and not be overcome.

That this is God's work and not man's should be apparent to all those who are acquainted with the history of the saints, their persecutions, their trials, their difficulties, and the marvelous means of their deliverance,—when dangerous and various untoward circumstances environed them.

My husband built a comfortable dwelling house on Parley Street in Nauvoo, but still we endured many privations, which in our own home in Ohio would probably never have fallen to our lot; but we always felt we must be thus tried to prepare us for future exaltation, and that we might be able to participate with those whom God had approved and owned, who "came up out of great tribulation."

Every one acquainted with the history of our people know the terrible results of the apostacy of "Bennett, Foster and the Laws." Joseph Smith had no peace, his life was sought continually by his enemies, and this was the occasion of constant anxiety and trouble to the saints.

The persecutions brought upon our people in Nauvoo and other places adjacent, by the wicked misrepresentations of such men as Dr. Bennett, William and Wilson Law, and others who had been members of our Church, increased rapidly. Every now and then Joseph Smith was arraigned before the magistrates on some pretext or other, and the Saints were threatened with mobs, and they felt there was no security for them because of their betrayal by designing and treacherous men.

In January, 1844, my youngest daughter was born. She was the first child born heir to the Holy Priesthood and in the New and Everlasting Covenant in this dispensation. I felt she was doubly a child of promise, not only through the priesthood, but through Joseph's promise to me when I gave him my eldest daughter to wife. He prophesied to me that I should have another daughter, who would be a strength and support to me to soothe my declining years; and in this daughter have these words been verified. My health was very poor, but I remained strong in the faith of the Gospel, and full of courage to persevere in the latter-day work. My two youngest children were frail little tender blossoms and required the most constant care.

During the ensuing summer a fearful and continuous storm of persecution raged, until it led to the massacre of Joseph and Hyrum Smith; and John Taylor, who, although pierced with bullets until his life scarce hung by a single thread, afterwards recovered. After this horrible tragedy, the people sorrowed and mourned for their Patriarch and Prophet. Indeed, the terrible grief and consternation which were the result of the untimely death of these noble men was beyond description.

The Gentiles, our opposers, thought they had destroyed our religion, overthrown our cause, and destroyed the influence of our people, and actually had accomplished all that was necessary to do away with Mormonism.

But God's work cannot be thus ignored; another prophet, Brigham Young, was raised up to succeed Joseph, and the work rolled on. We were not allowed, however, to rest in peace; those who had apostatized from us and were filled with a spirit of rebellion against the work sought by all their power and influence to stir up the authorities of government in the State of Illinois, and to drive us from the bounds of civilization. At this time the people were energetically at work upon the Temple, and President Brigham Young and his brethren of the Quorum of the Twelve, with the Bishops and all the leading men, were pushing everything forward towards completing the Temple, in order to obtain certain blessings and confirmations that had been promised to the Saints when the Temple should be so far finished as to enable them to work in it. The people were most of them poor, and they denied themselves every comfort they possibly could to assist in finishing the Lord's house. In the latter part of the fall of 1845 we commenced work in the Temple, and then I gave myself, my time and attention to that mission. I worked in the Temple every day without cessation until it was closed.

We were making preparations to leave Nauvoo and go into the wilderness. I had a large family, and my household cares and my many other duties were indeed arduous; I worked constantly day and night, scarcely sleeping at all, so great was my anxiety to accomplish all that was necessary and go with the first company who left in February, 1846, crossing the Mississippi River on the ice.

BATHSHEBA WILSON BIGLER SMITH

A biographical sketch of Bathsheba Smith appears in the letters section of this volume to introduce a letter she wrote to Phebe Woodruff. Letters are only a part of Bathsheba's written legacies. She also left a variety of other writings, including diaries, an autobiography, some reminiscences, and several articles for the *Woman's Exponent* and other church periodicals. She lived a long and eventful life, well documented in the literary trail she left behind.

For Bathsheba Smith, Nauvoo was pivotal in the formation of her faith and life as a Latter-day Saint. She frequently reflected on her experiences there, particularly on her association with Joseph and Emma Smith. She also often expressed how privileged she felt to have received the temple ordinances at the hands of the Prophet, to be instructed by him in the meaning of each step of the temple ceremony, and to enjoy his company in these private, sacred gatherings. Her first home as a young bride, the births of her two children, and the beginning of a joyous marriage were all part of her Nauvoo experience, which remained a happy memory for Bathsheba despite the upheavals and dislocations of the Church's final years in Nauvoo.

The reminiscence that follows is a short but complete narrative of Bathsheba Smith's life in Nauvoo. It is anecdotal and largely personal, focusing mainly on her marriage, her home, her children, and her husband. But when it shifts briefly from the private to the public, it seems consciously aimed at the reader, bearing witness of Joseph's prophetic calling, her own acceptance of plural marriage, and the validity of the claim of the Quorum of the Twelve to leadership of the Church after the death of Joseph Smith.

Despite its dispassionate style, Bathsheba's recollection is detailed and informative. Besides the personal conviction it conveys, it is also an entry into the personality of its writer, forthright, unequivocating in her convictions, and loyal. How poignantly in character was her last act before she left her beloved Nauvoo home: tidying up the rooms, sweeping the floor, and "putting the broom in its accustomed place behind the door," leaving a perfectly kept house for those who were driving her from it.

REMINISCENCE OF BATHSHEBA WILSON BIGLER SMITH*

In the spring of 1840 my family moved to Nauvoo Illinois. Here I continued my punctuality in attending meetings, had many opportunities of hearing Joseph Smith preach and tried to profit by his instructions, and received many testimonies to the truth of the doctrines he taught. Meetings were held out-of-doors in pleasant weather and in private houses when it was unfavorable. I was present at the laying of the cornerstone of the foundation of the Nauvoo Temple, and had become acquainted with the prophet Joseph and his family and I had a deep love and respect for his wife, Emma, which has never changed.

I had promised a young man that I would "keep his cabin" in Missouri and on the 25th of July 1841, I kept this promise and was married to George A. Smith the youngest member of the Twelve. Elder Don Carlos Smith [cousin of George A. Smith and younger brother of Joseph Smith] officiated. A year before my marriage I had not heard from the man I loved since he left for his mission to England until one day Lorenzo Snow joined him in London and gave him news of me and my family. One day a neighbor came to our house showing a letter addressed to Bathsheba W. Bigler and post-

*This autobiography, one of several versions, was edited by Alice Merrill Horne, a granddaughter of Bathsheba W. Smith. Original typescript is in possession of Harriet Horne Arrington.

marked Liverpool. He held the letter high to tease me, but knowing well who had written my name, I danced and sang for joy. Presently he burst into tears and gave me the precious letter. [When] George A. Smith returned I had six letters tucked away among my precious belongings.

My husband was born June 26, 1817, at Potsdam, St. Lawrence Co., New York. I first met him when a neighbor introduced him to my father saying, "I want George A. Smith to meet Mark Bigler because you two will so enjoy each others' stories." George A. Smith came to the Bigler home as a missionary. Each time he came to visit the farm we would kill a fat turkey. My husband declared he enjoyed seventeen turkey dinners around the Bigler hospitable board.

Mr. [George A.] Smith has received many honors and has been given various positions of trust. April 26th, 1838, he was ordained a member of the High Council at Adam-ondi-Ahman.

On April 26, 1839, while kneeling on the cornerstone of the foundation of the Lord's House in the city of Far West, he was ordained one of the Twelve Apostles. He immediately started on a mission to preach the Gospel in Great Britain from which he returned twenty days before our marriage. Two days after we were married we started, carpet bag in hand, to go to his father's who lived in Zarahemla, Iowa Territory, near the Mississippi River. We walked about a mile and a half to the river side. A skiff had just pushed off; we hailed it. The owner came back, took us in and rowed us across the river without charge. We were met by my husband's brother, John L. Smith, with a horse and a light wagon, who conveyed us to his father's house. There we found a feast prepared for us, in partaking of which my husband's father, John Smith [brother of Joseph Smith Sr.], drank [to] our health, pronouncing upon us the blessings of Abraham, Isaac and Jacob. I did not understand the import of that blessing so well then as I do now. I was indeed happy and all of our relations on both sides were well pleased with our marriage.

After living at father Smith's about a month we started housekeeping in a small log cabin close by. From the time I was in my teens I had been laying away linen and other articles, preparing myself to some day help furnish a home. Mother fitted me out with

furniture, earthenware, cooking utensils, beds and bedding. My
husband had china and earthenware which the Saints in
Staffordshire potteries had presented him. All of these blessings
added to our comfort and happiness. But the house leaked and the
chimney smoked. We next bought an unfinished log house. We fitted
it up and built a brick chimney, but that, too, smoked. Soon after this
my husband was counseled to move to Nauvoo. We did this and
rented a log house of Ebenezer Robinson, but it was open and that
chimney, too, smoked.

In a few weeks we rented a more comfortable room of Bp.
Vincent Knight. Then Brother Joseph gave us a lot which had a small
log house on it. My husband fixed up the place as best he could; but,
after all, it was the worst looking house we had yet lived in. I was
ashamed to have my acquaintances see me in such a looking place. It,
however, had the desirable qualities of neither leaking nor smoking.

My husband went to work with all the time he could spare and
soon had a storey and a half frame house put up, with four rooms in
it—two below and two above. By fencing and draining the lot, and
with great labor, we soon had a splendid garden, thrifty [thirty?]
fruit trees, flowers, vegetables and corn. I spared no pains nor effort
to make this home a place good to look upon.

As the 4th of July, 1842, came on Sunday we celebrated the 4th
on Monday. A military display by the Nauvoo Legion was followed
by a sham battle. My husband was chaplain in the general's staff.
Emma [Smith] and other ladies rode with the staff. At four o'clock
on the morning of Wednesday the 7th a son was born to us. Words
are feeble to express my joy. His father named him George Albert
[Junior].

In two months more, my husband was leaving for a mission. I
had but five pounds of flour, but there were vegetables and corn in
our garden and a cow supplied us with milk and butter. My brother-
in-law, Caleb W. Lyons, made me a large grater and I grated the corn
into meal on which we lived until my husband was able to send me
flour. He also sent me some pork, beans, and wild, dried grapes,
which lasted us the winter. Our garden supplied us bountifully with
vegetables. In two months Mr. Smith returned, having preached in

many of the principal towns in Illinois. The winter set in early and with severity.

When on his mission to England, my husband, while preaching out-of-doors in London, injured his left lung, causing occasional hemorrhages. This winter 1842-3 he took a violent cold, which settling on his lungs, confined him to his room for some weeks.

In the spring of 1843 Missouri renewed her wicked persecutions. Brother Joseph [Smith] was arrested in Lee County, Illinois, while on a visit to his wife's relations. Great effort was made by his brethren at Nauvoo to obtain his release. At great expense of time and means he was brought to Nauvoo and there discharged under a writ of Habeas Corpus. In this year, 1843, my husband went east as far as Boston, on a mission, preaching and attending conferences by the way. He returned in the fall. My son, George Albert, had been sick all winter with dysentery, which caused me great anxiety. He was now improving.

Soon after my husband returned, we were blessed by receiving our endowments and were sealed under the holy order of Celestial Marriage which order is for time and eternity and was revealed July 12, 1843.

I heard the Prophet charge the Twelve with the duty and responsibility of administering the ordinances of endowments and of sealing both for the living and the dead. My husband and I met with Joseph and many others in a room dedicated for the purpose and prayed with them repeatedly.[14]

I heard the Prophet give instructions concerning plural marriage.

In the spring of 1844, many elders went forth preaching. My husband, on the fifth of May, started to preach and lecture. He visited Illinois, Indiana and Michigan. Soon after he went a terrible persecution began in Nauvoo, which ended in the martyrdom of the Prophet and his brother Hyrum. I am unable to describe the sorrowing that followed. I cannot think of it without experiencing again those days of anguish and horror and mourning.

My husband returned August first and on the fourteenth a daughter was born to us and we gave her the name Bathsheba. I have always thought that her sympathy and her tendency to weep over another's distress was due to my harrowed feelings previous to her birth. The Twelve immediately returned and though the times were exciting, under their wise counsel excitement abated. The spirit of resentment gave way to mourning, from which the people emerged more hopeful and more determined that Truth should triumph. The Twelve, who were acknowledged as the presiding quorum of the whole church, immediately exercised all their influence to finish the Temple and the Nauvoo House in accordance with the Revelation of January 19, 1841 [D&C 124].

Not content with the cruel wrongs already inflicted, our persecutors continued to annoy us. Notwithstanding this, work on the church buildings was pushed until September 1845, when the burning, by the mob, of one hundred and seventy-five houses belonging to our people in Hancock County caused the sheriff, J. B. Backenstos, to issue a proclamation calling for two thousand men as a "posse commitatus" to disperse the house burners. My husband, in charge of the work, released four hundred workmen to compose part of this posse. The house burners, to avoid arrest, left the country, and work on the temple redoubled in zeal.

Governor Thomas Ford sent General John J. Harding at the head of four hundred militia to Nauvoo. He dismissed the sheriff's posse, but made no effort to arrest the house burners. General Harding informed the Saints in Hancock County that they could get no protection from the state. The mob was determined to drive the Mormons from the state and therefore, they must go.

Previous to this, a council of church authorities, had passed a resolution (which, as a matter of policy, was kept private) to send one thousand five hundred men as pioneers to make a settlement in the valley of the Great Salt Lake. This resolution was determined on and in accordance with the design and policy of the Prophet Joseph when living.

Those burned out of their homes fled into Nauvoo for shelter. Our house was filled with refugees. With every means available, Mr. Smith [George A.] pushed work on the Temple, so that in the fall of

1845, thousands received their endowments. I officiated for a time as priestess.

Mr. Smith and I believed firmly in Joseph Smith as a Prophet of the Most High. We believed that he had sealed his testimony with his blood. I became thoroughly convinced as well as my husband, that the doctrine of "plurality of wives" as taught by Joseph the Prophet, in our hearing, was a revelation from God; and having a fixed determination to attain to Celestial Glory, I felt to embrace every principle, and that it was for my husband's exaltation that he should obey the revelation on Plural Marriage, in order to attain to kingdoms, thrones, principalities and powers, firmly believing that I should participate with him in all his blessings, glory and honor.

In accordance with this purpose I had in the last year, like Sarah of old, given to my husband five wives—good, virtuous, honorable women who had gathered to Zion without their families.[15] Four of these women were considerably older than I and two of them older than my husband. They were all deeply religious. I was young, only twenty-three years old and Mr. Smith but twenty-eight, though I believe we were mature for our years on account of experiences gained amid the perilous times through which we had already passed. I was proud of my husband and loved him, knowing him to be upright in all things, a man of God, and believing that he would not love them less because he loved me more, I had joy in a testimony that what I had done was acceptable to my father in heaven.

The fall of 1845 found the city of Nauvoo one vast work-shop, for nearly every family was wagon building. Our parlor became a shop in which to paint wagons and, likewise, every other parlor in the neighborhood was put to some such use, in the general preparation for the winter exodus.

On the 9th of February, 1846, in company with many others, my husband took me and my boy of three and a half years and my little girl of one and a half years and some of the other members of our family (the remainder to follow as soon as the weather would moderate), and we crossed on the ice the Mississippi River and turned our faces toward the wilderness in which we were to seek out an abiding place.

We left a comfortable home, the accumulations of four years of labor and thrift and took away with us only a few much needed articles such as clothing, bedding and provisions. We left everything else behind us for our enemies. My last act in that precious spot was to tidy the rooms, sweep up the floor, and set the broom in its accustomed place behind the door. Then with emotions in my heart which I could not now pen and which I then strove with success to conceal, I gently closed the door and faced an unknown future, faced a new life, a greater destiny as I well knew, but I faced it with faith in God and with no less assurance of the ultimate establishment of the Gospel in the West and of its true, enduring principles, than I had felt in those trying scenes in Missouri. I, a girl of sixteen, had at that time declared to the weeping Saints, around the death-bed of David Patten, that God had established His church with the promise that it should never be thrown down and I testified that though we might some of us be called to give up our lives, yet the Kingdom of God should stand and His people would be preserved. Now I was going into the wilderness, but I was going with the man I loved dearer than my life. I had my little children. I had heard a voice, so I stepped into the wagon with a certain degree of serenity.

MARGARET GAY JUDD CLAWSON

Margaret Judd was ten when she and her family arrived in Nauvoo in 1841. Canadians who joined the Church in 1836, they had met one obstacle after another as they attempted to gather with the Saints. Finally they reached Nauvoo, only to be confronted with additional hardship. They shared with other newcomers the scarcity of housing and provisions, and each member of the family had a turn with malaria or some other sickness. In time, however, the family settled into a comfortable home, and life seemed more promising. Margaret's admiration for the resourcefulness and determination of her parents and her mother's commitment to the gospel is clearly demonstrated in the many homely incidents that make up her recorded recollections. Though written years after the events took place, they convey the sense of drama and community spirit that influenced her view of life as a young girl in Nauvoo.

Margaret Gay Judd Clawson

The Judds immigrated to the Salt Lake Valley with one of the earliest pioneer companies, and in 1850 Margaret joined with several other theatrical-minded people to form a drama company there. Hiram Clawson was one of the number. Their marriage two years later brought together two of early Utah's best-known thespians. They became the mainstay of the Deseret Dramatic Association and were regular participants in other theatrical ventures.

Margaret performed in the opening presentation at the Social Hall in 1853 and appeared on stage in Utah, usually playing comedic parts, many times over the next twenty-five years. She was a well-known and prominent member of Salt Lake City society at the time of her death in 1912.

The excerpt that follows, taken from a lively, expressive life history, shows Margaret Clawson's observant eye, impressionable memory, and a sensitivity to the human drama that unfolded in Nauvoo and her family's participation in it.

REMINISCENCE OF MARGARET GAY JUDD CLAWSON*

At last in the spring of 1841 we went to Nauvoo. How happy Mother was! She was a devoted Latterday Saint. Her one thought from the day she was baptized was to gather with the Church, and now she was in their midst. Well, when we arrived there Brother Noble who had gone right through found us and insisted on our family sharing part of his home until we could get a place of our own. Houses were very scarce Mother had her misgivings knowing Mrs. Noble too well. But "Necessity knows no law," so my parents accepted his kind offer, and things went along a little while But the lady of the house soon began to show the Cloven foot, she did not belong to the Church and was as bitter as gall, and very quarlsome and never let an opportunity pass without saying something disagreeable about the Church, and especialy about the Phrophet. All the apostate lies she could hear she took such pleasure in making mother listen to often. But Mother had made up her mind that she would *not* quarrel with her. But it was pretty hard to have to hear her sneers, insinuations and abuse continualy. I remember once mother had me sit down and read the Book of Mormon. That was too much! She took a cup of water, and dashed it over me and the book. Well,

---

* This version of Margaret Clawson's reminiscence is from a corrected typescript of the original holograph, which is in the LDS Church Archives.

things got from bad to worse until mother could stand it no longer. In the mean time, father had bought a lot. So he got some lumber and built a shanty and mother was delighted to get out of a comfortable house into all the discomforts of a shanty. When the Sun shone it was hot and when it rained it was wet, but mother never uttered one word of complaint. Not even that horrid woman could keep her from enjoying her religion. My parents were faithful attendants to the meetings in the "grove" to hear Joseph preach, I have seen and heard him many times. Strange as it may seem, in about a year that good brother Noble took his wife back to the state of New York where they came from and never returned to Nauvoo although before he came he sold out everything with the firm determination of spending the rest of his life with the Church, but her everlasting fault finding and complaining had the desired effect at last, & the old adage "A continual dropping will wear out a stone" was verified.

Soon after we got there brother Riley was taken with a white swelling on his knee. Poor boy, How he suffered. Mother used to be up with him night after night working so hard trying to releive his sufferings, but nothing seemed to do him any good, so she decided to have him baptized in the font [of the Temple]. Before going she told him that the Lord could heal him so he went with the greatest confidence. When they got there mother lifted him out of the wagon and carried him to the font, and an Elder took him in his arms and carried him down into the water. He could not tak[e] a step or put his foot to the ground without the most exc[r]uciating pain; but after he had been baptized and was carried to the steps[,] mother waiting to take him in her arms, all at once he called out, "Oh, Mother I can walk and sure enough he walked right up the steps, and from that time he had no more pain in his knee. The swelling gradualy went down, and he was soon running and jumping with his playmates as usual and never had any more trouble with his leg. How little I could then appreciate mother's feelings at the miraculous healing for there never lived a more tender devoted mother. Would that I could do justice to her great, good, and noble qualities. She was a natural born nurse and well did she magnify that gift. There was a great deal of sickness in Nauvoo at that time. How often and often she would go around among her sick neighbors nursing and helping them, and more than that she made me go with her. I was only a little girl, but I could give a drink of water to the poor things burning with fever, also wash dishes and many other little chores. Not inheriting any of mothers nursing qualities, it was a great hardship to me. How I did hate it! Wasn't it *bad* enough to wash dishes at home without going to the neighbors, and when any of them got well, I was delighted, *only* because I knew that I would not have to go there any more. Oh, the selfishness of human nature even in children. Father was working very hard at that time getting material to build us a house. He used to go to an island in the Mississippi to get lumber. He would go Monday morning and stay until Saturday evening getting out what was called shakes—our house and many others were made of the same. It was an all sumer job getting a little two room house built. I think it was about a mile east of the grove, a nice location on what was called the Bluffs. Then there were the Flats down by the river. What a beautiful view from above and the ever interesting sight of steamboats passing up and down the Mississippi with Joseph's home, the Mansion house, the center of attraction. I have heard mother tell of a little incident about the Prophet. Soon after we went to Nauvoo, she had occasion to do a little shopping, going to the store, she passed his home. He was standing on the lawn conversing quite earnestly with several very elegant, gintile gentlemen. As she passed along, very naturaly she looked at the Prophet. She knew him, but he did not know her. All at once he reached his arm over the fence and grasped her by the hand, and gave her a hearty shake. He did not hesitate in his conversation with the gentlemen and mother passed right on. I need not say she was delighted. I am sure he divined what a noble-spirited woman she was[.] Well when our house was done and we moved in my parents were delighted. It was their *own* home and in the midst of the Saints, where they expected to live the rest of their days. Our family consisted of father, mother, brother Riley, sister Phebe, and myself. Grandfather and grandmother Judd lived with us part of the time. My Grandparents were most welcome in our home. Mother and grandmother were always on the best of terms. Grandmother said "I would rather live with Teresa than any one I ever knew." Mother not being like many daughters-in-law who look upon their mother-in-law as their natural enemies. So their association was always most harmonious. I was very fond of my grandmother Judd. I have only a faint recollection of my grandmother Hastings as I never saw her after I was six years old, but I have heard Father say that she was a very kind, liberal-hearted, generous, woman. I think it was about in forty-two or three that the mob used to harrass the Saints very frequently and we often had quite exciting times. It was generally known when the mobs were prowling around outside of Nauvoo. The bretheren were advised to always be in readiness to meet them to protect their homes and families. One morning I saw something more than usual going on at one of our neighbors, an English family by the name of Thompson. So I ran over to see what it was. Well, the word had been brought in that the mob was coming and very near, to the Thompsons (he was a very small man) with others had been called to the war. His wife was hurrying to get her protecter ready to go. I was filled with patriotism, when I saw him staggering off under the weight of his lunch and gun. After bidding him good bye, she stood there and called after him As long as she could see him these encour[a]ging words, "Now, Thompson, stick to thy post and don't thee flinch." No doubt they stimulated him to greater deeds of valor, But the expected did not happen. It was merely a false alarm, the mob was not there, and Thompson came home, covered with glory and as brave as a lion and said what he would have done if the mob had been there, much to the admiration of his wife and myself. Times were very hard and provisions were scarce. Father was an industrious, hard working man and could work at two trades, but it seemed almost impossible for him to get the right kind of pay for his work to provide the ne[c]esaries of life for his family. So he want back to LaHarp [Indiana] to work. He used to send us flour, meat etc. Transportation was not as easy in those days as now it is, so father had to watch his chance for sending us provisions, and if he missed we ran short. Father often walked the 25 miles home to see his family. He was a splendid walker. He told us once when he came home of a mad dog

overtaking him. He was a terrrible sight, his eyes were blood red, his
tongue hanging out, and frothing at the mouth. Father was quite
pleased when he passed without a salute. In a very short time a lot of
men and boys with clubs and guns came running after the dog. They
said he had bitten a boy and several animals. In a little while, father
heard them yelling and the guns fired off, so he supposed they had
killed the dog. As I remember it now I suppose father had not had an
opportunity of sending us any provisions at that time so we got up
one morning to find ourselves without anything in the house to eat
except some shelled corn. There were five of us at that time mother,
grandmother, brother Riley, sister Phebe & myself. What were we to
do? We had heard of a woman who had a hand mill for grinding. She
lived about a mile from us, and as our only alternative was the corn.
So Mother said "Children, do you think you could take some and
grind it, and when you come back I will make a nice Johnny cake for
our breakfast". Of course, we could. So brother and I started out in
high spirits with all the corn we could carry, in high spirits and
feeling the importance of helping to support the family. Well, when
we got there she took us into the back yard, and showed the mill and
told us that we would have to pay her toll for the use of it. We had
heard that before. We started in real brisk, it did not seem so very
hard. We talked and laughed and encouraged each other. The meal
seemed to run out of the hopper quite fast and we thought Mother
would be so surprised to see us home so soon with such a lot of
meal. Well, when we had gotten nearly half of the corn ground that
harred [horrid] woman came out and took it all in for her share. Oh,
didn't our hearts sink! And did not that mill get awful hard to turn,
and then the handle slipped off and struck me on my finger nail and
hurt me dreadfully. Then it was Riley's turn to grind, so I could stop
and cry awhile. It was not long before the handle slipped again, and
knocked his finger nail nearly off. Poor fellow, how he did cry, and
how the blood run. He always got the worst of every hurt. I went into
the house and asked the woman for a rag to put around his bleeding
finger but she would not take the trouble to give me one, but said "It
would not hurt very long." So I tore a piece off my apron and
wrapped his finger up. Well, it was my turn to finish grinding the

corn. I could not expect Riley to work any longer with his aching finger. Everything must have an end and our grist was ground at last, & we started home, "wiser, but sadder children." When we came in sight of home there was Mother watching for us, and when she saw our bunged up eyes and sore fingers she could scarsely restrain her tears. I don't think she expressed herself half as strong as she felt, for her eyes were unusually bright and her cheeks very red. If mother had met that woman then there would have been quite a flow of eloquence. I think in a very short time mother had the meal sifted and the corn bread in the spider baking, and when it was done, oh, what a delicious breakfast. No sweeter morsel was ever set before a king than that hard earned Johnny cake was to us, As good luck would have it, father sent us some provisions from LaHarpe that very day. With all our poverty and hardships, I never heard Mother speak one word of complaint, she was so thankful to be with the Saints and hear the teachings of the Prophet. Father planted us a garden that spring. The vegetables grew very fast, but the weeds grew faster. Mother made Riley and I do the weeding (or some of it). We used to say if it was only shady, and we could sit down it wouldn't be so hard, But to go right out in the hot sun, and stoop over to pull the weeds We thought it awful cruel of Mother to have us do it. She often used to show [us] how to do it. It seemed *so easy* for her. Why she could pull more weeds in five minutes than we could in half an hour, and still she insisted o[n] *us* doing it. Oh, the hardships of childhood. I think it was the latter part of 1843, that my Uncle and Grandfather went to Springfield Ill, from there they kept writing to Father, Telling of what good times it was there saying coopers were getting higher wages than any other trade, and if he would come there for awhile that he could get a good start, and would not have to live from hand to mouth, as he was then doing. Altho' Father was hard working and industrious, he did not seem to get ahead at all. So after awhile, he decided to go. Mother was very loth to leave Nauvoo, hoping it would be for only a short time. There was quite a little branch of the Church there. In the spring of 1844, we went to Springfield, Illo. We had not been there more than two or three months when we got the news of the Prophet's death. Mother would not believe it. Said it was a false report. But when it was confirmed our house was a house of mourning. I don't think Mother could have felt worse if it had been one of her own family. Father got all the work he could do at fair wages, But with a family to support, and clothe and house rent to pay & he didn't get rich very fast. And there was another one added to our home. On New Years day, 1845 brother George came and that made us six in family. My Second great grief came on the fourth of October, 1844, when my dearly loved Grandmother left us for a better world. She was so pleasant and kind to all. Mother loved her as her own Mother. I shall never forget how dreadful I felt. It seemed the sun would never shine again. I was then thirteen and could fully realise our great loss. I could not eat and slept very little until Mother became quite worried about me. But youth and time obliterates sorrow. She was sick about two weeks and said from the begining that she did not want to get well again. After she was in her Coffin, one of my young cousins Came to look at her. As soon as he saw her he said, "Oh, Grandma is laughing["] and if that beautiful smile was an indication of her happiness, it was indeed supreme. After the Saints left Nauvoo, my parents redoubled their exertions to get an outfit to go to the Rocky Mountains. In the meantime, Father had one or two quite sick spells which put him back considerably. How well I remember what a hard time he had breaking in the animals to draw the wagon. There were six cows and two oxen. The oxen were well broken and quite sedate, But the cows were wild and unruly. He would get help to yoke them up, and then would start to drive them. All at once, they would run off in an opposite direction to where he wanted them to go, Or would run around to the back of the wagon, and get all tangled up. Well, this went on for days and days, and while Father was breaking the cattle, Mother was praying. She told me afterwards that many nights when we were in bed asleep that she would go out into the orchard at the back of our house, and there pour out her soul in prayer, asking the Lord to open the way for us to go with the Saints. She was willing to share their privations for the sake of being with them. Another source of anxiety to her was that I was in my teens, at the romantic age of seventeen, and Mother knowing the susceptibility of the human heart, was afraid that some young man might persuade me to think more of him than I did of her, and induce me to remain there. She could not live away from the Church, and she could not leave a child behind. So my parents said we must not stay here any longer. Well, after weeks of hard work, Father had gotten the cows broken so that he could drive them, And on the ninth day of May, 1849, my brother Riley's sixteenth birthday, we said good bye to our friends and relatives, got into our wagon, and started on our long, eventful journey. Oh, how Mothers countainance beamed with joy! What did she care for hardships, if she could only reach the goal. One of many little romances. The night before we left—My true lover, Henry Ridgley, came to bid me farewell, And under our trysting tree (a big tree close bye) we each vowed eternal constancy, for four years at least. For at the end of that time, he would be of age, and then he would come to claim me for his own, even if I was at the end of the Earth. Well, he did come to see me, but it was forty years after inste[a]d of four years. He had a wife and three children. I had a husband and was the mother of thirteen children. The romance of youth gone—the reality here. How we could talk of the long ago, and laugh at each others inconstancy. After a pleasant two weeks visit with us, he returned to Springfield and in five years after, I received a letter from his wife telling me of his death.

ELIZA CLAYTON MARGETTS

Eliza Margetts was a member of the Clayton family from Manchester, England, whose more famous member was her older brother, William. In 1850, after migrating to Utah, she married Henry Margetts. They became parents of a daughter, Alice, who remained their only child for ten years until their son, Henry, was born. Nine years later the Margettses adopted another daughter. Eliza and Henry loved drama and performed in local dramatic productions in Salt Lake City. Their daughter, Alice, early showed a theatrical bent and acted with her parents as a young child. The family also loved to travel, particularly to areas where they could immerse themselves in the theater and enhance their knowledge of the dramatic arts and theatrical experience.

In 1869 Henry and Eliza were called to assist in the settlement of Paris, Idaho, north of Bear Lake on the Utah-Idaho state line, where he was appointed probate judge. Paris became their permanent home. Though a long way from any cultural center, the family took their talents in drama and music with them to the Bear Lake Valley, producing and acting in numerous cultural presentations. Henry and Eliza both died in Paris, just three weeks apart: Henry in January 1901 and Eliza in February.

When her family emigrated from England to Nauvoo, Eliza Clayton was only ten years old, but her memories of Nauvoo remained vivid throughout her life. Living in Carthage, Illinois, at the time of the martyrdom of Joseph and Hyrum Smith, she was more than a casual observer; she visited the jail immediately after the murders, leaving a brief but graphic description. She also left an eyewitness account of the battle of Nauvoo and the miracle of the quails, one more testimony of these extraordinary events in Mormon history.

REMINISCENCE OF ELIZA CLAYTON MARGETTS*

At the age of ten years I, with my parents, emigrated from England, and arrived at Nauvoo in the fall of 1840, our family being large father was counseled by the Prophet Joseph to go into the country, we did so, and remained away from Nauvoo untill the Summer of 1841, when we moved back, in consequence of the persecution of mobocrats.

I have a distinct recollection of hearing Ruth, wife of Wm Clayton, talk of the organization of the Female Relief Society, on her return home from the meeting at which said organization took place.

We moved to Carthage in the fall of 1842, at which place we lived untill after the martyrdom of the Prophet Joseph and his brother Hyrum. In the forenoon of the day on which these atrocious murders were committed some of the neighbours, disguised and with painted faces, came to our house and told mother she had better get out of the way as they were going to kill the Prophet that day. A terrific storm arose that day, and in the afternoon we heard the firing of guns and soon after saw some of the murderers run away howling like fiends. My sister Lucy who was at this time living with the jailer's family, and was at the jail when the shooting commenced, came home and told what had happened. The next day I went with my sister Lucy to the jail, we found the doors and windows open and everything in confusion, as tho the people had left in great haste, we went up stairs to the room in which the Prophet and his brother had been shot, everything seemed upset, there were some Church books on the table and portraits of Joseph and Hyrum's families on the mantle piece. Blood in pools on the

---

*Photocopy of original letter, entitled "Reminiscences of Nauvoo," is in Special Collections, Harold B. Lee Library, Brigham Young University.

Carthage jail, from a painting by Frederick Piercy, ca. 1857

floor and bespattered on the walls, at sight of which we were overcome with grief and burst into tears. After becoming somewhat collected we gathered up what we supposed belonged to the inmates of the room at the time of the murder, and placed them together on a trunk that was in the room.

About three weeks after the massacre of Joseph and Hyrum, we moved back to Nauvoo. I witnessed the trying scenes the saints passed through untill they were driven from Nauvoo.

I remember a circumstance that occured during what is called the battle of Nauvoo. While at the well drawing a bucket of water, a cannon ball from the enimies guns struck the chimney of the house in which we lived, which so much frightened me that I got my finger fast in the well windless [windlass][16] and in extricating myself skinned my finger nearly the whole length.

"I was among the remnant of the sick and dying saints on the banks of the Mississippi, after the expulsin, when they were miraculously fed by quails that alighted in their midst." When the quails alighted they lit on our laps and every thing that was around[.] after we had caught enough to eat they flew towards the

west like a swarm of bees. Before this there were some young men
went out in the woods with there guns to find some game for their
famlies to eat and while they were gone the quails came and had
gone when they got back, they had bad luck while they were out and
killed nothing and had to come back with out anything to eat for
there families and great were their joy when they found every body
had plenty to eat.

MARY GIBBS BIGELOW

The brief autobiographical sketch left by Mary Gibbs Bigelow details her early life and marriage and ends abruptly at the close of her experiences in Nauvoo. As with many of the other autobiographical accounts, Nauvoo was central to her life history, and recapturing its memory somehow explained the life that followed. Mary's reminiscence reveals a woman who, within the narrow circumstances of her early life, lived fully and earnestly. Every homely detail gains significance and vitality through her vivid prose, especially the step-by-step account of making her wedding dress, from raising and picking the cotton herself, ginning, carding, and spinning it into a fine thread, weaving the thread into cloth, and bleaching it until it was pure white, to the final design and sewing of the dress.

Mary's early life was spent in Broom County, New York, where she lived until her marriage in 1826 to Nahum Bigelow, twenty-four years her senior, whom she had known since she was thirteen. He waited patiently until she was seventeen to marry her. Mary and Nahum had ten children, two of whom, Lucy and Mary Jane, became plural wives of Brigham Young.

The Bigelows heard the gospel when they were living in Lawrence, Illinois, and after joining the Church they moved to Nauvoo, settling in nearby Camp Creek. In the fall of 1844, while fighting for her life after she and her infant son were stricken with malaria, Mary had a remarkable vision. In it, she records, the Savior promised her that she would recover, but when she inquired about her baby, she was told only, "Your babe is in mine own hands." Three inquiries brought the same answer. Mary recovered, as did the baby, to her great delight. However, the following spring the child once again became ill, and this time the outcome was not as Mary had hoped. Though his death was difficult to accept, Mary wrote, "the same spirit rested on me as it did when I had the vision," and she soon felt the peace of reconciliation with God's will.

In the fall of 1845, after a quiescent period following the death of the Prophet the previous year, the Bigelows experienced the mob raids on the communities surrounding Nauvoo. Mary left a vivid description of the devastating personal toll of those depredations. Her son Hyrum, sixteen at the time, shouldered a major responsibility in protecting the family because of his father's illness.

The Bigelows eventually moved west and settled in Farmington, Utah, where Nahum died in 1851, leaving Mary with six children not yet married. She eventually moved to Provo. In 1888 she died in St. George, at the home of her daughter Lucy Bigelow Young, then living in Brigham Young's winter home. Mary's vivid and detailed account of her last days in Camp Creek and Nauvoo conveys the fear and apprehension of those uncertain times.

REMINISCENCE OF MARY GIBBS BIGELOW*

We moved to Nauvoo in the fall of 1843. We went to Brother Matthews, and then down by the levee. Bought land and began to farm. We were all taken sick, had a terrible sickness—fever and ague. We lived there through the massacre and I had a son born on the 4th of July, a week after the Prophet was slain. We called his name Joseph Smith Bigelow. He lived nine months and sixteen days and died.

The fall after he was born, at conference time, I was taken very very sick. All were very sick. We had sickness from the time we lived there until we left. While I was so very sick and was given up by everybody, and was thought to be dying even by myself, I sent to the

*This excerpt is taken from "Autobiography of Mary Bigelow (Maiden name—Mary Gibbs), June 26, 1809–April 10, 1888," typescript copy in the Marvin M. Witt Papers, LDS Church Archives.

field for my husband to come and put down the dates of the births of my children. He came in haste and taking the Record Book put down the names and dates of some whose record had not been made.

Then afterwards I had a vision. The Savior came to me and told me that I would get well. What about my baby, I asked, for he was also very sick. He answered me, Your babe is in mine own hands. With it I will do as seemeth me good. He then told me again that I would get well, for I had a work to do. Again I asked about my baby and received the same answer. The third time he promised me that I would get well, and again I asked about my baby, and again he gave me the same answer.

The baby got well and fat. This was in the fall. I got well also. But when the baby was so lovable in the spring it took the water on the brain and died suddenly. The same spirit rested on me as it did when I had the vision. I dedicated him to the Lord, and I never shed a tear until I had been to the grave and came back.

When we came back into the house Daniel stepped into the house first and clasping his hands said, O my little Dafie is gone, is gone. He was too little to speak plain. Whereupon we all burst into tears and lamentations. My sympathy was aroused, although I felt resigned to the will of the Lord, feeling it was all right.

My little Liola had the black canker which took his under jaw bone out and five teeth. I went the same summer to see my parents. Liola died while I was gone. He was so bad that the neighbors came in and sat up with him, and were also there after he died. He had spasms. When I came back I felt lonesome indeed. We had our blessings by President Young.

The next fall after the mob commenced to mob and burn houses, we were advised to move into Nauvoo from Camp Creek. We took all the honey we could and everything that we could, leaving the corn in the field. We took our cows, our horses and wagon and oxen and went into Nauvoo. We afterwards gathered corn and squashes.

We were in Nauvoo at the October conference held in the Temple in 1845.

Brother Young spoke that now the excitement and mobbing was allayed for the brethren to go back and secure their crops. My husband was not well when we moved back. He had the chills. We were among the first that moved back and being on a public road the mob noticed us.

On Monday evening after dark a posse of the mob came. They came and knocked on the door. Father was on the bed with a chill. The man said that he had orders to notify us to leave immediately. Father asked him, leaning on his elbow, "By what authority do you order peaceable citizens to leave."

He stuttered, "By orders of the Governor and other officers."

"It is not likely," Father said, "that the Governor will be giving orders for peaceable citizens to leave their homes. What is your name?" "Where do you live?" Father asked. He stuttered, "I live, live, all over—everywhere. I was from Carthage yesterday." They made a big noise out doors and voices called: "Come out, don't be jawing with no woman," as I had told him that I wasn't going to go. If I wasn't a Mormon they wouldn't order me out. ["]If you want to murder us, take us all out and leave us all together.["]

A young man that had been to school with one of my boys came in and said that, "We have not come down to parley with the women. We want to know if you are going to leave immediately." He spoke in a mad, savage and determined manner. Father said, "No, we are not going." Then he said, "If you are not going, you will be tumbled out and burnt up." Voices out doors said, "Stick a brand of fire in the house and that will start them"

He started for the fireplace and I started for him with the shovel or tongs. They called him out for another consultation. He came in again a second time, just inside of the door and said, "We will give you until Thursday night to leave or you will be tumbled out and burned up." They then rode off.

The next morning we started Hyrum off to Nauvoo to let President Young and Col. Markham know of the threats of the mob. While Hyrum made the statement about the mob President Young sat with his head in his hands and then rose up and said, "If the mob should come to burn my house I would defend it to the last. Go home and tell your father to make an affidavit and have it sworn to, and then send it to Carthage to Major Warren. He is stationed at Carthage to prevent mob violence, so it is right for your father to send a written statement to him, and if he won't do anything, come to Nauvoo and you shall have all the help that you need." Joseph Young gave a pistol to Hyrum and told him to give it to his father to defend himself.

Hyrum came home. Edgar Gimsley, who was his campanion, went with him to Carthage. They went across the bottom fourteen miles nearly to Carthage, staying all night, and in the morning rode into Carthage and got there about 10 o'clock. He rode up to the Court House yard and went into the house and asked for Major Warren. He called him out to the back door of the Court House and handed him the paper.

He said because of court being in session and having sent some troops to Lima he couldn't spare any troops, but could spare some the next day. Hyrum answered, "Next day the mob will have the house burned and leave us without a home." He next inquired where he lived. Hyrum told him on the road between Laharpe and five miles from Pontusie. He noted it down.

Hyrum went back to the horses and his companions. He felt very despondent and foreboding and anxious so he wheeled on his heel and went back to Major Warren and said, "The mob will very likely be there tonight and if you could spare but four men, it will probably keep the mob from burning our house."

He studied a moment but said he could spare none. Hyrum and his companions mounted their horses and started immediately for Nauvoo.

Then Major Warren about 1 o'clock had a consultation with Captain Morgan who said, "That is more important than all there is here to do. We have been notified and there may be trouble there." Consequently he sent a Lieutenant and three men who went around to Laharpe and came down to our house. It was a long way around to Laharpe, perhaps 24 or 25 miles, which brought them to our house about nine o'clock.

Hyrum and companion arrived at Nauvoo between sundown

and dark and rode by the Temple to the little guard house west of it. Joseph jumped off his horse and inquired for Col. Markham. One answered, "I don't know where he is." What do you want of Col. Markham, where do you live, where do you come from, was asked at once.

"I live at Camp Creek but am now from Carthage. We went there to tell Major Warren about the mob threatening to burn our house, and he couldn't send anybody and was told to come here and Col. Markham would send all the help that was needed." Then he gave Hyrum to understand that Col. Markham and possee had gone up to Pontusic on a little steamboat landing on the Mississippi river and not seeing anything going on returned that night to Nauvoo.

As Hyrum had had no dinner and the horses had had nothing to eat he went down to President Young's and had supper, fed the animals and started home. He arrived home about 1 o'clock.

When the troops [the Lieutenant and three soldiers from Carthage] were within a mile of our house they got a jack Mormon, Mr. Dickson, to pilot them.[17] Asked first for Squire Logan and then for Mr. Bigelow. He [Dickson] was friendly and came to the yard, saying, "They live in here," and then turned back.

When Mary Jane and I saw someone coming, I said, "Here they come!": Mary Jane came running in and said, "Four are coming, and I don't think Hyrum is with them" Father was in bed with his night cap on.

One of them outside said, "You stay here and I will go and see." Father said, "That's not Hyrum," took his gun, expecting the mob and went to the door.

One [of the soldiers] stepped to the door asking, "Does Mr. Bigelow live here?" "Yes that's my name" answered he, "What do you want?" "Let me in and I'll tell you," said the outsider. "In the name of common sense, what do you want?" asked Father. "What's the use to be so particular," said the one on the outside.

Then my husband, as he [the soldier] was pushing his way in, shot off his pistol and shot him in the left breast. And as he turned he said, "Boys, come to my assistance, I'm shot." Then he shot him again in the right side and cut his sword belt.

The men cried out, "We are from Carthage, we came to protect you;" then one caught his foot in the stirrup and fell. One came running and fell over the sawhorse. Father said, "Why didn't you tell me so before, I wouldn't have shot you any sooner than I would my wife or children."

Father had let go of the door and had challenged him three times, and pulling the pistol had shot him in the left breast. And as the man turned and spoke, he took the gun and shot him the second time, because he did not tell his business as he ought to have done.

When the candle was lit, the Lieutenant come up to the table and unbottoned his coat and said, "I came to protect you and see how you've hurt me." "Why didn't you tell me," Father said, "I wouldn't have shot you any more than I would my wife or one of my children." His coat was thickly padded and was smoking, but the pistol was too near, too much lead and too little powder so that he lived. He soon became so faint and exhausted that we got him on the bed and he bled profusely. All were alarmed lest he should die. The three men came in and readily understood that it was owing to his stupidity that he was shot.

Then Dickson came back, came into the house and got excited. One of the soldiers was dispatched to Carthage for Dr. Barnes and the Lieutenant's brother.

The Lieutenant said, "It is my own fault. I ought to have told him, but I did not think the old man was so smart, so courageous. But I will make an affidavit that whether I live or die, it will clear your father."

The firing of the gun was the signal for the mob to gather and the mob hearing the firing began to come.

The arms and saddles were in the house and one man said, stretching out his arms, "I will shoot both pistols into the crowd."

Dickson went out the back door and told the mob that the soldiers were there and then the mob rode away and left us in peace, save for our anxiety for the Lieutenant.

One of the soldiers had come running in saying, "There's a possee of men gathering around here." He gave his orders. Do your duty. Take my pistols. They went out of one door and Dickson went out of the other. Asa [another Bigelow son] was out with the soldiers.

Hyrum sat up with the Lieutenant and me. Father went to bed as he was sick. The Lieutenant let Hyrum take his $200 Gold watch to keep him awake. It gave an alarm or played a tune every half hour and was amusing.

I got supper for the men. A little before daylight the doctor came with the Lieutenant's brother. Dr. Barnes talked to father in a wicked way and said, "such a man as you ought not to be at large." But the wounded Lieutenant Everett said, when the children felt bad, "Don't feel bad for my statement will clear your father."

The names of the soldiers were Bush and Hedges. The Lieutenant had said to the soldier that had been sent off, "I don't know whether I will die before you come back or not." A school teacher, Mr. Caldwell, came that morning and talked with the doctor and found out the truth, but being bitter against the Mormons he went away and raised a great excitement against Mr. Bigelow all over the country.

I got breakfast and after breakfast Hyrum hitched up the team, putting a straw bed and bedding and a buffalo robe, and Mr. Bigelow got in to go off to trial.

The Lieutenant was comfortably fixed in the doctor's carriage and went to Pontusic, where he made out an affidavit that Mr. Bigelow was not to blame, and then took a steamboat to his parents' home in Worsaw, I[llinois]. Mr. Bigelow and Hyrum went down to Pontusic. One soldier remained with us, knowing that danger threatened Mr. Bigelow.

I heard parties passing, looking at Mr. Bigelow laying sick in the wagon and saying, "let's take him out and flay him alive. This is the old codger that did the deed. Let's take him out and tie a stone around his neck and throw him into the river." The soldier Hedges heard such expressions and said to us, "They intend to get away with him," but he kept by us and no one interfered.

The Lieutenant gave his affidavit to the soldier and we went on to Carthage. I had taken lunch with us and we ate at Pontusic. While going over the prairie we went by the ashes of a house that had been burned down. It was Leonard Rice's house, in the prairie settlement, and by a place where one of the mob was killed. He was a hostile, savage wicked fellow. The Lieutenant's brother went with Lieutenant Everett to his home, and the doctor and carriage was with our cavalcade.

Between daylight and dark we drove into Carthage. My husband and myself were taken to Hamilton's Hotel, and Hyrum went to the barracks and stayed with the soldiers who had a stag dance. I slept upstairs; had a bedroom to ourselves. At 10 o'clock we went to the Court House. They took the pistol and gun and Mr. Bigelow went to be examined.

Lawyer Babbit, I think his name was Almon, one of our brethren who was acting attorney for the Mormons, came and whispered to my husband that he would assist him if he needed him in a legal defense. He accepted him thankfull, but there was no trial. Major Warren and Captain Morgan came next saying that he suggested sending the men, and that four men were sent. Hedges came next and gave a correct and favorable statement of losing their way and arriving at Mr. Bigelow's house late at night and what happened there. The written affidavit of Lieutenant Everett was then read by the clerk. It praised him as he was sick and old and yet so brave and shrewd, and that the mob did come afterwards, and being so favorable it cleared my husband.

The Judge decided then that according to the testimony he did not consider any need for further action in the case. He said the case ought to be a reminder to the people to be cool and calm, and not to be rash, and then he dismissed the case.

My son Hyrum saw the jail in which Joseph Smith was incarcerated and the window where he was shot. Mr. Bigelow was taken in a wagon to the Court House and helped into the room, but was unable to sit up but a little while there. After the case was dismissed we got into the wagon again, and started home. On nearing the house Mary Jane and Lucy met us telling us that James Porter and another man had told them that our lives were not safe, that the mob was coming to kill us all.

We got home a little before night and I was so glad to see my lonesome little children who had been tormented with fear on our account and who were glad that we got home safe and alive. We had samp mush[18] for supper.

James Porter who was living on my husband's farm and another man from Musgusto Creek came and told us that the mob was coming to burn the house and had threatened to kill old Bigelow and all his family. We did not feel safe, so one of the boys took Lavinia to Sister Gunsleys, as she coughed so bad, and we hid everything that was valuable and took our bedding and went and made our beds in the corn, near the bean patch where we had pulled up the beans. We took all of the children in bed with us, never undressing them, and having everything dark about the bed so that the mob wouldn't see us. It was cloudy. I was very sick with the sun pain. My husband administered to me and I felt better. After prayers we laid down but had but little sleep as we felt like watching. In a very little while we heard the firing and whooping at the house and were glad that we were hid. My husband said, "lay still and pray, children." We all prayed silently.

They yelled and set the bloodhounds on our track but the Lord preserved us from them. We could see them loping around, and heard the mob racing through the corn field in search of us. The corn was hardly ripe and not gathered. We got up in the night and moved our bed in the hollow, and then my husband and Hyrum went and leaned on the fence and watched proceedings. When the mob dispersed they came back and went to bed.

The mob came about 10 p.m. and went away at 3 a.m. They had ranted around until then. We were the only family in Camp Creek that was molested, which we wondered at. At last daylight came and my husband got up, bidding us to lie quietly until he came back and he would see if the mob was completely gone. The November night was gone and the sun was up before he got back. He found the house still standing but the windows were broken. The tracks of horses feet were all around the house. We went back and my grown daughters commenced picking up the hidden things.

I wanted to get breakfast and sent my fourth child, my second son Asa, to the beautiful large spring that was under the porch of the milk house. The spring ran off into the milk house, where we kept milk and butter pans, churn, etc. Asa went down for water. He brought the water to the house, but said he believed the spring was poisoned as there was a glistening green scum on the water. He poked it away and got another pail full and it was the same. I felt that the child was inspired by God, and as the water stood the scum rose again. I said, "Don't use it, but let it stay until Father comes, and go to another place to a Branch for water a half a mile away."

When Father came back he put some of the water in a bottle to take to Nauvoo, and have Dr. Willard Richards and others analyse it. When it was taken the doctor said it contained four ounces of arsenic and would have killed ten men. We got some good water and had joint mush and milk which we had every meal. The corn meal was made by shaving off the corn with a jointer or plane. The corn was still soft.

We washed up the tin cup and spoons. A man with a broad brow came along who had lost his way and came to our house to inquire the way. When he found out about the mob, the Lieutenant, the poisoning of the spring, he entreated us to move into Nauvoo and told us he would help us all that he could. We harnessed up and put our things into his wagon and our own and started for Nauvoo. We got there safe but were all wet, as it rained all day. We went to an old Dutchman's by the name of Stuedevant. Hyrum used to go back to Camp Creek and help get the stock and crops. He boarded at Porters. Sometimes Mr. Bigelow went out, but it was after a while as he was afraid of being ambushed.

At the time he was poisoned about Christmas. He had been out once before but this time my husband, myself and Hyrum went out home to get a grist of corn ground, and not considering it safe for my husband to go near Pontusic on the Queens mill road he stayed at Porter's home working in the cornfield. James Porter, who always had breakfast, came over and kindly invited Mr. Bigelow to come to breakfast. He did not wish to go as he had provisions with him and wanted to get his own breakfast at home, but Porter insisted, and begged so and as he had always been friendly my husband went. No children were visible. They were not up, but were still sleeping. At breakfast he was offered coffee. He felt as if he ought not to take it but drank it. It was poisoned with white vitriol but he felt no effects of it then.

Hyrum stayed and gathered the corn. We took down some squashes and Hyrum quit staying at Porters. When Porter came over in the morning he wanted to buy some big iron kettles that we scalded pigs in. He was bribed to poison Mr. Bigelow and that was why he kept his children in bed so that they wouldn't get poisoned, and entreated Mr. Bigelow to go to breakfast. My husband felt queer after breakfast and while going home, I drove the team. That afternoon while fixing a wagon tongue he commenced trembling and turned pale around the mouth. He sat down on the wagon tongue. Hyrum went for an Elder who got Brother Patten, brother to David W. Patten, to come. It was snowing. They came in and sat down and looked at Father. He was screaming with pain. They administerd to him, spoke in tongues saying that he should get well. He had been poisoned by the hand of an enemy. Father vomited up some very green stuff, probably enough to have killed ten men.

After Brother Patten had spoken in tongues he said that my husband should get well and go to the Rocky Mountains and establish his family. He stayed about all night, and he [my father] surely got better and was healed.

SARAH LOUISA NORRIS DECKER

Though married to a well-known member of the Church, Charles Decker, who supervised much of the road building and many of the colonizing expeditions when the Church moved to Utah, Louisa Norris Decker lived a quiet, relatively obscure life as one of his plural wives. But she left a striking and moving account of her family's experience in Nauvoo. Three years after her birth in New Jersey, her parents accepted the gospel and made plans to join the members of the Church in Missouri. The death of Louisa's sister and other setbacks delayed the Norrises in their move west, and they were not able to gather with the Saints until 1842 in Nauvoo, when Louisa was seven.

Like the accounts of Margaret Judd Clawson and Eliza Clayton Margetts, Louisa's reminiscence gives an adult's recollection of a child's experience in Nauvoo. The families of all three remained in Illinois after the exodus began in February 1846. Like others unable to leave then, they faced the hostility and violence of the mob in what has come to be known as the battle of Nauvoo, which occurred later that summer. Louisa's family, particularly, felt the cruelty of the impatient mob. Her father was killed during one of the skirmishes, and her mother died in childbirth in Garden Grove, Iowa, shortly after they were forced to leave Nauvoo.

Left an orphan to cross the plains, Louisa was assigned to the Abraham O. Smoot company, under the direct care of a Brother Kinyon, the captain of ten. When his wife gave birth to a baby at the Green River, the infant became a comfort to Louisa and someone to love. The Kinyons never seemed to perceive, Louisa wrote, how much "the orphan girl longed for the kind words they so freely gave their own."

Upon reaching the Great Salt Lake Valley, Louisa lived with her sister's mother-in-law, Sally Murdock, until she was eighteen and then lived with her sister Mary until her marriage to Charles Decker in 1858. She gave birth to seven children, only two of whom survived beyond birth. Her daughter moved to San Francisco, but her son remained in Utah. Louisa died at his home in 1914.

The detailed account that follows, written in simple, direct prose, reflects the immense impression these childhood experiences made on Louisa. Only in such private narratives is the story of the last days of Mormon Nauvoo and the human cost they exacted fully comprehended.

REMINISCENCE OF SARAH LOUISA NORRIS DECKER*

My parents David and Louisa Norris were born in the state of New York; when they married moved to the state of New Jersey, where their four children were born.

About 1837, a traveling Elder, Ball by name held a meeting at their house the subject being of faith, repentance and baptism. My mother lay sick in the back room listening and was so convinced of the truth that she asked to be administered to and was baptized in a river where the ice was cut away to perform the ceremony, that restored her to perfect health. She was wrapt in a quilt over her wet clothes and rode a mile home, changed her clothing, and cooked dinner for the Elder and her family.

This testimony I have heard her repeat several times. My father did not join the Church at this time, but a short time after my eldest brother Nathaniel had taken a severe cold and was becoming very deaf; mother being of great faith sent for Brother Ball and asked him to administer to my brother; when he arrived he said Sister Norris do you have faith that he will be healed? she answered certainly we have

*Excerpt is taken from *Woman's Exponent* 37 (March 1909): 41–42.

those promises. Then he repaired to the woods back of the house evidently to seek the Lord in prayer. Returning in about an hour he administered to my brother, who was immediately healed and was never afflicted afterwards. Then my father joined the Church, sold his possessions and started to join the Saints; got as far as Kirtland when the baby sickened and died; which detained them so late that he thought best to stay over one year and work at his trade blacksmithing. There he loaned out his money and failing to get it, we were kept back two more years which was a great worry to my parents, as they had started for Missouri and a great part of those left in Kirtland were weak in the faith, or had left the Church altogether. The last year we were there 1841 and 42 we lived in the house of our Prophet Joseph Smith near the Temple. My brother Nathaniel and sister Mary had been baptized. Just before we left there I now being eight years old I was baptized. The Saints had now settled in Nauvoo at which place we arrived in 1842; father built a house and blacksmith shop on corner of Parley and Granger Street near the homes of many of the leading members of the Church, and three blocks from the Prophet's home thus he was blest at last to associate with the tried and true; he joined the Quorum of the Seventies, also the Nauvoo Legion and became one of Brother Joseph's body guard. Mother joined the Relief Society. Emma Smith being president; we now had an opportunity to get well acquainted with the Prophet and his family. My sister and I went to school with his children in the new seventy's hall a block west of our house (the teacher named Kelsey boarding at our house).

The Temple was being built and each one seemed to desire to help, and many sold things that they could scarcely spare to put the means towards the building. I can remember of my mother selling her China dishes and fine bed quilt, to donate her part.

About this time there began a spirit of apostacy among a few that had been the Prophet's trusted friends, and with the ill feeling of the out side influence caused him much sorrow and this bitter feeling grew, urged on by our Missouri enemies. There was a paper started to keep the bitter feeling stirred up something after the style of the "Tribune" here.[19] It became necessary to keep night watchmen out to prevent a surprise or an assassination, there were false charges gotten up to get possession of the Prophet and take him away from his friends which was finally accomplished as is well known by all.

The Nauvoo Legion wished to go with him but in his last talk with them; he said brethren stay at home and also said "I go as a Lamb to the slaughter." Brothers Hyrum Smith, John Taylor, and Willard Richards and some others accompanying him on the way going with him; the Church history records the dreadful tragedy; my father was on guard that night, he came in early in the morning with the sad news, that caused the greatest sorrow and mourning ever felt throughout the city.

There was no breakfast eaten in our home that morning before the burial of Brother Joseph and his brother Hyrum: the Saints had the privilege of passing through the Mansion house and taking a last sad look at them. And when I saw where the bullet had pierced the face of Brother Hyrum that had caused his death it made a lasting impression on me that I never can forget; the burial soon followed using great caution as there were spies on the watch to betray. I go sometimes and listen to the trusted old man that dug the graves at night, he is still living among us and his face lights up with joy when he says "and I never told a living soul" until asked by one having authority. "Where was my father buried?" he also told me he was drummer in the Nauvoo Legion and cut stone on the Nauvoo Temple.

Not satisfied yet those opposed to us began a series of persecutions; also a great apostacy took place and jealousy arose as to who should lead the Church. Sidney Rigdon, Lyman Wight and Strang had their followers but when a meeting was called and Brigham Young arose and spoke with power, it was as if the Prophet Joseph's very voice spoke through him. I heard my father and mother when they returned from meeting testify to this, and many others since then. I believe it was the largest attended meeting ever held in Nauvoo. So many among us now drawing away from the Church and the opposition from outside made very trying times for us and a night guard had to be kept. My father and many of the Nauvoo Legion were called to this duty. Father working at his trade through the day and standing guard at night. Now commenced a system of getting up false charges against our leading members to have them arrested, to take them away as they had done our Prophet and often they were seen by the guard prowling around the homes of the Apostles until it was not safe to stay in their own homes.

There were an old couple named Simons living across the street from us that made them welcome in their up stairs rooms.

* * * * *

*Persecution and Expulson of the Mormons from the City of Nauvoo,"
from an old lithograph*

Now the necessary preparations were being made for the journey west. The Twelve and others that were in the greatest danger from outside influence going first. Those staying aiding in helping them. This was father's busy time the blacksmithing being in great demand. He worked on a good part of the 42 wagons that carried the first company out; working early and as late as ten o'clock at night. Mother staying up to get father an extra supper and then going on guard in his turn. The Temple being partly finished in the winter of 1846 the work there was being hurried through. My father, mother, brother and sister received the ordinances. My sister was married to John Murdock and journeyed with his people westward.

All this time the persecutions never abated. Men that had work outside of city limits were caught and unmerciful whipt. One night Uncle Phineas Young and his son S. H. Young came late at night to our house, said they were riding with a brother that was coming in with his team. They saw some of these desperadoes hurrying after them. They run and hid in the grass but were near enough to see the man with the team caught stript tied to his wagon wheel and whipt until his groans ceased when he fainted. They then crawled through the grass until a safe distance to run. This is only one of the cruel things that was happening right along on the out skirts of town. Women and helpless children were carried from a sick bed and laid on the ground while their house and goods were burned. Wheat, haystacks and barns were burned and the cattle driven off. Many families that had depended on their land for a living had to come into the city for protection. I have watched the smoke arise and knew more homes were being burned. Companies and single families were crossing the river all summer camping on the other side or pursuing their journey west. Some getting work to feed their families, a few were staying hoping to sell for a little. There were some strangers coming into secure cheap homes. I think my father sold his five roomed house for a yoke of oxen but do not know as his records and the account of the work he did in helping the brethren off (for they were in no condition to pay at that time) the papers were lost at winter quarters, but all those debts were later forgiven.

Later on about the first of August, 1846, father was ready to start on his journey. By this time the mobbing and driving every Mormon out of the city was the plan of our enemies. Father felt it his duty to stay, saying he could not desert his brethren in their great need. And when hundreds of the mob came with their guns and cannons and camped near the city, our people gathered there men and boys and camped out making ready to resist the enemy that so greatly out numbered them, that it looked like almost a hopeless task, then camped out about a week, there were the musket shots fired and cannon shot at our people. Saturday they moved up to close range, then there was a hard fought battle so near that we could see clouds of smoke arise and hear the roar of cannon while listening I counted

72 cannon shots fired, not realizing that one of these shots had deprived us of a kind father's care but the news was already on the way and my mother's cry of anguish was so distressing that the messenger, a strong man, wept. We never knew how many of the enemy were taken off. Our people lost three, Brother Anderson and son. My father David Norris was instantly killed by a cannon ball. The late Henry Grow stood by his side and when the order came to them to march to the front of a field where the enemy had started to come in back of our people [and] surround them cutting off a chance of retreat. Henry Grow was walking in father's footsteps. In telling me this he said one step more and it would have been him. Providence calls one and leaves another. Later in the day a flag of truce was carried over and a treaty made that all that did not renounce their religion should cross the river in three days. Should stack their guns and ammunition in the Temple. And they came Monday and took possession of the city and searched the houses to see there were no weapons hidden. Father's body was brought home at dusk. My brother was released from duty, we had not seen him for a week, he lay down in mother's room up stairs. Mother had been in poor health most of the summer and was now prostrated with grief. My little brother Benjamin, five years old, had cried himself to sleep. This left me alone down stairs with the dead. A tallow candle for light, the blood dripping, dripping from the body all night and lay on the bare floor in a puddle. My brother before he lay down to rest said he expected two men to come for the night, but they were called away on duty. The city was guarded to keep from being surprised. We knew by sad experience the enemy could not be trusted. My brother said if I heard the horn blow or bells ringing to call him that would be the signal that the mob were coming. Once the horn blew but it was a false alarm. I did not call him, I thought he had done his part. He was in his 17th year and I was 12 years old and a very timid child, and the night was lonely. I, only going to the foot of the stairs to speak to mother a time or two, a man came in the morning with team and a hasty made coffin, in which he was laid, wrapt in a sheet. There was no time to make a robe nor any one to make it. My mother still bed fast was left with her little boy. While the funeral

procession, consisting of Brother Nathaniel, myself and a Brother Coulay followed the wagon to the grave just west of the Temple, a short prayer was said and his body was laid to rest.

It was now our task to get our wagon ready, Nathaniel getting a permit to go on the field to bring the front wheels of the wagon that had been used to mount a cannon. The city was now in possession of the enemy and parties were searching for ammunition and guns that might not have been delivered. Our trunks and boxes were emptied on the floor, and as I followed them from room to room, I said, "These are the men that make our homes desolate."

Now we made all haste to cross the river. We helped mother to her seat in the wagon, Nathaniel driving and I following with the one horse wagon that father had used to deliver his work.

We traveled slow and stopped with some camp of Saints at night, as there were many all along the road. There was much sickness in these camps, and the fall rain made the roads bad. Some had camped where the men could get a few days' work.

We got as far as Garden Grove, where a few had settled. We found a family that we knew in Kirtland by the name of MacKinney. They received mother in their house, where she gave birth to a baby boy, which only lived a few hours; and mother passed away on the morning of the 5th of November.

Here we found kind friends to see that mother and babe were properly dressed, one neighbor, Brother Whipple, made the neat pine board coffin that held mother and babe.

NANCY NAOMI ALEXANDER TRACY

"Not a hundredth part hath been told," Nancy Tracy wrote as the concluding statement of a life sketch that she hoped would be read "with some degree of interest" by her children's children. She was right in her assessment. Although her reminiscence is remarkably detailed and observant, it provides only the contours of the peaks and vales that comprised the whole of her long life. Nonetheless, she has mapped the major landmarks along her life journey clearly enough that the reader never misunderstands their significance or puzzles over the direction she chose to take.

Nancy Naomi Alexander Tracy

Her early life promised comfort, peace, and security in the familiar, familial setting of Jefferson County, New York. After her father's death, she was raised by loving grandparents who provided her with schooling, domestic skills, and a strong religious character. But she resisted associating with any single denomination.

Soon after Nancy's marriage to Moses Tracy in 1832, Mormon missionaries brought the gospel to Jefferson County. The sermon of David Patten made the gospel "plain and beautiful and easy to understand," she remembered. "I believed with my whole soul and I could see that I had been preserved from uniting with other creeds."

After their conversion in 1834, she and her husband traveled to Kirtland, where they witnessed the marvelous events attendant to the dedication of the temple and hoped to make the city their permanent home. But Missouri beckoned, and the Tracys made the "long and toilsome journey" a thousand miles to the west. They shared the sorrows and depredations of the other Mormons in Missouri and once again packed up their dwindling supply of belongings to make a new home in Illinois.

The first sentence of Nancy Tracy's reminiscence notes that her life was filled with "hardships, poverty, and persecutions ever since [she] embraced the Gospel in the year 1834." Her experiences in Missouri, in Illinois, in the trek west, and even in Utah attest to that self-appraisal. After losing two sons in Nauvoo, she despairingly noted that "it seemed almost impossible to raise a child there." The trials of the journey to Utah and efforts to create a new community took their toll. Her husband died in 1858 after a long, disabling illness, and being left to manage their family and farm alone, this forty-two-year-old widow with ten children understandably felt "worn down with toil and hardship." A second marriage, though it brought her motherhood for the eleventh time, eased many of her burdens. She lived a long and faithful life until her death in Marriott, Weber County, Utah, in 1902.

"Through all my sufferings I never doubted," she wrote to her children, "but felt to cling to the Gospel." Experiencing the spiritual manifestations in the temple in Kirtland and receiving her endowments in the temple in Nauvoo gave her, she believed, the spiritual strength to endure. Living near the temple site in Nauvoo, Nancy watched the progress of the building's construction, and she found it as difficult to leave the temple as to leave her home when the Saints were driven out of the city. "But the hand of the Lord is over us," she affirmed, "and so we shall find a resting place."

REMINISCENCE OF NANCY NAOMI ALEXANDER TRACY *

Winter passed and spring came but with wet, stormy weather. However, the Saints left [Missouri] as fast as they could, going east. We started in March [1840], about the middle, I think. Imagine our feelings in leaving our homes and starting out not knowing where we were going and leaving our Prophet and leaders in prison at the mercy of those bold fiends of human shape. Notwithstanding our afflictions, the hand of the Lord was over His people, and they found a place of rest for the season.

As I said, we took up our march towards the rising sun. It stormed continually. Our outfit for the journey was a meager one. It consisted of one horse attached to the two wheels of a wagon with bed sheets for a cover. The box was seven feet long; so sometimes at night we could make a bed in the cart by taking things out. But we would make our bed outside when the weather would permit. It was tedious traveling. When we got on the Mississippi bottom, it was terrible. It was 9 miles across and took two days to cross. At last we landed in Quincy, Illinois, and found the people very hospitable. They seemed willing to do all they could to alleviate the condition of the Saints. We traveled on up the river about 40 miles and stopped to see what we should do. This was in Adams County. There, five families of us, 3 families named Tippets and Gustavus Perry and ourselves stopped. We found some empty cabins which the owner let us go into. The place was sparsely settled, but we were glad to get shelter. It was 7 miles to the little town where there was a store and other public buildings. The Saints in general traveled on up the river, but we stayed here one year and raised corn, turnips, and other garden stuffs. Brother John Tippet's wife died here in child birth. Her babe also died, which cast a gloom over us. She was a good woman, and we sadly missed her. I suppose her grave is still alone and unmarked to this day.

In the spring following, we made another move north. Our

---

*"Life History of Nancy Naomi Alexander Tracy Written by Herself," typescript copy in Special Collections, Harold B. Lee Library, Brigham Young University.

horse having died, Brother Tippet loaned us one to go on with. The Saints had located a place to settle still farther up the river called Commerce. It was a very sickly place, but the only one we had to go to. When we got up there, lo and behold! there was Brother Joseph in the midst of the Saints. I will not attempt to describe his miraculous escape from prison, suffice it to say he got safely to his family and the bosom of the Saints. So Mr. Clark was greatly mistaken when he said we should never see Brother Joseph again.[20] The Lord worked out the deliverance after the Saints had all left the state.

Well, here we were again to start anew to make another home with nothing but our hands and brains to begin with. We were not conquered in spirit but determined to live our religion and stand by the principles of the Gospel and help to build up the kingdom of God on the earth. The people of Illinois seemed willing to give us a resting place. It was really a beautiful place to build up a city with the grand Mississippi rolling down past, her steam boats playing [plying] up and down. It was sublime! They called the City Nauvoo, the beautiful.

We got a city lot just below the brow of the hill where the temple was to be built. We built us a good log house, fenced in the lot. One full acre had a picket fence in front of it, and it began to look like really living again, although we had to live very close, both for food and clothes.

My fourth son was born in this house on the 22nd of June, but he was a sickly child and died when he was twenty months old. It was a hard place to raise children for a great many died of summer complaint when teething.

We lived in this house about two years and then sold the place to Brother Wilford Woodruff. We got another lot farther west on another block and this time built a frame house with two good sized rooms. After we moved into it, I took up a school for three months and so passed the summer.

The work on the temple was progressing, Elders were being sent out to the nations to preach the Gospel, emigrants from different parts flocked in, and everything prospered. About this time the Relief Society was organized with Emma Smith, president, with two counselors, and Eliza R. Snow, secretary. This was for the relief of the poor and for every noble purpose that came within woman's sphere of action. I united with this society. There was much valuable instruction given in these meetings. Sometimes Emma would bring the prophet in to give instructions. One in particular, I remember, he opened the meeting by prayer. He was so full of the Spirit of the Holy Ghost that his frame shook and his face shone and looked almost transparent. This was about the time that the order of Celestial marriage was given by revelation to him. He had taught it to a few who would hear it, but I heard him say at one time when he was preaching (turning to those that sat behind him), "If I should reveal to these, my Brethren, who now seem to be my bosom friends, what God has revealed to me, they would be the first to seek my life." And it was so. Even when this law of Celestial marriage was taught, these very men, William Marks, the Laws, and others, turned vipers against him. The clouds had begun to gather. It was not all sunshine now in Nauvoo. The opposing element was at work. The prophet was harassed with false brethren and apostates trying to prefer charges against him and bring him before the courts, but they could not prove anything against him. And for what reason was this tirade against him? It was because he was a prophet of the living God and because he had chosen to lay the foundation of the kingdom of God on the earth in this last dispensation. This has been the case in every age of the world when there has been a prophet to lead the people of God. They have been persecuted in like manner, and this is still another testimony of the divinity of this work.

Again I turn to our temporal affairs. Again we had a chance to sell and better our conditions. An old couple came from the east and wanted a home. We sold this home of ours to them for $225. Then my husband went up on the hill near the temple and bought a small lot and built another house with three rooms and a basement and with a brick fire place and an old fashioned brick oven by the side of it. This was a beautiful location; fronting the east was the public square and to the south just one lot and a street separated us from the temple. Here we hoped would be our permanent home. My husband did his own carpenter work and also helped to work on the temple. Out of my bedroom window I could see the masons at work and could hear the click of their hammers and hear their sailor songs as they pulled the rock in place with pulleys. It was grand to see. Notwithstanding, trouble was brewing and work on the temple was being pushed ahead.

One day I looked over toward the temple and saw a large crowd gathered with some two or three women present; so I thought I would go over. I put on my bonnet and shawl and made my way over. Brother Joseph was there and seemed busily engaged over something. Finally, he looked up and saw us women. He said for the brothers to stand back and let the sisters come up. So they gave way, and we went up. In the huge chief corner stone was cut out a square about a foot around and about as deep lined with zinc, and in it Brother Joseph had placed a Bible, a Book of Mormon, hymn book, and other church works along with silver money that had been coined in that year. Then a lid was cemented down, and the temple was reared on the top of this. It made me think of the prophets in ancient days hiding up their records to come forth in some future generation. At any rate, it was for some wise purpose, but I never heard any explanation of it.[21] The building progressed rapidly, and I was present when the cap stone was laid and heard the last ring of the trowel. The Saints turned out enmass. The address on that occasion was pathetic and grand, being delivered by Brigham Young.

There was much to contend with during the raising of that house for the evil one was stirring up the hearts of the people for he knew blessings would be poured out upon the Saints in that house. However, the Lord held the enemy at bay for the present.

Previous to this, Brother Joseph had written his views on the powers and policy of the government. It was printed and came out in pamphlet form. The Elders that were sent out on missions were counseled to take this work with them and present it to the world.

My husband had been in the employ of Amos Davis, a merchant in Nauvoo, for one year, and I had been teaching school. At this time, my husband was one who was chosen to go and preach the Gospel and also produce this pamphlet wherever he went. He was to go the state of New York. Consequently, he would go and visit his birth place. I got an idea that I would like to go with him and see my relatives. I had been away about ten years, and I had now four children. It seemed quite an undertaking, but I felt equal to the task; so my husband asked counsel of Brother Joseph. He told him to take me along, and I would prove a blessing to him. Therefore, we prepared to go; my husband went to Mr. Davis and got his wages, and besides, Mr. Davis made him a present of a nice suit of clothes, a hat, and fine boots and gave to me a dress pattern.

When we were ready, we went down to the landing. There were quite a number of elders going. Brother Joseph and Hyrum were at the landing to see the brethren off. The Church owned the steamboat. Her name was Osprey, and we were going as far as St. Louis on her; then we were to take a larger boat, the Robert Fulton, from St. Louis to the mouth of the Ohio river and up that river to Pittsburgh. But when we got to this river, we got in shallow water and ran aground. They could not move her, and so we had to wait until another boat came along and took us off. This one was called the Clipper. We could step right off the Fulton's lower deck onto the Clipper's upper deck, as she was so close along side and was a smaller boat.

From this point, we went to Louisville, where we had to go through the locks for there was great fall in the river. From there, we went on up to Pittsburgh and thence by sail and canal until we came to Buffalo. Then we went down Lake Ontario to Sackets Harbor, and we were now within 16 miles within Father Tracy's and 10 miles from Samuel Mattison's, my husband's brother-in-law. I stayed at the hotel, and he walked to his brother-in-law's and got him to go and bring us to his house. We stayed that night with them, and he took us next day to father's where we received a cordial greeting. It had been 3 weeks now since we left Nauvoo. We were tired and had to have a rest. We visited for a while and then father Tracy took us to Polaski, about 15 miles away, to see my mother and sister, and also my brother Eli. My brother Albert was in Canada teaching school and was a Methodist minister. When he heard we were there, he dismissed his school for a few days and came over to see us. We taught him the Gospel, but he was satisfied with his religion and would not listen to the message we had to bear. At last he went back, and it was the last time I ever saw him although we corresponded with each other. He is now in Missouri and has a family.

We ended our visit for this time with my relatives, not forgetting to preach to them the Gospel and give them Joseph's views on the policy of the government. We then returned to Ellisburg, my husband to start out on his mission. When we got back, we received the heart rending news that our prophet was slain in Carthage jail. We were horror stricken. My husband sobbed aloud, "Is it true? Can it be true, when so short a time ago he set us apart to fill this mission and was all right?"

The story of how they came to their death has oft been told. Joseph and his brother Hyrum had had the faith of the state pledged to them that they would be protected if they would give themselves up to be tried, but it was concocted beforehand to murder these innocent men. They knew they could prove nothing against them, and so they resorted to strategy to take their lives, thinking they would put an end to Mormonism. But the day of reckoning will come when vengeance will be taken. The Lord says to leave it with him, that he will repay. His plans are not to be frustrated by the puny arm of man.

Well, this, of course, cast a dark gloomy shadow over Nauvoo and all the Saints near and far, for they loved the Prophet of God. But Mormonism was not dead. Neither was it going to die. The Lord could raise up another to build on the foundation that was already laid. These wicked men did not comprehend the predictions of the ancient prophets that in the last days God would set up His kingdom, no more to be thrown down or given to another people.

My husband continued in his mission during the summer and fall. He baptized two and bore faithful testimonies wherever he went. In the winter months he stayed at his father's and labored in the branch that remained in Ellisburg. He belonged to the Seventies' quorum and had authority to make some things right that were not altogether in order in the branch.

Winter passed. Many of the twelve and other elders that were not on missions were called home.

In the spring, we made preparations to go back to Nauvoo. We bore faithful testimonies to those of our friends who had not obeyed the Gospel, bid them farewell, and then father took us to Oswego and there we took steamboat up to Lake Ontario. We stopped to view Niagara Falls, which was a grand sight. Our route home was the same as when we went. When we got to Pittsburgh, we went on board a river steamboat named "Sarah Ann." It was an old boat. When we got to Louisville, they chose to go over the rapids instead of through the locks. It was very risky, as the boat was so old. The shore was lined with people watching. Everything was so quiet on the boat you could have heard a pin drop. Everyone held his breath until she got safely over; then there were cheers from the shore and wavings of hats and handkerchiefs. The boat steamed on until we got to the mouth of the Ohio river. Then we came out onto the grand old Mississippi. We were now 500 miles below Nauvoo. The time seemed long, we were so anxious to get home to the city of the Saints.

We arrived on Sabbath morning, but oh how lonely and quiet everything seemed.

When we were in Louisville, I had left the boat as she lay at the wharf and had gone into a store and purchased some things, among which were a nice bonnet and veil. I could not get at my trunk, and so I tied them up in a large handkerchief and hung them up on a hook in the roof of the boat. When we got to the Nauvoo landing, I forgot all about them in our hurry and they went on with the boat and I never saw them again.

Our house had been rented while we were away. As soon as we arrived, we went right home and prepared to go to meeting for that day was appointed for us to choose a first presidency to lead the Church. The saints convened in a grove. Sidney Rigdon and his followers were on hand to contest their right to be the leaders of the Saints. At one time he was one of Brother Joseph's councilors, but he was not righteous, and Joseph shook him off saying that he had carried him long enough and he would carry him no longer. Therefore, it was out of the question to have such a man lead the people.

Brigham Young was the man chosen and sustained by

unanimous vote to be the mouthpiece of God to the Saints. I can testify that the mantle of Joseph fell upon Brigham that day as that of Elijah did fall upon Elisha, for it seemed that his voice, his gestures, and all were Joseph. It seemed that we had him again with us. He was sustained by the voice of the people to be the prophet, seer, and revelator.

Soon after this, my youngest child was taken sick and died in two weeks. His name was Theodore Franklin and he was two years and two months old. Now I had two little boys laid side by side in the burying ground, their little graves the same size.

Well, the Temple was so far completed that fall that the Lord accepted it at the hands of the Saints, and it was dedicated. The Saints began to receive their blessings. Therein we had our endowments in that house.

The evil one saw that the Saints were getting power from on high. Of course, he raged and stirred up the feeling of enmity against us, and the people again determined to drive us from our homes. So during the winter months preparations were made and some had already left their comfortable homes and crossed the river on the ice to go into the wilderness beyond civilization we know not where only as the hand of the Lord shall lead us. O liberty! thou precious boon that our Fathers shed their blood to gain, whither hast thou fled? But the hand of the Lord is over us, and so we shall find a resting place.

On the 15th of March, 1845, my sixth son was born.[22]

About the last of May, previous to our departure from Nauvoo, I was aroused from my slumbers one night, hearing such heavenly music as I had never heard before. Everything was so still and quiet when it burst upon my ear that I could not imagine where it came from. I got up and looked out of the window. The moon shone bright as I looked over at the Temple from whence the sound came. There on the roof of the building heavenly bands of music had congregated and were playing most beautifully. The music was exquisite! And we had to leave all this; the Temple, our homes, and the pleasant surroundings and bid farewell. It was to your tents, O Israel.[23]

"Emigrant Train Crossing the Plains," painter unknown,
from the Relief Society Magazine (1917)

At another time, fire caught in the roof of the Temple. How it
caught, I never knew, but for awhile it seemed that the house would
be destroyed. Men, women, and children came out and formed a
bucket brigade. The wells were drained and finally they went with
wagons and barrels to the river for water and at last succeeded in
putting out the flames. The damage was considerable. It seemed that
if the evil powers could not harass the people one way, they would do
it in another.

But now the time had come for us to take up the line and march,
this time far away to the west where white man's foot had never trod.
We were going to find a resting place among the red men of the
forest. Our journey had been delayed some time on account of my
confinement, but as soon as I was able to travel we started out. So
farewell to beautiful Nauvoo. May the Lord have mercy on our
enemies' souls for their cruelty and wickedness to an innocent and
law abiding people. But we are to be a tried people and to be made
perfect through suffering.

NOTES

1. In some early religious traditions, principally the Puritans and Friends, in order to become members, women were required to keep a daily account of their spiritual awakening and progress. Other women were impelled by their own desire to mark their spiritual journeys, their diaries becoming a permanent record of these "spiritual pilgrimages." See Carol Edkins, "Quest for Community: Spiritual Autobiographies of Eighteenth–Century Quaker and Puritan Women in America," in Estelle C. Jelinek, ed., *Women's Autobiography, Essays in Criticism* (Bloomington: Indiana University Press, 1980), 39–52.

2. Like Sarah Rich's effort, Rachel Woolley Simmons also felt impressed to write a journal "for her own satisfaction." Modestly disclaiming any great merit in its style or content, she nonetheless believed it would also bring pleasure to her children. See Rachel Woolley Simmons, "Reminiscences and Journals, 1881–1891," holograph, LDS Church Archives.

3. In the late nineteenth century, even though she published her autobiography, the Duchess of Newcastle nevertheless included the disclaimer that "it is to no purpose to the Reader, but it is to the Authoress, because I write for my own sake, not theirs; neither did I intend this piece for to delight, but to divulge; not to please the fancy but to tell the truth . . . " in "A True Relation of My Birth, Breeding and Life," *The Lives of William Cavendish, Duke of Newcastle, and of his Wife, Margaret Duchess of Newcastle,* ed. Mark Antony Lover (London: John Russell, 1892), 309–10, as quoted in Domna C. Stanton, "Autogynography: Is the Subject Different?" in Domna C. Stanton, ed., *The Female Autograph, Theory and Practice of Autobiography from the Tenth to the Twentieth Century* (Chicago: University of Chicago Press, 1987), 14.

4. See Edkins, "Quest for Community," 39–52.

5. Elizabeth Ann Whitney, a counselor to Emma Smith in the Nauvoo Relief Society, had received her endowments with her husband, Newel K. Whitney, from the Prophet Joseph before the temple was completed.

6. Her brother Robert died of consumption, with which he had suffered for a number of years, in 1841.

7. When first taught, vicarious baptisms were not arranged by gender, many women performing the ordinance for their deceased relatives of both sexes. Brigham Young later regulated the procedure.

8. Emmeline B. Wells, "L.D.S. Women of the Past," *Woman's Exponent* 37 (June 1908): 2.

9. Andrew Jenson, *L.D.S. Biographical Encyclopedia*, 4 vols. (Salt Lake City: Andrew Jenson History Company, 1914), 2:373.

10. Augusta Joyce Crocheron, *Representative Women of Deseret* (Salt Lake City: J. C. Graham and Company, 1884), 28.

11. "In Memoriam," *Woman's Exponent* 22 (October 1, 1893): 44.

12. "A Leaf from an Autobiography," *Woman's Exponent* 7 (February 15, 1879): 191.

13. See Minutes of the Female Relief Society of Nauvoo, June 9, 1842, LDS Church Archives.

14. Bathsheba is referring to the group of men and women to whom Joseph administered the temple ordinances while awaiting completion of the temple. It was sometimes known as the Endowment Group or the Holy Order.

15. These five women were, in order of marriage, Lucy Meserve (1844), Nancy Clements (1845), Zilpha Stark (1845), Sarah Ann Libby (1845), and Hannah Maria Libby (1846). Later, in 1857, George A. married Susan Elizabeth West.

16. A windlass is a cylinder-like device around which a rope is wound by a crank that lowers or raises a bucket from a well.

17. The term "jack Mormon" originally referred to sympathetic non-Mormons.

18. Samp mush, or porridge, is made from coarse hominy.

19. The Salt Lake *Tribune* was established in Salt Lake City in 1850 as a voice for non-Mormons in Utah.

20. She is referring to General Clark of Missouri, whom she remembered announcing, after the arrest of Joseph Smith, that "we need never expect to see our leaders again for their fate was fixed and their doom sealed."

21. Records do not show that documents were placed in any of the cornerstones for the Nauvoo Temple. Later that same year (1841), when the cornerstone of the Nauvoo House was put in place, Joseph Smith placed a manuscript copy of the Book of Mormon in a "square cut chest" that measured about ten by fourteen inches and eight inches deep and was "cemented around the edge with lead that had been melted and poured in the seam." Nancy might have been confusing the two events. See Dean C. Jessee, "The Original Book of Mormon Manuscript," *BYU Studies* 10 (Spring 1970): 265.

22. Her recollection may be faulty here, or the date incorrectly recorded, since the Saints left Nauvoo in 1846 rather than 1845.

23. The temple was dedicated privately on April 30, 1846, and publicly during the following three days in May. The concert of "heavenly music" that she heard coming from the roof of the temple may have taken place during the first part of May rather than the end of May.

INDEX

⤳

of, prepares to leave Nauvoo, 243–44; father of, is murdered, 245; begins exodus to west, 246

Derby, Erastus H., 54

Deseret Dramatic Association, 214

Diaries: reasons for keeping, 39–41; importance of, 258n.1

Dikes, George P., 79

Douglas, Ellen Briggs (Parker), 35n.83, 95; impression of Nauvoo, 6–7; biography of, 108–9; letter of, to parents, 109–12; 1843 letter of, to family, 112–15; describes husband's death, 113; poem of, 114–15; 1844 letter of, to family, 116–19

Douglas, Judge Stephen L., 130

Edkins, Carol, 258n.1

Edmons, P., 72

Ellison, Jo, 111

Ellison, John, 114

Ells, Hannah, 9, 107

Emmett, James, 179

Emmons, Judge Sylvester, 123, 125

Endowment Group, 259n.14

Farnsworth, Julia, 16, 175

Fielding, James, 194

Fielding, Joseph, 98, 101, 193

Follett, Louisa, 15, 27

Ford, Governor Thomas, 131, 173, 211

Free, Emiline and Eliza, 77, 78

Frost, Olive Grey, 58

Garner, Mary Field, 4, 12, 28

Gilbert, Sidney, 197

Gimsley, Edgar, 231

Goddard, Sister George, 191

Granger, Lydia Dibble, 154n.19

Granger, Oliver, 153n.12

Green, John P., 69

Grow, Henry, 245

Hackett, Samuel, 183

Hall, Jane, 118

Hancock, Levi, 75

Harding, John J., 211

Harris, Emmeline. *See* Wells, Emmeline B.

Harris, James, 43, 44

Haven, Charlotte, 94, 95; is impressed by Nauvoo midwives, 12; on Sunday evening cottage meetings, 18–19; biography of, 123–24; letter of, to family, 124–29; describes party at Rigdon home, 126–28

Haven, "H" and Elizabeth, 123

Haven, John, 123

Haven, Maria, 123

Hawworth, James, 119

Hendricks, Drusilla Dorris, 19, 159; chinked own log house, 7; worked to provide for family, 9; biography of, 161–62; reminiscence of, 162–68; hardships of, in Quincy, Illinois, 162–67

Heward, Elizabeth Terry Kirby, 159; was nurse, 11; recalls prayer meeting, 18; experiences manifestations of Spirit, 19; contributes to Nauvoo Temple fund, 20–21, 180–81, 185; remarries, 34n.66, 183; biography of, 178–79; reminiscence of, 179–88; patriarchal blessing, 181; poem of, 182; daughter Rachel dies, 186; gives money from property sale to Church, 187; leaves Nauvoo with Saints, 187–88

Higbee, Charles, 123

Higbee, Elias, 60

Hinkle, George M., 54, 88n.6

Holmes, Elvira, 77

Holmes, Jonathan H., 57

Huntington, Caroline, 81

Huntington, Dimick, 55, 69–87 passim

Huntington, Henry, 72

Huntington, Oliver, 72

Huntington, William, 69–87 passim

Hyde, Elizabeth Howe, 26

Hyde, Orson, 72, 74, 187

Ives, Mary, 9, 93

Ivins, Rachel, 16

"Jack Mormon," 259n.17

INDEX

Jacobs, Henry, 67
Jacobs, Isaac, 76
James, Jane Manning, 3–4
Jolly, Sarah Pippin, 23
Jolly, Susan, 94
Judd, Margaret, 11

Kane, Elizabeth, 124
Kelly, William, 147
Kimball, Heber C., 72, 75, 108, 137, 187;
letter from wife to, 138–39
Kimball, Hiram, 103, 125, 153n.12, 189,
199
Kimball, Mary Ellen, 21–22
Kimball, Sarah Melissa Granger, 16,
153n.12, 154n.19; on organization of
Relief Society, 25, 191; biography of,
189–90; Relief Society activities of,
189–90; was suffragist, 190; reminis-
cence of, 191–92;
Kimball, Vilate, 16, 22, 105, 175; on
death of Joseph Smith, 26; biogra-
phy of, 137–38; letter of, to Heber C.
Kimball, 138–39
King, Timonth, 183
Kington, Hannah Pitt, 7
Kington, Thomas, 31n.16, 55
Kirby, Elizabeth. See Heward, Elizabeth
Terry Kirby
Knight, Vinson, 53

Lambert, Mary, 14
Law, William, 153n.13, 154n.21, 204
Law, Wilson, 54, 154n.21, 204
Leavitt, Cornelia, 75
Leavitt, Leonora Snow, 55, 63, 88n.7
Lensink, Judy, 39
Leonard, Abigail, 19
Lewis, Melinda, 7
Libby, Hannah Maria, 259n.15
Libby, Sarah Ann, 259n.15
Lightner, Mary Rollins, 8
Lindsay, William, 76
Lyman, Amasa, 55, 86
Lyons, Caleb, 209
Lyons, Sylvia, 75, 77

Margetts, Eliza Clayton, 159–60; biog-

raphy of, 223; reminiscence of,
224–26; describes martyrdom scene,
224–25; witnesses miracle of quails,
225–26
Markham, Hannah, 71
Markham, Stephen, 62, 66, 82, 86
Marks, William, 58, 77, 251
Marriage, plural, 17, 44, 176–77, 195,
201–3, 210, 251
Maughan, Mary Ann, 11–12
McConoughey, Eli, 88n.8
McDugle, Margret, 76
McFate, Elizabeth (Richards), 176
Merick, Fanny, 78
Meserve, Lucy, 259n.15
Mikesell, Hiram, 81
Millet, Alma, 186
Mississippi River, 13
Mobs in Nauvoo. See Nauvoo
Morley, Isaac, 64, 196
Morley, Lucy, 64
Moss, William and Betty, 111, 114
"Mother in Israel," 34n.34
Mummies purchased by Joseph Smith,
75, 89n.19
Murdock, Julia, 8
Murdock, Sally, 240
Murray, Fanny Young, 36n.95

Nauvoo: establishment of, 3; housing
conditions in, 4–7, 217; economy in,
7–10, 149, 152, 165–67, 185; sickness
in, 11–12, 116–17, 217; social activities in, 12; steamship and boat
arrivals at, 13–15; women's activities
in, 16–18; spiritual life of women in,
18–24; reaction of Saints in, to death
of Prophet, 27–28; "battle of,"
28–29, 225; mobs in, 86–87, 139,
142, 174, 186, 230–38; descriptions
of, 110–11, 250; post office at, 125;
Charlotte Haven describes party at,
126–28; described in petition to governor, 131–33; persecutions in, 204,
210; after martyrdom, 174–75, 211,
228, 243–45; exodus from, 175,
187–88, 211–12, 245–46; child's
death in, 186

Terry, Elizabeth and Timothy, 180
Terry, Jacob D., 186
Thompson, Elizabeth Barlow, 24
Thompson, Mercy Rachel Fielding:
    biography of, 193–94; reminiscence
    of, 194–95; temple worker, 193–94;
    traveled to Palestine, 194; dream of,
    195
Thompson, Robert, 193, 195
Thornber, Hannah, 111
Thornber, Henry, 114
Thornber, John, 112
Tippet, John, 249
Tracy, Nancy Naomi Alexander: patri-
    archal blessing of, 4; describes
    Prophet's sermons, 26; biography
    of, 247–48; reminiscence of, 249–57;
    describes exodus from Missouri to
    Illinois, 249; settles in Nauvoo, 250;
    home of, 251–52; travels to New
    York with husband, 252–53; returns
    to Nauvoo by steamer, 254–55;
    receives ordinances in temple, 256;
    hears heavenly music at temple, 256;
    describes fire in temple, 257
Turley, Frances, 105

Walker, Lucy and Jane, 15
Weld, Dr. J. F., 123, 124
Wells, Daniel H., 44
Wells, Emmeline B. Harris, 10; left
    alone by husband, 15; on Eliza R.
    Snow's temple service, 22; on
    diaries, 39; biography of, 43–45;
    diary of, 45–49
West, Susan Elizabeth, 259n.15
Whitney, Elizabeth Ann Smith: on
    plural marriage, 17; special spiritual
    calling of, 19, 167; daughter of, born
    under covenant, 22; becomes plural
    wife, 44; temple worker, 138, 197;
    biography of, 196–98; Relief Society
    leader, 197, 198, 200–201; reminis-
    cence of, 198–205; trials of, in Mis-
    souri, 198; family of, moves to Illi-
    nois, 198–99; remembers prophecy

of Joseph Smith, 200; learns about
    and enters plural marriage, 201–3;
    receives endowments from Prophet,
    258n.5
Whitney, Newel K., 44, 57, 60, 66,
    258n.5
Whitney, Sarah Ann, 8
Wight, Lyman, 242
Wilkinson, Margaret, 117
Williams, Alexander, 164
Williams, Electa, 5
Wilson, Harmon T., 62
Winters, Mary Ann Stearns, 5
Woodruff, Phebe Carter, 6, 16, 103,
    175; letter to, from Leonora Cannon
    Taylor, 106–7; biography of,
    134–35; letter of, to Wilford
    Woodruff, 135–35; letter to, from
    Bathsheba W. Smith, 145
Woodruff, Wilford, 7, 57, 106n., 250
Woolley, Rachel, 11

Young, Brigham, 50, 67, 72, 73, 187;
    sermons of, 75–76, 82-83; married
    Mary Ann Angell, 140; letter to,
    from wife Mary Ann, 141–42; leads
    Saints after Prophet's death, 168,
    174, 185, 204, 230, 242, 255–56;
    description of, by Jane Snyder
    Richards, 174–75; warned about
    mob by Hyrum Bigelow, 230–31;
    regulated procedure of vicarious
    baptisms, 258n.7
Young, Joseph, 10, 80, 84, 231
Young, Lucy Bigelow, 228
Young, Mary Ann Angell, 6, 94; biogra-
    phy of, 140–41; letter of, to Brigham
    Young, 141–42
Young, Zina D. H., 10; was midwife,
    16–17; on death of Joseph and
    Hyrum Smith, 27, 70–71; on com-
    munity of women, 30; biography of,
    67–69; diary of, 69–87; rejoices at
    meeting in temple, 79–80; describes
    mob actions, 86–87